D0087712

Teacher Development and Educational Change

Teacher Development and Educational Change

Edited by

Michael Fullan
Andy Hargreaves

RECEIVED

JUL 2 1 1993

MSU - LIBRARY

 The Falmer Press

(A Member of the Taylor & Francis Group)
London • Washington, D.C.

UK   The Falmer Press, 4 John St, London WC1N 2ET
USA   The Falmer Press, Taylor & Francis Inc., 1900 Frost Road, Suite 101, Bristol, PA 19007

© Selection and editorial material copyright Michael Fullan and Andy Hargreaves 1992

All rights reserved. No part of this publication may be reproduced, stored in a retrieval system, or transmitted, in any form or by any means, electronic, mechanical, photocopying, recording, or otherwise, without permission in writing from the Publisher.

First published 1992

A catalogue record for this book is available from the British Library

ISBN 0 75070 010 6
ISBN 0 75070 011 4 (pbk)

Library of Congress Cataloging-in-Publication Data are available on request

Jacket design by Caroline Archer

Typeset in 11/11½ Bembo by
Graphicraft Typesetters Ltd., Hong Kong

Printed in Great Britain by Burgess Science Press, Basingstoke on paper which has a specified pH value on final paper manufacture of not less than 7.5 and is therefore 'acid free'.

LB
1707
. T4
1992

10-8-93
ℓ𝓂𝓁
85047879

Contents

v

Contents

Acknowledgments

We would like to thank the Faculty of Education, University of Toronto, the Ontario Institute for Studies in Education, and the Social Sciences and Humanities Research Council for supporting the International Conference on Teacher Development. This book was developed as a result of the conference held in Toronto in February 1989.

Chapter 1

Teacher Development and Educational Change

Michael Fullan and Andy Hargreaves

For something as obvious as the need to relate teacher development and educational change, it is surprising how little systematic attention has been devoted to understanding the topic and taking appropriate action.[1] In fact, the focus on the link between teacher development and educational change is barely fifteen years old. In this chapter we want to trace this development briefly, indicate the unfinished agenda, and illustrate how the chapters in this book contribute to what has only very recently become a rapidly growing knowledge base.

We divide the period of research on teacher development since 1975 into two broad phases. The first phase analyzed the relationship between teacher development and successful implementation of innovation—we call this the *innovation-focused period*. The second phase takes the matter more deeply by considering *the total teacher and the total school*.

The Innovation-Focused Period

In some ways the logic and evidence linking teacher development to successful implementation of innovations is relatively straightforward, although there are a number of subtleties and complexities in the process. In a review in 1977, Fullan and Pomfret marshalled considerable evidence that demonstrated how teacher development and successful implementation of innovations were related. We observed that effective implementation consists of alterations in curriculum materials, instructional practices and behaviour, and beliefs and understandings on the part of teachers involved in given innovations. Put more simply, successful change involves learning how to do something new. As such, the process of implementation is essentially a learning process. Thus, when it is linked to specific innovations, teacher development and implementation go hand in hand.

At the time we learned that teacher development should be innovation-related, continuous during the course of implementation, and involve a variety of formal (e.g. workshops) and informal (e.g. teacher-exchange) components. We also confirmed that most innovation attempts did not incorporate these characteristics.

Since 1977, significant advances have been made in spelling out the processes involved in these relationships. Huberman and Miles (1984) captured these processes in their twelve case studies of school districts.

> Large-scale, change-bearing innovations lived or died by the amount and quality of assistance that their users received once the change process was under way...The forms of assistance were various. The high-assistance sites set up external conferences, in-service training sessions, visits, committee structures, and team meetings. They also furnished a lot of ongoing assistance in the form of materials, peer consultation, access to external consultants, and rapid access to central office personnel...Although strong assistance did not usually succeed in smoothing the way in early implementations, especially for the more demanding innovations, it paid handsome dividends later on by substantially increasing the levels of commitment and practice mastery. (p. 273)

Huberman and Miles, along with others, also contributed new insights into the process of teacher learning, which included: the universal presence of early implementation problems in all cases of success, the role of pressure and support, the way in which change in practice frequently preceded change in beliefs and understanding, and the time-line of two or more years of active assistance during implementation.

Stallings (1989) in a series of experimental studies also demonstrated how staff development was connected to change in teacher practice, and in turn to increases in student achievement. Stallings found that teachers are more likely to change their behaviour and continue to use new ideas under the following conditions:

1 They become aware of a need for improvement through their analysis of their own observation-profile.
2 They make a written commitment to try new ideas in their classroom the next day.
3 They modify the workshop ideas to work in their classroom and school.
4 They try the ideas and evaluate the effect.
5 They observe in each other's classrooms and analyze their own data.

6 They report their success or failure to their group.
7 They discuss problems and solutions regarding individual students and/or teaching subject matter.
8 They need a wide variety of approaches: modelling, simulations, observations, critiquing video tapes, presenting at professional meetings.
9 They learn in their own way continuity to set new goals for professional growth. (Stallings, 1989:3–4)

The corner-stones of the model, according to Stallings, are:

- Learn by doing—try, evaluate, modify, try again.
- Link prior knowledge to new information.
- Learn by reflecting and solving problems.
- Learn in a supportive environment—share problems and successes. (p. 4)

Joyce and Showers (1988) in their well-known theory-demonstration-practice-feedback-coaching model have shown rather conclusively that staff development is central to instructional change involving teaching models. In a more thorough test of the approach in Richmond County, Georgia, Joyce *et al.* (1989) provide further confirmation of the link between staff development, implementation, and student outcomes. After eighteen months of intensive training and follow-up with teams of teachers focusing on models of teaching, Joyce and his colleagues were able to claim considerable implementation in the classroom, which in turn was related to a dramatic impact on student achievement and student promotion rates (p. 7).

Other large-scale studies show time and again that staff or teacher development is closely related to successful change (Mortimore *et al.*, 1988; Fullan, 1991). However, there are some unsettling issues within these approaches which require explanation, and which eventually lead us to consider a radically different approach to teacher development. First, it is worth emphasizing that the initiatives examined by Huberman and Miles, Stallings, Joyce and Showers, and others required great sophistication, effort, skill and persistence to accomplish what they did. They work, but they are exceptions. More typical is Pink's (1989) litany of problems in the projects he examined. He identified twelve barriers to innovation-effectiveness:

1 An inadequate theory of implementation, including too little time for teachers to plan for and learn new skills and practices
2 District tendencies toward new skills and practices

3   Lack of sustained central office support and follow-through
4   Underfunding the project, or trying to do too much with too little support
5   Attempting to manage the projects from the central office instead of developing school leadership and capacity
6   Lack of technical assistance and other forms of intensive staff development
7   Lack of awareness of the limitations of teacher and school administrator knowledge about how to implement the project
8   The turnover of teachers in each school
9   Too many competing demands or overload
10 Failure to address the incompatibility between project requirements and existing organizational policies and structures
11 Failure to understand and take into account site-specific differences among schools
12 Failure to clarify and negotiate the role relationships and partnerships involving the district and the local university— which in each case had a role, albeit unclarified, in the project. (Pink, 1989:22–4)

We believe that these types of 'typical' barriers will always eventually take their toll on existing pockets of success because the innovation-focused approach is too narrow and too weak an intervention to impact on more basic institutional conditions that must be altered if teacher development is to flourish.

Second, and more fundamental, the success stories we referred to above 'worked' in only a narrow sense—some specific instructional innovations were implemented, but we have little idea of how they relate to the wider context of the teacher, the school and the district. As we have noted elsewhere, schools are not in the business of simply implementing specific single innovations one at a time (which is difficult enough); they are in the business of managing *multiple innovations simultaneously* (Fullan, 1991). It does not tell us much to know how one particular innovation fared. Nor do we know enough about the relationship of these innovation experiences to the teacher's sense of purpose, the teacher as a person, or the contexts and conditions under which they work (Hargreaves, 1991). Do experiences with innovation make teachers more or less dependent? Do they result in a more or less developed sense of efficacy and self-esteem? Are the selected innovations the right ones for that teacher, those students, this situation? Does the school as an institution improve i.e. provide better working and learning conditions for all teachers and all studies, as a result of becoming involved in particular innovations? Do the expert's and the administrator's voices drown out or inhibit the development of the teachers' voices?

The Total Teacher and the Total School

These questions lead us to the conclusion that the innovation-focused paradigm is useful but fundamentally limited for understanding teacher development. For the latter we need a more comprehensive framework. We have written elsewhere that such a framework must take into account four main elements (Fullan and Hargreaves, 1991):

1 The teacher's *purpose*
2 The teacher as a *person*
3 The real world *context* in which teachers work
4 The *culture* of teaching: the working relationship that teachers have with their colleagues inside and outside the school.

We can only comment briefly on the importance of each of these components. Because teaching is a moral craft, it has purpose for those who do it. There are things that teachers value, that they want to achieve through their teaching. There are also things that they dis-value, things that they fear will not work or will make matters worse. In this sense teacher development means enabling teachers to develop, to voice and to act on their sense of purpose. We are not saying that the teacher's sense of purpose is sacrosanct: only that it is neglected and underdeveloped as a source of innovation and effectiveness. Teacher development then, must actively listen to and sponsor the teacher's voice; establish opportunities for teachers to confront the assumptions and beliefs underlying their practices; avoid faddism and blanket implementation of favoured new instructional strategies; and create a community of teachers who discuss and develop their purposes together, over time.

The teacher as person has also been neglected in teacher development. Most approaches to staff development, for example, either treat all teachers as if they are the same (or should be the same), or stereotype teachers as innovators, resisters, and the like. In more recent research, we are seeing that age, stage of career, life experiences, and gender factors—things that make up the total person —affect people's interest in and response to innovation and their motivation to seek improvement. Most strategies fail to take these differences into account, and consequently fail to be effective for many teachers. We are beginning to see some development along these lines. Huberman (1992) draws out several different implications according to stage of career; Krupp (1989) does the same for age and gender; induction programmes address the special needs of newly-hired teachers. But these are recent exceptions. And most approaches still fail to value (and consequently fail to involve) the veteran teacher, and they fail to appreciate the nature of the varying life circumstances of different teachers as these relate to the teacher as a person.

Third, the contexts in which teachers work must be taken into account. Grade levels present very different contexts as do elementary compared to secondary panels, inner city as opposed to suburban and rural communities, the degree to which curriculum and testing is mandated, and so on. Many attempts to improve instruction take little account of the social contexts in which learning and teaching take place. The price of ignoring the context of teaching is failed idealism, guilt and frustration at not being able to meet the standards, criticism of teachers who fail to make the changes, and erratic leaping from one innovation bandwagon to another.

Finally, the culture of teaching and the culture of schools loom increasingly as keys to teacher development. Initial teacher education is widely regarded as weak and wrong-headed, reinforcing habits and conditions virtually contrary to continuous individual and collective development (Goodlad, 1990). School cultures, with only a few exceptions, continue to allow, if not foster individualism at the expense of teacher growth (Rosenholtz, 1989). Collaborative work cultures that actively promote ongoing teacher development are very much in the minority, and are held together only by the extraordinary efforts of a few. Ironically, individuality is also thwarted by the superficial forms of interaction and absence of support evident in most schools. As we and others have observed, only the simultaneous renewal of both universities and schools/districts will create the conditions for long-term teacher development (Fullan, 1991; Fullan and Hargreaves, 1991; Goodlad 1990).

Implications

Our overarching conclusion is that teacher development must be conceptualized much more thoroughly than it has been. Its relationship to educational change is not just a matter of better implementation of selected innovations (although it includes this) but more basically a change in the profession of teaching, and in the institutions in which teachers are trained and in which they work. Teacher development is thus tantamount to transforming educational institutions. Fortunately this is becoming the agenda of the 1990s, although it is unlikely to receive the deep and continuous attention it requires. It is beyond our mandate and space to map out here a set of strategies for teacher development. We have elsewhere recommended a set of twenty-four strategies or guidelines for action for teachers, principals and those working outside the school (Fullan and Hargreaves, 1991). Goodlad (1990) formulates a systematic agenda for reform of teacher development, and provides a hypothetical case study illustrating its enactment. Our purpose in this introductory chapter is to focus the agenda.

Each of the chapters in this book (and in its companion piece, Hargreaves and Fullan, 1992) advance our knowledge in understanding teacher development and in pointing to directions for reform and the improvement of practice. Together the chapters in this book draw on empirical work in Canada, England and the United States. They address both micro and macro issues of educational change. The chapters can be divided conveniently into four sets dealing with (1) individual teacher experience and development (Aitken and Mildon, Sikes, Grimmett and Crehan); (2) school-level conditions for teacher development (Leithwood, Stoll, Wideen); (3) policy issues (Hickcox and Musella, Little); and (4) school/district–university partnerships (Rudduck, Watson and Fullan).

Aitken and Mildon in a study of pre-service teachers continuing into their first years of teaching provide insights into the new teacher as person, and illustrate the incredibly personal nature and tension of early teacher development. Sikes, in her chapter, follows teachers in their career experiences, especially in relation to 'imposed change'. She argues that imposed change is increasingly a reality in many countries and states. She acknowledges its potential value in addressing issues of equity, but argues that imposed change is doomed to backlash and failure if it doesn't take into account the career situations and cultures of teachers affected. Grimmett and Crehan show how very complex the relationship is between individual teacher personalities and a range of collegially-intended supervision practices. Using case studies of three teachers and their principals, Grimmett and Crehan explore the differences between administratively-imposed collegiality, and organizationally-induced collegiality. Using specific episodes in the relationships over time, Grimmett and Crehan are able to identify some of the conditions under which interdependent collegiality and teacher development are more likely to occur.

Leithwood makes an important contribution by conceptualizing three dimensions of teacher development: professional expertise, psychological development, and career-cycle development. He then outlines four guidelines for how school principals can foster development along the three dimensions. In Chapter 6, Stoll draws on her research with Mortimore—in which they found twelve key characteristics of effective schools. Stoll describes how one school district is proceeding to implement an effective schools project using this knowledge base. Unlike most other work on school effectiveness, Stoll makes explicit links to matters of teacher development. Similarly, Wideen reports on a case study in which a school staff, supported by the district, created a setting in which teacher development occurred. School improvement or school effectiveness projects do not always result in teacher development, so Wideen's study is particularly instructive about how this occurs within an improvement project mode.

As we move to the policy level, Hickcox and Musella juxtapose the purposes of staff development and performance appraisal and find some overlap, but also considerable incompatibility and divergence. Since both procedures are purportedly related to teacher development,

Hickcox and Musella conclude that changes are needed in both, if teacher development is to benefit. They find that some of the newer forms of supervision for growth, coaching and mentoring and similar approaches incorporate features that help reconcile traditional conflicts between appraisal and staff-development approaches. In a state-wide study in California, Little found that the prevailing patterns of staff-development policy and practice in the thirty districts in her sample were not conducive to sustained teacher development. Despite substantial monetary investment in teacher development, Little reports that the most common form is 'service delivery'. Although one-shot staff development was not as prevalent as reported in earlier research, classroom-based follow-up was rare. Nor of course, did the service-delivery mode at all address the basic issues of teacher purpose, person, context and culture we discussed earlier.

The final two chapters report two examples of one of the more powerful strategies for teacher development, namely, school/district–university partnerships (see also Sirotnik and Goodlad, 1988). Rudduck reports on a potentially powerful partnership between one local education authority and a university in England. The key strategy was to release teams of teachers full time to work in improvement projects or 'commissions' drawn up by their schools. Two or three days a week were spent at the university, and two or three days at the school. Rudduck derives several valuable positive and negative lessons about the conditions and benefits of the partnership. Watson and Fullan describe the Learning Consortium partnership in Ontario which involves four school districts, and two institutions of higher education. Their study also shows that such partnerships are powerful because they attempt school renewal and university (teacher education) renewal in concert. Both chapters show how the cultures of the university and the school systems are different, how sustained efforts over many years will be required to make them work (or to put it another way, how fragile these partnerships are as social experiments), and how schools and faculties of education need each other if serious teacher development is to occur.

In conclusion, it is only in the last few years that teacher development as a concept has come under scrutiny. In so doing, it has become clear that previous assumptions about linking staff development and effective change confined to specific innovations were too limited. We now begin to see that comprehensive career-long teacher development, and institutional reforms in faculties of education and school systems is the real agenda. Teacher development is thus positioned to take a central role in educational reform in the 1990s.

Note

1   We will not attempt to define the term teacher development at this stage of the chapter. As will become clear we use it both to refer to specific develop-

ments through in-service or staff development, as well as to more thorough advances in teachers' sense of purpose, instructional skills and ability to work with colleagues.

References

FULLAN, M. with S. STIEGELBAUER (1991) *The New Meaning Of Educational Change*, New York, Teachers College Press; Toronto, OISE Press; United Kingdom, Cassell.

FULLAN, M. and HARGREAVES, A. (1991) *What's Worth Fighting For: Working Together For Your School*, Toronto, Ontario Public School Teachers' Federation.

FULLAN, M. and POMFRET, A. (1977) 'Research on curriculum and instruction implementation', *Review of Educational Research, 5* (47), pp. 335–97.

GOODLAD, J. (1988) 'School–university partnerships for educational renewal: rationale and concepts', in K. SIROTNIK and J. GOODLAD (Eds.) *School-University Partnerships in Action*, pp. 3–31, New York, Teachers College Press.

GOODLAD, J. (1990) *Teachers For Our Nation's Schools*, San Francisco, Jossey-Bass.

HARGREAVES, A. (1991) 'Cultures of teaching', in HARGREAVES, A. and FULLAN, M. (Eds.) *Teacher Development and Educational Change*, Basingstoke, Falmer.

HARGREAVES, A. and FULLAN, M. (1992) (Eds.) *Teacher Development and Educational Change*, Basingstoke, Falmer.

HUBERMAN, M. (1992) Teacher development and instructional mastery', in HARGREAVES, A. and FULLAN, M. (Eds.), *Teacher Development and Educational Change*, Basingstoke, Falmer.

HUBERMAN, M. and MILES, M. (1984) *Innovation Up Close*, New York, Plenum.

JOYCE, B. and SHOWERS, B. (1988) *Student Achievement Through Staff Development*, New York, Longman.

JOYCE, B., MURPHY, C., SHOWERS, B. and MURPHY, J. (1989) 'Reconstructing the workplace: School renewal as cultural change', Paper presented at the annual meeting of the American Educational Research Association, San Francisco.

KRUPP, J.A. (1989) 'Staff development and the individual', in CALDWELL, S.D. (Ed.) *Staff Development: A Handbook Of Effective Practices* (pp. 44–57), Oxford, Ohio, National Staff Development Council.

MORTIMORE, P., SAMMONS, P., STOLL, L., LEWIS, D. and ECOB, R. (1988) *School Matters: The Junior Years*, Somerset, United Kingdom, Open Books.

PINK, W. (1989) 'Effective development for urban school improvement', Paper presented at the annual meeting of the American Educational Research Association, San Francisco.

ROSENHOLTZ, S. (1989) *Teachers' Workplace*, New York, Longman.

SIROTNIK, K. and GOODLAD, J. (Eds.) *School–University Partnerships in Action*, New York, Teachers College Press.

STALLINGS, J.A. (1989) 'School achievements effects and staff development: What are some critical factors?' Paper presented at the annual meeting of the American Educational Research Association.

Chapter 2

Teacher Education and the Developing Teacher: The Role of Personal Knowledge

Johan Lyall Aitken and Denis A. Mildon

Educated men and women, even when they most violate principles, act from their reason, however perverted, and from their affections, however misplaced.

Henry James

I   Background

Genesis of Project

This research project began in September 1987 at the Faculty of Education at the University of Toronto. The class studied was one section of the Junior/Intermediate division. Sections are given numerical designations: this one happened to be 'Section 11'. The senior author of this chapter was one of several professors assigned to teach this group. After over two decades of experience in teacher education, she was, in the words of Ezra Pound, 'dying a little of my ennui' concerning the effectiveness and value of this pre-service course as it was then constituted. There was at the time, however, a hint of hope-in-the-air in the form of blueprints for reform in teacher education and development. In Ontario the most promising of these was the Fullan-Connelly Report on Teacher Education (1990) which described and discussed not only 'current practice' but also 'options for the future'. This ray of hope, combined with the sense of urgency and commitment evinced by the Section 11 group, ignited the project.

It seemed important to find out as much as possible about the role of the immense personal knowledge the candidates brought to the pre-service programme, both in their motivations to become teachers and in the ways in which they responded to the in-faculty and practicum experiences. Did personal knowledge determine what could be learned? Did personal knowledge constitute a deciding factor in suc-

Table 2.1:   *Characteristics of Section 11 Participants*

Total of participants, October 1987:   28 (23 women/5 men)

Ages: Average age – 30

under 25	7
25–29	8
30–39	10
40–46	3
	28

Graduate Studies: 8

Previous teaching experience:

Actual teaching	14
Related experience	14

Additional language(s)

None	6
One	15
Two or more	7
	28

Parents: 9

Married   (as of December 1988):   16

Teaching positions (as of December 1988):

Roman Catholic schools, Ontario	12
Public schools, Ontario	12
Supply teaching or teacher-related work	13
Graduate school	11
	48

cess in teaching? How did the candidates themselves view the intertextuality of their own personal narratives and knowledge and their pre-service teacher education?

Description of Class

In Section 11, some members were chronologically old enough to be parents of some of the others (see Table 2.1). They differed not only in age, but in sex, ethnicity, socio-economic background, life experience, religious affiliation or allegiance, marital status, level of formal education, ethical concern, exposure and commitment to the arts, interests in sports and recreational activities and, perhaps most dramatically, level of literacy (including ability to read out loud, to comprehend a variety of texts, to speak, to listen and to write). More than half the class had a considerable degree of proficiency in at least one language other than English. A significant number played at least one musical instrument with a professed degree of accomplishment. Many were entering teaching after what seemed to be successful first or second careers, such as law, chartered accountancy, home-making and child care, instruction at the Canadian Ballet school, or an executive post in an oil company. Approximately one-third of the class were parents.

Objectives of the Study

The long-range objectives at the outset were:

- to determine how each candidate's personal narrative influenced the motivation to become a teacher
- to assess the extent to which the biography of pre-service teachers seemed to fit them for teaching
- to assess the extent to which their life experiences and reflections may have prepared the Section 11 members to teach prior to any formal training
- to discover the ways in which previous vocations (e.g. business careers, parenting) conditioned perceptions of both programme of study and the practicum component
- to learn from these student teachers the aspects of the teacher-education programme they deemed extraordinarily useful, appropriate or detrimental to their development as teachers and to check out these impressions at various points during their teaching careers
- to discover how these student teachers viewed their practicum, their impressions of classroom practice, and themselves as beginning teachers in the context of elementary and secondary schools
- to note similarities and differences between their views of their performance in the practicum and those of their associate teachers
- to observe the capacity of this group to tolerate the frustration of assignment load, to meet the demands of practice teaching, to integrate theoretical and research studies with classroom practice, and to extrapolate theory from classroom practice (including field trip and outdoor educational experiences)
- to identify changes in reflection and critical practice
- to note the subsequent placement of students and any additional qualifications taken to improve their knowledge base and/or to better fit them for their teaching.

Sources of Data to February 1988

Data collection began in the third week in September 1987. The resources included curriculum vitae, a record of in-class participation and interaction, 'Junior Placement Practice Teaching' journal, 'Then and Now' report (childhood memory and adult reviews of a significant childhood text), an analysis of a recently-published junior-level novel, a workshop presentation, including written preparation, self-evaluation and peer evaluation as well as researcher's notes, written responses to the final practicum session, practice-teaching evaluation sheets, notes from interviews with the professor—both those initiated by the professor and those initiated by the student/teacher—post-practice teaching interviews in October or November 1987, December 1987 or January 1988, and March 1988, phone interviews from October 1987 to August 1989, first-term entries in 'wisdom of practice' journals distributed at Symposium One, August 1988, phone interviews during October/November 1988 and January/February 1989.

From Symposium One, August 1988, the following sources of data were collected: transcripts of personal narratives, written auto-biographical sketches and researchers' field notes. From Symposium Two, 2–3 December 1988, transcripts of all workshops, written responses to Connelly/Aitken workshops, questionnaire on current teaching practices and researcher's field notes were collected.

Collaboration

The research was collaborative from the outset—the beginning teachers working as co-researchers and the research assistant interviewing, and being interviewed by, many of the participants. Influenced in part by the work of Cole (1985) that out-of-school interviews are more effective than those conducted on site, interviews have taken place not only at the faculty, but in the OISE cafeteria, in restaurants and pubs, in the researcher's home, in the beginning teachers' homes, and on the phone.

The class began with thirty students. After seven weeks there were twenty-eight (one had changed divisions, one had dropped out of the faculty programme altogether). These twenty-eight, according to present faculty criteria, 'successfully completed the course'. Participation had been entirely voluntary and could be dropped at any time. With varying degrees of intensity all class members stayed on until the final class. At that final class the beginning teachers/researchers were asked for a written 'yes' or 'no' regarding future participation. Two class members elected to drop out at this juncture. The other twenty-six 'signed on' with an understanding that they had two-way tickets and that the commitment, while serious, was by no means binding.

At our first symposium, of 26–27 August 1988, all but two who could physically be there, were there. Postcards from China and messages from Northern Ontario honeymoons were accepted as evidence of continuing commitment. Two, however, have been off the project since that time. We have no communication with one student but the other still phones occasionally declaring interest but consistently 'too busy' to participate.

At the second symposium, twenty-two beginning teachers appeared for at least the Saturday session and nineteen were there for the entire session. There are two students whom we cannot accommodate within our present symposium structure. They illustrate the clash between personal and professional obligations and the primacy for many teachers in their decision-making of the demands of what Beck (1971) calls 'the inner group'. One of these teachers is married and the mother of four teenaged children. Her Friday evenings and Saturdays must regularly be devoted to religious observances with her family. The other eager but absent beginning teacher is prevented from coming by parental restrictions.

II Four Journeys Toward Becoming a Teacher

Part Two of the paper considers the first steps of the journey toward becoming a teacher—the journey described by Connelly and Clandinin (1988) as 'history, anticipation and experience'—the one that begins in the pre-service, induction and apprenticeship period and continues for the rest of our teaching lives. In Section 11 there were (by October 1987) twenty-three women and five men, seven under twenty-five, eight between twenty-five and twenty-nine, ten between thirty and thirty-nine and three over forty (see Table 2.1). Each of these four age-groups is represented in this paper. Three women and one man have been selected, in an attempt to provide a variety in class background, choice of socio-economic group in which to begin teaching, as well as a mix in racial and ethnic backgrounds. While each individual story of becoming a teacher is unique, an attempt will be made, where possible and appropriate, to identify ways in which each one is in some ways representative of a larger population. All names are pseudonyms and all beginning teachers discussed have given their permission to have their words and experiences used in this paper.

In two case studies an effort is made to contextualize the beginning teacher's story written in some of the pertinent 'literature' on teacher education and careers as well as personal narrative. In the delineation of the other two, where there are obvious parallels, no attempt is made to repeat contextual references.

Samantha

Samantha entered the Faculty of Education at age twenty-three with an honours degree in French which included a year at a university in France. Both her parents had once been teachers and she grew up in an affluent urban district. Her poise, physical presence, and rich vocabulary augured well for her success in teaching. In addition she possessed a thorough and confident knowledge of her discipline.

In her first Section 11 class, Samantha recited the following 'background information' to the group: 'I hated all my French teachers until fourth-year university. Then I got one I liked, like really loved, and decided to go into teaching French to make it better.' Samantha seemed to have a sense of mission to make amends for the wrongs she believed had been done to her. When asked by other group members why she had continued to specialize in French in spite of her alleged hatred of her teachers through three levels of schooling, she hesitated and then said, 'I like French and anyway I always wanted to show them.' It was the first hint of the difficult struggle she would have integrating her interpretation of her personal history to which she clung fiercely with her anticipations and theories about teaching, and the actual experiences and opportunities for learning in the pre-service programme. Samantha's personal history, as told by her, seemed to ground her sense of possibility and simultaneously to limit her will to act upon new conceptions of teaching and learning. Samantha spoke frequently of her hate for all teachers in her growing-up years and felt often during practice teaching sessions that she was hated by students as an inevitable outcome of simply 'being a teacher'. Indeed 'hate' was a word that clanged with disturbing regularity in both her spoken and written accounts of both past and present school experience. Being hated for being a teacher, Samantha connected readily with both her personal experience and her socio-economic background. She spoke of 'very, very negative memories of school', 'never feeling any emotion for any teacher ever', 'solely indifferent to teachers'. This is overshadowed and contradicted by her blunt claims that she 'hated all teachers...just because they were a teacher I hated them'. To her frustration, however, she found herself early in her pre-service year inclined to imitate the very teachers she professes to have hated. Ironically, she returned to the comfort she believed could be obtained in a classroom through rigid control.

> I'm more frustrated with myself because I don't, I'm falling back on teaching I had. I'm falling back on somebody standing up in front of the classroom, writing things on the board and saying 'write this down, copy this' and that's what I fall back on a lot.

Samantha appears to have carried forward into her pre-service year interpretations of her experience which shaped a distinct and limiting notion of 'teaching'; one in which teachers were to be authoritarian and students were to be in rows copying. She found optional models in her faculty classes and in her first practice-teaching session. The highly individualized and relaxed approach of her first associate seemed to her 'sensitive to children's needs'. She admired this practice in which peer tutoring and conferencing were emphasized, though she expressed surprise that conferencing is considered teaching. *Real* teaching, for Samantha (as for many beginning teachers) seems closely, often solely, connected to the transmission model. She claimed interest in various teaching styles but as the year unfolded she felt anything other than transmission was increasingly beyond her capabilities.

After this first session, by which she judged all further practice-teaching experience, Samantha wrote in her journal:

> Much to my amazement, I discovered that I actually enjoyed teaching...well maybe not so much the 'teaching', but certainly being with children was a very rewarding experience...I think because of my feelings of confidence that many discipline problems didn't manifest themselves, simply because the children sensed that I wouldn't put up with them. This unfortunately was also a shortcoming that I sensed because I felt a need to be in control all the time. I think that this will change as I become more secure with teaching and with my teaching style and more able to relinquish some of the strict control of the class.

Samantha never got to a point in the practicum sessions where she felt in control in spite of the reassurances of her associates and faculty professors. Simultaneously she resisted the idea of taking control. She seemed trapped self-consciously between the most vivid role-models she had from her past, and her resentment about the experience she feels was, and is, generated by these very models. Her limited definition of *teaching* was common among her peers. Two aspects of teaching seemed not only outside of, but even alien to, 'teaching' in her mind. Co-curricular programmes and the extended life of the school as an institution seemed to her separate from teaching. She and other classmates considered these to be interferences and interruptions rather than genuine learning opportunities organically connected with classroom experiences. More significantly, child advocacy and caring for children seemed at odds with control and class management. In this respect, Samantha and many of her classmates exemplified Lortie's findings (1975). After her third practicum, she says:

> I made a lot of mistakes with the kids because I wanted to be nice to them and you can't be nice, you can't be as nice as I

wanted to be. Like I wanted to just talk to them and reason with them and you can't...

She resisted and resented even mentioning the words 'discipline' or 'classroom management' in describing her struggles to teach, and seemed particularly conscious of students whom she felt were not getting a fair deal from the associate, the programme, and especially from herself: 'I had to kick one girl out because she was laughing too much, which I felt awful about doing. I swore I'd never do that but I couldn't get her to stop...and so she hated me for the rest of the time that I was there.'

After her fourth practice teaching session, she speaks about a 'mixed up' girl of thirteen who 'reminded me so much of myself, and she hated me and I wanted her to know that I really understood, only I couldn't. You couldn't because it just wouldn't work.' In spite of some evidence that there were ways to reconcile caring and control demonstrated by associates and discussed in faculty classes, Samantha's claim was always, 'I didn't know how to, what to do with it, no one teaches us how.' The sense that teacher education may have little impact on teaching (Hargreaves, 1981) seemed all too pertinent. This desire to nurture and care for children, which was always spoken of as outside the act of teaching for Samantha, seemed to be distorted somewhat by her personal resentments about her own background, a resentment fairly vivid in her description of her approach to an elementary school in an upper middle class district.

> I can't deal with their attitudes. I don't like upper class. I don't like them because I went in...with the opinion that they would all be running around in Treehorn running shoes and Cotton Ginny and Roots and they all were...and I didn't give them a chance to be nice. They weren't, they weren't nice kids. They didn't like me and I didn't, I tried not to dislike them but it's very difficult to deal with hostility from people you don't even know who just hate you because you're there.

Samantha deliberately chose to be employed for her first year of teaching in one of the most demanding high-density/low-income elementary school districts in the Metropolitan Toronto region. She claimed that the kids there were 'more real' and it seemed probable that in her choice there was an attempt to deny, reject or compensate for her own background and schooling. Her alleged goal remained as it had been seven months earlier: to improve the quality of teaching. Samantha, as most Section 11 members, exemplified Jackson's (1986) conviction that

> It is perfectly clear that the knowledge culled from prior experience in school is there as a potential resource to be drawn

upon by all who face the demands of teaching...it provides a set of norms for the would-be teacher, a veritable scrapbook of memories about how teachers in the past have acted and, therefore, how one might oneself act in a similar situation.

Student-teachers have spent a very long time in classrooms as students and many have rigid notions that prevent clear observation and reflection about the classrooms they visit in their new capacity as teachers. In teacher education there is often an assumption made that students will be able to 'read the classroom' but an accurate reading may be blocked by prior experience and the personal interpretation of that experience.

Samantha's conviction that 'it was just me standing up there totally out of control' did not jibe with the associate teachers' assessments which included such comments as 'well-prepared', 'good rapport with students' and 'sensitivity to the needs of individual students'—all evidence of a degree of 'readiness' to begin the first year. Samantha, like many student teachers, was reluctant or unwilling to probe any further in discussion with an associate teacher who had given her the 'good assessment' she deemed necessary for employment. It seems that Samantha's vision of 'control' was more absolute than that of her associate teachers. This absoluteness, paradoxically combined with her resistance to undertake responsibility for power in students' lives, is vividly portrayed in her description and interpretation of one difficult moment in her third session.

> But there are kids with chips on their shoulders and they're not going to like you no matter what you do. There was one boy who did badly on a math test and you can't be subjective about marking a math test. You either do well or you don't and it's not a question of grey areas where maybe he could have gotten another mark but he just, he hated me and he was such a problem and I couldn't reason with him, like I couldn't make him see that he had failed the math test, it wasn't me it was him, but no, it was my fault that he had failed the math test, and because I'd failed him, he couldn't be a prefect for the school and he couldn't, like he blamed me for everything and it got to the point where I couldn't even have him in my class, like he'd come in and I'd say, 'George, get out' without any or very little provocation and it was hard 'cause I'd never been disliked by a kid before this.

When Samantha was asked to describe moments when she felt successful, they turned out to be times when she exerted considerable authority to the apparent satisfaction of her students. Once she made an unruly class sit and read with complete quiet for half an hour and 'they all just thought it was wonderful and that was the very nicest moment'. In a particularly 'difficult grade seven enrichment class':

> I came in and said, 'There are things I will not tolerate. I won't tolerate noise when I tell you to work'. . . and it would take an hour to get them on tasks. And then the second hour would be marvellous. When they were on tasks they were very into what they were doing. . .

By the end of the pre-service year, Samantha gave a blunt assessment of her own readiness:

> I really really feel not equipped to go out next year. And every practice teaching I feel less confident. . . Next year when I'm a teacher, people will expect me to be a part of this school and to know things and I know nothing. I don't know anything.

Samantha had a very difficult Fall term as a first-year teacher. Indeed she seemed well on her way to catching 'the debilitating disease of teaching' (Hargreaves, 1978). While she admits to herself that there were young teachers doing well with classes as difficult as hers, she felt more defeated and conspired against by the school system than enabled by it. By October she was meeting for an hour every morning with the vice-principal. She often began the day in class after these sessions had brought her to tears. She felt penalized for asking for help. Nevertheless, it is during this period that she began to establish some clarity about her personal history and her teaching style.

At the second symposium Samantha announced that she had resigned from her teaching position and that indeed her resignation had been requested by her Board. She responded to our questionnaire about current practices:

> Most of my class is teacher-directed. I don't understand how to implement discovery/activity-centered learning. . . Transmission seems to be my 'safety' mechanism. I fall back into it when I feel that things are out of control. It is not how I want to teach, I just don't know how else to do it. . . I was starting to view my kids as obstacles to my happiness rather than as children who were suffering from my trauma.

> Part of the reason that I am having so much trouble is that I am not *ready to see myself as different from my students*. I have discovered that in order to survive, *you have to become a teacher—play the role—and I am not comfortable with it*. (emphasis in original)

The phenomenon, often referred to in the lore of teacher education as 'getting to the other side of the desk' was particularly difficult for Samantha. Much of her talk about 'hating' was probably generated by a clash of perceptions. Samantha continued to see herself as a student, identifying with students 'against' teachers. Associates saw her as a beginning *teacher* and students wanted and expected her to behave as a *grown-up*, a teacher who knew what she was about. This transition is exaggerated in the case of Samantha but one that is difficult for many young teachers resisting not only the mantle of teaching but the more general, and sometimes terrifying one, of adulthood with its attendant responsibilities. What Levinson *et al.* (1978) call 'entering the Adult World', personally and professionally is frequently extremely difficult for young beginning teachers such as Samantha.

Samantha has been doing supply teaching since the beginning of January and she is finding it a restorative and healing process in which she is discovering a much broader range of classroom environments. In addition, she is learning to interact with other professionals as a colleague rather than as a student. It seems that she was not only driven by her own history but restricted by it. Her sense of practice was derived from the constructions by which she made sense of the pre-service experience. These constructions were clearly limiting. Samantha exhibited many of the skills considered necessary for effective teaching. For instance, one associate describes her as a teacher with 'a warm, friendly manner, who gave positive encouragement and constructive criticism'. Her 'pupils were treated with respect, kindness and fairness at all times. She worked successfully in whole class and small group and individual situations'. It appears, however, that Samantha's personal credo would not allow her to make much use of her capacity to impose order in the classroom. Her repeated resistance to this awareness led her to feel out of control and lacking other methodology in her teaching repertoire. Lortie (1975) has suggested that young teachers need to take more cognitive control over prior experiences. How could the pre-service programme have moved Samantha toward this goal? Samantha represents the group of students perhaps most in need of a developmental and cohesive practicum experience with much talking time with professors and associates as helping colleagues. Samantha has seriously considered leaving teaching but her supply teaching experience is giving her a chance to study herself and to experiment with methodology in environments in which the stakes are not so high as in a full-time position. As Maeroff (1988) observes:

> A stronger and surer knowledge base and a greater command of methodology contribute to a teacher's power. They lend authority of the sort that allows a person to teach with confidence and to command the respect of students and col-

leagues. This is not power of the sort that makes people jump when fingers are snapped; rather it is the power that will enhance the education of students coming in contact with such a teacher.

Samantha entered teacher education with a sound background in her subject of specialization and in general academic knowledge as well. What she lacked, as most beginning teachers do, was a command of methodology. Unfortunately tensions largely unresolved from her own experience as a child and as a student and the personal meaning she extracted from those experiences blocked her from much learning that would have been possible in her pre-service year. Now, after considerable trial by fire, she has, by joining the supply-teaching contingent, put herself in a position to develop more self-awareness and some command of methodology. At the time of writing Samantha planned to resume full-time teaching.

Shelagh

Shelagh appeared from the beginning to be a promising candidate for a collaborative enterprise: many of her forty-five years had indeed been spent in various kinds of collaboration. She had been consistently enthusiastic about the Section 11 project, was pleased that her story was to be shared and regretted that her real name and some of the identifying factors in her pilgrimage toward teaching must be withheld. There are a number of ways in which Shelagh's personal practical knowledge seemed to enable her to learn and even reflect in the pre-service year. 'Reflection', as *Reflection in Teacher Education* (Grimmett and Erickson, 1988) demonstrates, is amenable to many interpretations. Sometimes it seems to indicate reviewing experience and human interaction with the aim of understanding or unpacking its meanings. One element that seems fairly consistent in all the uses of the word 'reflection' is a certain distancing in time or space from an event, or continuum of events, with a view of gaining a clearer and perhaps more profound perspective. In spite of what Selman (1988) calls Schon's 'rather ambiguous terminology' and in spite of the emphasis, justified at least in part, upon skills in pre-service education, 'reflection', among *some* pre-service teachers, appears to take place with some degree of sophistication. Speaking of pre-service teacher education, Gilliss (1988) claims that 'the more subtle discussion of whether or not a particular behaviour is appropriate must come later'. This may not always be the case. A considerable propensity for reflection upon practice is evident in some of the journals and interviews of student teachers whose own personal narratives to date predispose them to reflection on practice in teaching and in other aspects of life, such as parenting.

Shelagh very early presented herself not only as a committed student teacher determined to 'get all that is going out of the Faculty' but also as an enabler of her classmates. She was consistently support- ive of others and able to help and collaborate in a manner which, in spite of her clearly rich personal background and experience, did not seem to threaten or antagonize her peers. 'Our stories are the masks through which we can be seen, and with every telling we stop the flood and swirl of thought and someone can get a glimpse of us' (Grumet, 1987). The following information was volunteered by She- lagh on the first day of class. The aspects of her life she chose to share on that occasion were, like everyone else's, highly subjective and selective.

> I taught kindergarten in Jamaica for three years. My mother is in her eighties and still teaching. I have taught ESL in schools and especially to my husband who is Italian and used to threaten to go back to Italy. Now that our house is all reno- vated and beautiful—he did a lot of it himself—and the com- pany he owns is doing well, I know he's free of that nonsense. My son is 12 and my daughter is 10. They are a delight and fully supportive of my finally getting a chance to do my own thing. My favourite avocations are, and always have been, reading and listening to music.

Some of the 'background living' Shelagh did *not* mention early on include her BA from an American university and her MA in French from a Canadian one. Also unclaimed was her work experience as a remedial-reading teacher to adults with learning disabilities, as an accountant in a well-known Toronto firm and as an administrative assistant in a manufacturing company. During her junior placement, Shelagh wrote a long descriptive journal. She missed only one day when she described herself as exhausted with her 'own kids getting on her nerves'. On all other evenings she wrote expansively, often ques- tioning herself as to why she had done certain things when she 'knew better' and deliberating as to how to improve the following day. These contemplated improvements interestingly were not exclusively in regard to class management, timing, or control but often reminders to 'thank' a child for assistance or to try to 'reach' another youngster she felt had not participated. A sensitivity to individual students and a tendency to call them by name when discussing programme, routines, and curriculum enlivened her journal. In her effort to bring the dis- parate experiences of attendance at the Faculty of Education and the practicum together, Shelagh filled countless pages describing in in- finite detail the layout of the school, its smell and feel, the interaction among staff members and between staff members and students. She explained with precision not only the programme but the extra- curricular activities. She brought photographs of the school and 'her children' back to the faculty so that her co-researchers could picture her in context. Whether or not Shelagh is familiar with the feminist slogan that the personal and political must conflate, she exhibits a strong need to blend her personal and professional lives—past and present.

> I was privileged to have my mother as my teacher and the enthusiasm she generated made me want to learn. I have children of my own and the glee in their eyes when they finally understand a problem makes me realize that I can make a difference. This, to me, is what teaching is about.

Shelagh tended to define teaching in terms of learning: her learning under her mother's tutelage, her children's and students' learning with her as guide. During her junior placement, the only faculty member who visited her school hailed her in the corridor and said, 'Hi. How's it going?'. He did not stop long enough for a reply. Faculty professors are often running from school to school as frenzied fire extinguishers: they are 'on call' during the practicum and often, with the best will in the world, do not manage to have many meaningful times in schools with associates and student teachers. The appreciation of both Shelagh and her associate in words and later in letter on the one occasion in another placement when a professor visited, seems convincing evidence of the crying need to 'bridge the gap' and integrate faculty- and school-based experiences.

Shelagh's journal and her practice-teaching reports reveal a high correlation between the content of journal writing and the school-based associate's reporting. The main differences between the two documents revolved around Shelagh's performance. In both the junior and intermediate placements Shelagh was more adversely critical of herself than were the associate teachers whose reports tended to consist, for the most part, of undiluted praise: 'Mrs Bluebird always gets the best from my students. She has an uncanny way of sensing what's going on with each class. Everything is well-planned but she's not inflexible.'

This was a typical entry. All ended with comments such as 'She'll make a great teacher', or 'I wish she would join our staff'. Shelagh herself was less than satisfied with certain aspects of her teaching. This was a fairly representative response among the older student teachers who often had unrealistically high standards for themselves. Whether these high standards were engendered from the larger context of their lives in which they saw themselves defined; from a habitual habit of modesty peculiar to their generation and culture; or from a fear that having been away from formal schooling for a number of years, they were rusty and out of date; or from a combination of these or from other factors entirely, one can only conjecture. The key may be nothing more complex than the inflation in grades that has occurred over the past decade. It could be that associate teachers measure the performance of older students with fuller life experience and often well-developed critical thinking skills against a backdrop of the student teacher who has recently completed his or her first degree. Much more research is needed in this regard. After all, Samantha was harsher on herself during the pre-service year than were her associate teachers. These estimates were only reversed when she entered her first year of teaching and did not have an inherited classroom into which to fit.

In all assignments throughout her pre-service year and in the eight months which then ensued, Shelagh used the personal experience of family not only as the portal through which to enter teaching but also as the support system which made her confident and determined to remain in her chosen profession. Throughout her time at the faculty, Shelagh made regular reference to mother, children, husband and mother-in-law virtually as co-travellers on her educational journey toward becoming a teacher. In Symposium Two, she once again identified her mother as her inspiration to become a teacher and more generally as her touchstone when her determination faltered.

> As you all know, my mother taught us until we were ten and then we had to go to high school at a boarding school. I remember she took us to the school, it was about four hours from home and the last thing she said to me was 'You're a big girl now, you will survive'.

> The scene was repeated at the airport as I left for university: 'You're a big girl now, you will survive'. Now as my classes are large and as I'm leaning more to written work as the kids are bad at group work and as I find myself yelling when there's chaos and things get out of control and I wonder what I'm doing there, 'You're a big girl now. You will survive.' Those words are my pride and joy. Not in a literal sense any more but symbolically. When I get down and low with the quantity of work, the number of children, the lack of control, I think of my mother's words and I brace myself for the future.

Shelagh's comments in her own home over coffee (18 February 1989) sum up her perception of herself and her work at the present stage.

> It is so much harder than I thought. And we run into more roadblocks and difficulties than I thought possible. I'm so much more tired when I get home than I anticipated. I'm cheerful by nature but sometimes I get mad having so many classes to deal with and the kids—*nouveau riche* Italian—like mine, I guess, obstinately praying in Italian—not French the

way they're supposed to. I need my mother's courage and I need my mentor. The principal just showed me my room and didn't tell me anything. He was completely indifferent to me and I'm not used to that. Then I found this wonderful old teacher who knows everything and who took me under her wing. She showed me a way, a loophole in the timetable, where I could get 40 minutes some days with classes and miss them entirely the next day so I have fewer kids per day and can get to know them better. I'm so lucky to have this amazing woman. I've written to my mother in Jamaica about her. She and the project of course have saved my sanity and I'm determined never to quit but it's not easy.

Finally, Shelagh is one of several in Section 11 who entered the faculty in midlife and were generally positive about their experiences there and in the schools. They have led us to question the terminology of Sikes *et al.* (1985). She refers for example, to 'late entrants' as if there were some kind of normal or proper time to enter teaching. For some people entering teacher education in midlife may be 'right on time'. Midlife entrants rarely seem to conform to descriptions of their age-mates in studies such as those of Sikes *et al.* (1985), or Huberman (1989). In addition, some older (not necessarily 'late') entrants did not seem to follow the celebrated sequence of concern for self, concern for curriculum, and finally concern for students as central to their teaching view (Fuller, 1969). Rather all three concerns seemed to be interwoven and operating in concert in their motivation, behaviour, practice and reflection upon that practice.

Jason

Jason was eager to talk about himself from the beginning and he told what he called 'his story' or parts thereof at every opportunity. He confirmed the well-documented stereotype that in gender-mixed classes, males speak much more frequently than females. It was difficult to silence Jason; he was enthusiastic about the process of becoming a teacher and well-liked in Section 11 in spite of his repeated interruptions when others spoke.

This is a very small excerpt from what he said to the group on the first day:

Me? Well, I love food, the outdoors, and my wife. I think I want to be a teacher as much as I want to be a father which is a helluva lot. I think that like if you give kids a chance they'll come through for you. I worked in a band and sometimes they'd goof off but if you got through to them they'd sure show up next time.

This was the first of Jason's recitals about his 'fitness to practice.' He was twenty-nine and said 'I've got no time to lose. I've gotta make up for the time I wasted.' 'Look, I've got no time for bitching: I'm here to learn something.' These were typical refrains in his conversations in class, in interviews and in written work.

In spite of his obsession with time past and time wasted, he did not, like so many of his classmates, consider the faculty year 'a waste of time'. He described the first practicum with a shrug:

> Rough, but pretty OK I guess. The kids were great. The associate was a bit of an ass hole but he meant well and you gotta run into those once in a while, ya know.

> I don't care how any of you moan—we need at least two years in this place to get ready. I think there are great people in this place. My associate don't agree—he says all you ever learn you learn in the field. Well that's bullshit. Just think about it. I taught this guy a thing or two. Like he thought silence was golden. Language Arts—you know but no real language, no talking or stuff—the poor kids they were dying to talk and when I took over they got lots of chance to talk (laughter from the group).

In general, Jason approved of his associates, calling one a 'great lady' and another an 'awesome woman who just knew everything—I mean everything about those kids'. He tended to view the practicum as a two-way street—readily conceding that he had much to learn yet confident that he had an important contribution to make. On Monday morning after his third and, from his point of view, least satisfying, practicum (the associate wrote that Jason was 'barely ready for teaching'), Jason told the group:

> Look, of course we're not ready for teaching. We're kidding ourselves but the way the system is we gotta pretend we're ready—just go and do it. Anyway, I've had better associates and I can tell you one thing—my classroom environment is gonna be better than the one I was just in.

Jason had an overwhelming desire to 'feel good' about himself and he wanted everyone else to 'feel good too'. In aid of 'feeling good' and cheering up about jobs (the faculty was pulsating with the fear of signing on 'too early' and missing a more desirable position or leaving it 'too late' and getting nothing 'decent'), Jason organized a Christmas-season party and most class members and some professors (all who taught Section 11 were invited) attended. After this event several class objections, such as 'he always interrupts', 'he swears too much: he can't do that next year' and 'his grammar stinks I wouldn't want him teaching my kid', ceased. His ability to engender a cohesive feeling, his home-made wine generously shared, succeeded in breaking down the barriers against him which some class members had begun to erect. After the final practicum Jason said:

> I couldn't have hit a better spot. I'm really torn now. I know we need more training here but I want to get my feet wet: I want to get out there. Anyhow—I've got no choice—we're pregnant, I think.

It appeared that Jason's desires for fatherhood and teaching expressed on day one were about to be fulfilled in tandem.

Jason asked questions about how to educate teachers—recognizing that 'one year was too short' on the one hand and expressing his eagerness to be 'in the school with the kids where it's really at' on the other. He made every effort to bridge the gap between faculty classes and practicum but his struggle pointed to the need for some very different 'options for the future' (Fullan and Connelly, 1990). As the year progressed it became increasingly difficult for reflective faculty members to defend the 'status quo' in teacher education in the face of the honest struggle, openly expressed by student/teacher/researchers such as Jason.

While Jason talked and wrote a great deal about what he considered his aptitudes and attitudes, and provided infinite detail about practice teaching in journal form, in class discussions and in interviews, he did not say much about his own past until the August symposium.

Listening to others, as he had eventually learned to do quite well, he began to clarify for the group, and perhaps more consciously than before for himself, some of the sources of his obsessive desire to teach.

> OK—I never told this before—I wasn't ashamed—or was I? I can't really say. However—a lot of you—the guys anyway—and some women too I think would rather be doctors or lawyers or something society values more but not me. Teaching is it for me. No 1 and the next 9 too. I've got a lot of stuff to settle and teaching's where I can do it. I'm no 'A' student—well that part I've told some of you before and while I'm very deep, I'm not what you'd call an intellectual but I'm a helluva lot closer to it than I used to be. I dropped French— OK—in Grade 10 and the teacher stopped me in the hall and said—'Hey you dropped French, eh? I didn't expect that!' That's all. Curtains. No—please come back—nothing. So at the beginning of Grade 12 I just stopped going entirely to anything—nobody called—nobody cared—then I just got a letter saying you are officially withdrawn. Game over. End of

show. I never felt so alone. If somebody would've listened to me, talked to me I would have stayed on. And I don't think it was for the best and I don't think I learned more knocking around. I've got a hang-up on this age thing. I wasted a lot of my life. The women who are older here have done worthwhile things like have kids or be a lawyer but the only worthwhile thing I did was go back to night school and take it from there. My parents are worse off, my wife's worse off, all that. I'm happy now. At last I'm happy. In fact from the minute I got accepted to the faculty I've been happy. That's why none of you know I didn't used to be happy—I never fit in anywhere. Not dumb enough to put up with jobs I could get. Not smart—read that enough university credits—to get anywhere else. Well—what I can do with my life is a lot now. It'll break my heart if a kid drops out and if their parents are working class and don't care. I'll be there for them and the really troubled kids with ambitious parents off in Hawaii neglecting their kids—those are the ones I can help. You don't learn a damned thing in the school of hard knocks—just that you screwed up.

Afterwards, in explaining that 'he felt better', 'he'd come clean', 'he was on a high', he added thoughtfully:

I'd never have told you guys any of this at the faculty or anywhere near that building. We had to get out of there. Here, where we're together in a different setting it just seemed natural to tell you. We're not in competition any more. We're all friends—we're all off on this journey together. And even Jill and Julie and Andrew who decided to do something a bit different, decided to do that, they had job opportunities and they're here today and they're all going to teach full time soon. [Two demurred at this point, but Jason continued undaunted.] I can't believe how we lucked into this project.

At Symposium Two Jason told the group that he'd never been so tired or so happy. He'd chosen to teach in an area that turned out to be much like Samantha's in terms of student population. In other ways the school climate and his position in it were entirely different.

Hey, what is all this about evaluation? Nobody's come into my class yet. The principal and a couple of teachers have asked, 'How's it going?' and I say, 'Great' and that's it. Now a bunch of you know it's not always that great cause I phone you for moral support and stuff and you always come through for me and I hope I come through for you. Like—how could we manage without that support system? I'm not telling any-body at school about my problems. Do you think I'm nuts? The kids like me, the parents, the ones I've met, like me and I just keep my door shut. The kids come to me about all sorts of personal stuff and I love that and I tell them personal stuff too. They all pooled money and bought the baby a teddy and wrote poems for the baby and are all caught up in my life too. Isn't that great?

Now I see everyone else has this wisdom of practice thing and I've only got a page and a half, double-spaced cause I had no time to write but I hope this time I can just do my research on me with my pictures. I've got separate pictures of me with each kid and then group pictures and each kid is in at least one group picture so you can see them in action and yeah the hospital baby pictures too. I'll write something for next time though and even today I'll write 'cause I take this research stuff really seriously.

The isolation described by Fullan (1982) is expressed forcefully by this teacher/researcher. Nobody ventured to ask serious questions or come into his class and he wasn't taking any chances. He was suf-ficiently elated and discouraged by turns that he had need of group members with whom, as many of them say repeatedly, 'It doesn't matter how dumb we look, we know each other. It's safe, not like in your own school.'

The need to stay in touch with peers and faculty members is clear but the need for on-site mentoring rather than threatening early eva-luation may be desperately needed too. Samantha's response to Jason's assessment is telling:

How could you be so lucky? That damned woman (the vice principal) never got out of my room. It's like she didn't trust me and the kids picked up on that and they thought they could get away with anything with me 'cause I wasn't a real teacher or something.

Jason and most members of the group gave Samantha strong support. They were all 'down' on that 'damned woman' who had hurt their colleague. Jason's 'story' thus far may sound like a success story but it raises many questions. He clearly revels in the 'social work' side of teaching. What is the significance of this aspect of his interaction with kids? He does not have the confidence either in himself or in the support and/or professionalism of the other teachers or administrators to discuss, let alone collaborate, with them. How healthy a situation is this? What kind of non-threatening intervention might be helpful?

Felicia

Felicia was thirty-five when she came to the Faculty. She speaks and writes beautifully, has taught dance, sings in two choirs and is in her own words 'in love with art'. She is the mother of four and said the first day:

> I don't feel guilty about staying home with my children. I've really loved the years when they were small and all the adventures we've had together. I know I love kids. I know from experience and from teaching dance on the side. I know the satisfaction I get from teaching other children besides my own and sharing in their sense of accomplishment.

Felicia never pushed her opinions on the group, was a good listener and wrote and illustrated a detailed and thorough journal about her junior placement. One of her practicum placements was in a school she had attended as a student and she had the class in sympathetic laughter when she described the ghosts, most of them 'fairly friendly', from this experience.

Felicia's practice-teaching reports were full of praise. This is typical.

> Ms Redbird prepares carefully and researches the topic. She encourages each child. While she is gentle and speaks fairly quietly, the pupils respond well to her. They didn't want her to leave at the end of two weeks. She says she's weak in math but it didn't show in grade six work. She's very good in language and drama. She knows lots of rhymes and poems off by heart and just works them into her lessons. The pupils were impressed and actually want memory work now so they can do what Ms Redbird does.

In retrospect, the only hints in any recorded or written work that Felicia might have any more than the usual difficulties when she began teaching came from single lines, one from each of two practicum reports: 'Ms Redbird is a perfectionist which she may have to curb', and 'Ms Redbird had a little trouble controlling the grade eights when I was out of the room.' Neither of these is a particularly negative statement but they are the only adverse criticism she received from the practicum sessions.

It was with astonishment that we received calls in October from Felicia stating that she was in 'grave difficulty'.

> The parents don't want me and even though the principal likes me, he won't stick up for me and they've got me under some kind of review and the superintendent is after me and I don't

think there's any sense in going to Federation because they'll have been there first and if they want to get rid of me perhaps I should resign first but even if I do I may have the same trouble again because the worst thing about me apparently is that I'm a first year teacher and nobody wants their kids with a first year teacher especially in a split grade and I'll have to be a first year teacher sometime if I'm ever going to teach and they always give split grades to first year teachers so what am I going to do?

Felicia described herself as 'holding on until Symposium Two'. She told her story in great detail, her eyes often filling with tears, but with a great effort to heap the responsibility for what she viewed as abject failure upon herself.

You know when I was young my father was very, very strict and I would get the strap for the tiniest thing. I have tried not to be strict with my own children and I like to reason and discuss things with my class. The parents are so very ambitious for their kids, however, that they don't want them in a split grade, especially the higher of two grades, grade six, because as they tell me 'Sara will be doing grade five work again and that's a waste of time'. When I try to explain my programmes which I really believe I have worked out very carefully, a parent will then say something such as 'This is nothing against you personally but I want my child to have the best education possible and he's not going to get it from a first year teacher. I warned the principal that if he put Karl with a first year teacher, I'd make trouble and there's no excuse for split grades, not with the property taxes we pay.'

After many examples, Felicia turned to us in tears:

What am I going to do? My nerves are shot. I can't sleep. I look back on my old life at home with the children and teaching dance twice a week and reading, acting in amateur plays, seeing my friends and just living. But how can I go back? My oldest is 13—they're all getting older—they won't be there for ever. I want a career of my own. I loved my practicum sessions: everyone says I was fine then. What's wrong with me? What should I do next?

Felicia's first term had several alarming elements in common with other beginning teachers' experiences. The perceptions that no parent wants her or his child with a beginning teacher and that first year teachers get the toughest classes become all too familiar. The feeling among many experienced teachers that they 'had it tough' and that new teachers have to 'win their spurs' or 'slay their own dragons' seems disturbingly prevalent.

Some Tentative Conclusions

It may be possible to learn in two or three years the kind of practice which then leads to another twenty years of learning. Whether many of our colleges get many of their students on to that fascinating track or whether the schools are geared to a thoughtful support of such learning by their teachers is another matter. (Hawkins, 1973:150)

One of the touchstones of the present research has been hope for the 'fascinating track' suggested by Hawkins. The Section 11 project at this point yields at worst discouraging, and at best uncertain, indications about the present ability of faculties of education and schools working in concert to provide educational and experiential programmes to get beginning teachers on this track. The present study suggests a number of changes in the present structure and climate of teacher education.

First, the need for a cohesive pre-service component to teacher education. The burden for making connections between the faculty programme and the practicum is too heavy and unwieldy for most student teachers. The physical separation of mentors (professors and associates) fragments the programme. Student teachers describe themselves as 'falling between two chairs'. They often find conflicting views of teaching/learning embodied in their mentors representing systems ignorant, or at least unsupportive, of each other's imperatives. Beginning teachers often struggle to reconcile opposing philosophies and face another 'great divide'. An exception to this brutalization of the pre-service year was expressed by one student the day she returned from a practicum:

I finally got a placement in the kind of school *our* professor talks about and for the first time, it turned out that half the teachers actually knew our teacher from the faculty and from workshops 'n stuff. It was fabulous! The two parts of my world came together. I never thought it would happen.

That the student herself had to do the 'connecting', that this experience happened more by chance than design, and that it is rare, an exception, are travesties of our trust. Zeichner (quoted by Fullan, 1982) reminds us that we 'need to study the characteristics of placement sites'. And we need to connect in-faculty studies as closely as possible with practicum experiences. Beginning teachers' self-evaluation differed from the associates' evaluation in the following categories:

—competence in the subject fields
—skill in communication
—planning, organization and teaching methods
—pupil/teacher rapport and pupil involvement
—classroom management

'Planning, organization and teaching methods' was the most contentious category and it was in this area that the most painful and dislocating stories were told. Interestingly enough, however, there was not a high frequency of unfavourable reports from associates in this category. By far the most numerous and dramatic discrepancies were found between actual classroom interaction and practice and a utopia many beginning teachers actually carry around in their heads of the ideal classroom with the ideal, generally unruffled teacher confidently presiding while students strive zealously for success with the work at hand—whatever it may be. This ideal in the head is very often the background against which beginning teachers measure both the reality of classrooms in which they are placed and their own performance and behaviours in these classrooms. It would seem that closer connections among all participants—beginning teachers, faculty associates, school administrators and faculty members—are needed to clarify everyone's perceptions of expectations and behaviour in school settings.

Secondly, the need for the practicum not only to be integrated with the faculty programme but to be developmental (Gilliss, 1988). Not only were the practicum experiences largely isolated from faculty ones, they were disparate one from the other. Four students in this study considered dropping out during the final week of the practicum which was described by all four as 'the worst experience of their lives'. Only the memory of earlier successes and more compatible teaching climates sustained them.

Thirdly, the need for ongoing peer sharing during the first years of teaching. For beginning teachers any personal reflection about their own classroom practice is impeded by their lack of understanding of the possible meanings of what they observe in themselves and others. They need to talk to more experienced teachers, to their professors from the faculty and, as information gleaned at the Symposium in August emphasized, to their classmates from pre-service education with whom they began the journey towards becoming teachers.

In the fourth place, the need for an experienced on site mentor and planned induction and apprenticeship periods for at least the first two years of teaching. Samantha's ever-present authority figure did not seem to help her or her situation but a genuine mentor might have done so. The lack of professional peer conversation, let alone a mentor, left Jason entirely too isolated behind his closed door. The lonely floundering of Felicia and many others spoke eloquently of the need for mentoring and Shelagh's description of the difference locating a mentor has made to her personal and professional journey was typical of the fortunate few who were helped by a 'special' and experienced colleague on a regular and dependable basis (see Fullan and Connelly, 1990).

Finally, this examination of the role of personal knowledge in teacher education and development leads to the conclusion that, as William Faulkner remarked, 'The past is not lost: it is not even past'. 'Eventually there are likely to be changes in the way that those headed into teaching are educated, certified and licensed' (Maeroff, 1988). The findings of the Section 11 project to date add to the general body of evidence that fundamental rethinking of teacher education is overdue. The establishment of a system of collegial mentors, induction and apprenticeship programmes during which beginning teachers would carry smaller loads, and any innovation that will render the road to becoming a teacher more sane and more humane, deserves consideration.

References

BALL, S.J. and GOODSON, I.F. (1985) *Teachers' Lives and Careers*, Lewes, Falmer Press.

BECK, C. (1971) 'Profiles in practical education (3)' in *Moral Education In The Schools*, Toronto, The Ontario Institute for Studies in Education.

COLE, M. (1985) 'The tender trap: commitment and consciousness in entrants to teaching', in BALL, S.J. and GOODSON, I.F. (Eds.) *Teachers' Lives and Careers*, Lewes, Falmer Press.

CONNELLY, F.M. and CLANDININ, D.J. (1988) *Teachers as Curriculum Planners: Narratives of Experience*, New York, Teachers College Press.

FEIMAN-NEMSER, S. (1983) 'Learning to teach', in SHULMAN, L. and SYKES, G. (Eds.), *Handbook of Teaching and Policy*, New York, Longman.

FULLAN, M. (1982), *The Meaning of Educational Change*, Toronto, OISE Press.

FULLAN, M. and CONNELLY, F.M. (1990) *Teacher Education in Ontario: Current Practice and Options for the Future*, Toronto, Ontario Ministry of Colleges and Universities, Queen's Printer.

FULLER, F. (1969) 'Concerns of teachers', in *Harvard Educational Review, 6*, pp. 207–26.

GILLISS, G. (1988) 'Schon's reflective practitioner: A model for teachers?', in GRIMMETT, P. and ERICKSON, G. (Eds.) *Reflection in Teacher Education*, The University of British Columbia, Pacific Educational Press.

GRIMMETT, P.A. and ERICKSON, G.L. (1988) *Reflection in Teacher Education*, The University of British Columbia, Pacific Educational Press.

GRUMET, M.R. (1987) 'The politics of personal knowledge', *Curriculum Inquiry, 17*, 3 pp. 321–9.

HARGREAVES, A. (1978) 'Towards a theory of classroom coping strategies', in BARTON, L. and MEIGHAN, R. (Eds.) *Sociological Interpretations of Schooling and Classrooms*, Driffield, Natterton Books.

HARGREAVES, A. (1981) 'Contrastive rhetoric and extremist talk: Teachers, hegemony and the educationalist context', in BARTON, L. and WALKER, S. (Eds.) *Schools, Teachers and Teaching*, Lewes, Falmer Press.

HAWKINS (1973) 'Learning to teach' in SCHOLMAN, L. and SIKES, G. (Eds.) *Handbook of Teaching and Policy*, New York, Longman.

HUBERMAN, M. (1989) 'Teacher development and teachers' careers', Paper presented at the International Conference Teacher Development Policies, Practices and Research Meeting at OISE, Toronto, February.

INGLIS, F. (1981) *The Promise of Happiness*, Cambridge, Cambridge University Press.

JACKSON, P.W. (1986) *The Practice of Teaching*, New York, Columbia University, Teachers College Press.

LE GUIN, U. (1979) *The Language of the Night*, New York, G.P. Putnam's Sons.

LEVINSON, D.J., DARROW, C., KLEIN, G., LEVINSON, M. and MCKEE, B. (1978) *The Seasons of a Man's Life*, New York, Knopf.

LORTIE, D.C. (1975) *Schoolteacher: A Sociological Study*, Chicago, University of Chicago Press.

MAEROFF, G.L. (1988) *The Empowerment of Teachers*, New York, Columbia University, Teachers College Press.

MITCHELL, W.J.T. (1981) *On Narrative*, Chicago, The University of Chicago Press.

SIKES, P.J., MEASOR, L. and WOODS, P. (1985) *Teachers Careers: Crises and Continuities*, Lewes, Falmer Press.

Chapter 3

Imposed Change and the Experienced Teacher

Patricia J. Sikes

Introduction

A fundamental purpose of education is to prepare young people for life in society, and since societies throughout the world are constantly changing and developing, education can also be expected to change.

There is nothing new about educational change, indeed, change can be seen as the norm, the stable state. What is new though is the rate and frequency with which changes are being introduced and imposed through governmental and state legislation; the way in which these changes reflect a worldwide trend towards centralized control of education; the extent to which they challenge 'the prevailing ethos and assumptions about how education should be delivered' (Broadfoot *et al.*, 1988:266); and the degree to which they directly affect, or at least have implications for, the careers of all teachers, heads/principals, and local authority/district advisers, superintendents and officers. As the Organization for Economic Co-operation and Development (1989) put it:

> [The] contemporary educational and political language is one of 'change', 'reform', and 'improvement'. Scarcely has one set of reforms been formulated, let alone properly implemented, and another is in genesis. (p. 110)

These 'changes', 'reforms', and 'improvements' impact primarily upon teachers.[1] They are the people who have to implement them, even though in the current educational *Zeitgeist* they are unlikely to have been involved in their formulation. What is more, teachers are in the rather strange position of being simultaneously both the subject and the agent of change (Dale, 1988:44; Walker and Barton, 1987:viii). They are required to change themselves and what they do to meet specifications laid down by policy makers who neither know them or the contexts in which they work. They may even be required to make changes which they believe, on the basis of their professional experience, to be inappropriate or impossible. And, inevitably, the very fact that they are required to implement these imposed changes means that their professional freedom and autonomy is further curtailed. Apple (1981, 1987) refers to this as the 'proletarianization' of teachers.

Imposed changes have their origins in a variety or a combination of such factors as economic trends, historical events, different political parties coming into power, social and cultural developments, demographic trends, or technological advances (see Levin, 1976). However, behind these factors and motivating all changes lies the assumption (which may or may not be justifiable) that all is not well and that students are not receiving the best education because teachers and their teaching is inappropriate or inadequate. The interpretation commonly placed on this is that teachers are lacking in knowledge, skills, competences and even sometimes, as Hargreaves (1988) records, personal qualities. The changes are, therefore, introduced in order to remedy the 'deficiencies' in the teachers and their teaching, and are ostensibly to help teachers to 'develop' and 'improve', i.e. they are compensatory. However, it is important to note that teachers are a convenient scapegoat. There are a lot of them and they do, undeniably, play a part in the task of preparing the young for the world. Nevertheless, surely it would be over-emphasizing their influence to lay all ills at their door.

Official sources express recognition of the complexity of teaching at the present time. For example, HMI in England and Wales noted that: 'The school teacher's task is increasingly complex and demanding' (DES, 1983); and OECD ministers issued a press communiqué stating that;

> The tasks of teachers are today more complex and demanding than in the past. They have to respond to the wishes of parents regarding educational outcomes, the social need for wider access to education, and pressures for more democratic participation within the schools. (1985:46)

Even so, further changes add to the complexity and teachers are continually required variously to alter their administrative and organizational systems, their pedagogy, curriculum content, the resources and technology they use, and their assessment procedures. And in so doing they are required to acknowledge their 'inadequacies'.

What do these imposed changes mean for teachers, for their perceptions and experiences of teaching? And what are the implications for the realization of the changes themselves?

Attempts to impose change on teachers, teaching and the nature and processes of schooling have been notoriously unsuccessful (Hargreaves and Dawe, 1989; Huberman and Miles, 1984). I am going to argue that this is because they have usually taken a generalized, 'hyper-rational' (Wise, 1977) approach and have failed to take a realistic view which acknowledges that (a) teachers are, first and foremost, people, and (b) schools are social institutions. (I would also suggest that they have failed because they have not addressed the root cause of the 'problem', because that is not always teachers—but that's another story.)

Fullan (1982:24–6) notes that the crux of change is how individuals come to terms with the reality of the change in the context of their familiar framework of reality. In other words, their interpretation of what the change means for them influences what they subsequently do and how they do it. 'Educational change depends on what teachers think and do—it's as simple and as complex as that' (Fullan, 1982:107). Thus, in order to gain some understanding of what the change means to teachers and their inclination to adapt to (or accept or be motivated towards it) it is necessary to find out how they see and experience their work and 'how much importance they attached to (it) in the first place' (Tipton, 1988:5), i.e. prior to the change. This is especially significant given the number of people who work in even a small school. Each one has their own personal perception and experience of their work and of the school. Consequently each experiences their own version of change, to a greater or lesser extent (Gray, 1980; 1988). As Westoby notes, educational institutions are 'riddled with intentions, through, with and against which they must operate' (1988:x). Any imposed change is subject to the effect of these intentions which means that there is often a great gulf between rhetoric and reality, between what is intended by the authors of the change and how the change actually turns out (see Barker-Lunn, 1970; Dale, 1988; Sharp and Green, 1972; Troyna, 1985). Realization changes the change as the change changes the situation in which it is realized.

What Imposed Change Means for Teachers

Imposed change may focus upon various areas of school life and, thereby, on various aspects and combinations of teachers' working conditions, practice, knowledge, skills, expertise, beliefs, understandings and qualities. Yet as I have suggested, it is not a one-way process, for the implementation of change is influenced by the teachers' ideologies: in other words, by the beliefs and values, the body of ideas which they hold about education, teaching, the schooling process in particular and life in general. This means that it is not possible to attempt to change one aspect without affecting all the others. As Hargreaves wrote, 'changing the teacher...involves changing the person...(and, therefore) changing the life' (Hargreaves, 1988). Those responsible for imposing change have usually failed to recognize this. They have failed to recognize the nature of teaching, that lives are not neatly compartmentalized and the fact that teachers comprise a heterogeneous group in terms of their lives, beliefs and values.

What I want to do in this section is look at four areas which I believe are especially significant when it comes to understanding what imposed changes mean to teachers. These areas are predicated on a particular view of people which, to quote Hargreaves:

> rests upon a regard for the importance of the active, interpret-ing self in social interaction; for the way it perceives, makes sense of and works upon the actions of others and the situation in which it finds itself; the way it pursues goals and tries to maximize its own (often competing) interests; the way it pur-sues these things by combining or competing with other selves; the way it adjusts to circumstances while still trying to fulfil or retrieve its own purposes (1988:216).

Following this view teachers can be seen as people who make up their own minds; people who are pro- rather than re-active; who choose a particular course of action or strategy because it seems to them to serve their purpose. The areas are:

1 Teachers as people
2 Teachers' aims and purposes
3 Work context and conditions
4 Work culture

Traditionally these areas have been considered in isolation, both by researchers and by policy makers. However, a holistic approach is essential to what is, after all, a holistic situation. A compartmentalized approach will prove inadequate and problematic. Having said that, I am now, somewhat contradictorily, going to look at the areas indi-vidually, not because I see them as separate but for ease of presenta-tion and as a framework for comprehension. I shall then put the areas together and consider specifically what imposed change can mean for the life experience of mid-career teachers.

1. Teachers as People

The teachers I am considering here are *people* who happen to be teachers. Teaching is their job of work, their paid occupation. What-ever their motives for entering the profession, and these vary (Lawn and Ozga, 1981; Lortie, 1975; Sikes, 1986; Sikes, Measor and Woods, 1985), teaching and being a teacher is a part, not the whole, of their lives. It fits in, affects and is affected by other parts.

The things that happen to us throughout our lives have an in-fluence on the sort of people we become, upon our perspectives, understandings and attitudes, our beliefs and values, our ideologies and philosophies, and the actions we take. Obviously, life experiences influence the sorts of teachers people become, and the sorts of teachers they want to be and be seen as being (Butt, *et al.*, 1986; Crow, 1987a and b; Denscombe, 1985; Hatton, 1988; Invargson and Greenway, 1984; Knowles, 1988; Lacey, 1977; Lortie, 1975; Nias, 1984; 1988; Smith, *et al.*, 1986).

Life experiences are of different kinds. There are those which are idiosyncratic and personal, dependent upon the sorts of circumstances we individually live in: for example, experiences springing from our family and domestic backgrounds. Others have a more definite and obvious historical determination, such as a war or a particular *Zeitgeist* (Huberman, 1988; Sikes, 1988a and b).

Educational ideologies and philosophies are rooted in history and go in and out of fashion. Initial teacher education reflects these fashions and, as pupils in school, future teachers experience the fashions of previous years (Dale, 1977; Denscombe, 1982; Sachs and Smith, 1988; Zeichner and Grant, 1981). Different generations of teachers, therefore, come into contact with different ideas which can be expected to have some influence on their ideologies and approaches to teaching, and on their expectations of what a teaching career involves. This is not to say that teachers get struck in time-warps, they do change their ideas if it seems appropriate and beneficial (see Ball, 1981; Holly *et al.*, 1987; Troyna, 1985), but rather to acknow-ledge that certain experiences can be formative.

Many life experiences are associated with the particular life-cycle stage we have reached. Various approaches to the study of the life-cycle have demonstrated that different ages have their associated biological, psychological and social aspects and characteristics (see Levinson *et al.*, 1978, for example).

While at no time do I intend to suggest that teachers are a straightforwardly homogeneous group, research shows that there is a teacher life-cycle (see Ball and Goodson, 1985; Huberman, 1988; Mil-ler *et al.*, 1982; Peterson, 1964). Teachers of a similar age and sex share similar experiences, perceptions, attitudes, satisfactions, frustrations and concerns, and the nature of their motivation and commitment alters in a predictable pattern as they get older. There are variations relating to the ethnic group of the teacher, and such differentiating characteristics as type and location of school, subject area, and man-agerial regimes but even so, aspects of this professional life-cycle are common to teachers working in different education systems in differ-ent countries at different times.

Imposed changes can be experienced positively or negatively, depending on how they affect an individual's life experiences. Taking a negative view they can mean that:

- a teacher's initial reasons for being a teacher no longer apply, that their expectations cannot be met, and that their commitment comes to seem misplaced;
- the initial grounding teachers receive and the ideas which underlie their educational ideologies and philosophies go out of fashion and are viewed unfavourably, meaning that teachers are faced with the idea that they have been wrong and may even have disadvantaged their pupils in some way;
- professional and personal life-cycle needs and expectations are not met.

Alternatively and more positively the reverse can be the case.

2. Teachers' Aims and Purposes

Quite obviously teachers' aims and purposes are important influences on their perceptions and experiences of their jobs. Teachers see their role in different ways. For instance: some see their chief purpose to be getting children through examinations; some see themselves as custodians and purveyors or transmitters of particular knowledge or skills or cultural mores; some aim to 'socialize' youngsters; others have an instrumental orientation and see teaching primarily as a means of earning a salary. Most probably subscribe to a mixture, with an emphasis on the aspects they personally value the most.

Although perfect match is rare, teachers ideally find jobs in schools which match their ideologies and philosophies and where they can be the sort of teacher they want to be and be seen as being (see Smith *et al.*, 1986).

Imposed changes which affect the things they value most can mean that teachers can no longer find a match between their aims and purposes and those prevailing in schools. The introduction of comprehensive education in England, for example, was very difficult for many teachers (Beynon, 1985; Riseborough, 1981; Sikes, 1984) to come to terms with. Similarly, some teachers have found it difficult to reconcile the contemporary, often imposed emphasis on vocational training with their aims and purposes as 'liberal educators'. In such cases teachers may feel themselves to have been 'deskilled' (Apple, 1981; 1987); though, alternatively, others may feel 'upskilled' (Ozga and Lawn, 1988:323).

This is not to say that teachers' values are necessarily 'right' or for the greatest good of the greatest number of people. Nevertheless, whatever the case, their perceptions and experiences will be influenced by the extent to which there is congruence between their aims, purposes and values and those pertaining in the systems where they are employed.

3. Work Context and Conditions

> I visited schools where the rain dripped into a bucket on the
> classroom floor, where the teacher reported, 'We sweep the
> mouse droppings off the desks in the morning', where there
> were no staffrooms, or where toilet facilities were archaic and
> cramped. (In one school I was locked in the lavatory but was
> swiftly released by a child who said, 'It always does that so [the
> headmaster] says the person nearest the door in our classroom
> must listen hard and let the teachers out if they get stuck'.)
> Some schools were cold or ill-ventilated, many were dirty or
> badly in need of decoration. To look out of the windows in
> some schools was impossible; in others it was depressing.
> (Nias, 1989:111)

Teachers believe that working conditions adversely affect what they
do, or more precisely what they are able to do (see Hargreaves, Nias,
1989; Poppleton, 1988; Riseborough, 1986). Many teachers face the
daily battle of having to manage with inadequate resources, in inadequate and inappropriate accommodation—Nias' report rings true
for anyone who spends any time visiting schools in Britain. More
significantly and more commonly, *time* is usually at a premium, and
this is especially true when changes are imposed. It is in the nature of
imposed change (as a fast response to a perceived problem) that
teachers are rarely given much (i.e. 'sufficient') time in which to
acquaint themselves with the change and to plan and prepare for it.
Yet time, as a component of conducive conditions, is crucial. As the
OECD (1989) put it:

> (it is not axiomatic) that teachers are to blame if and when
> disappointments arise about educational performance or the
> speed of change. Teachers are the necessary, indeed the most
> necessary, ingredients of quality but still not sufficient to
> guarantee it. They should be given, and should accept, a large
> measure of responsibility but they cannot be held solely
> accountable. Their contribution must be understood in terms
> of the curricular, organizational, and social context in which
> they work. *It needs to be prefaced too by the understanding that that
> contribution depends upon the establishment of conditions conducive to
> sustained high levels of morale and motivation and the full exercise of
> professional development.* (Chapter 1, emphasis added)

(Hargreaves and Dawe, 1989, and Hoyle, 1972, make a similar point.)
   Poor conditions carry messages about the value that is placed
upon the work teachers do. Many teachers believe that if the polit-
icians and administrators valued education they would put more
money in to improving the conditions, thereby enabling teachers to

improve the quality of their teaching. Some, benevolently or naively, put the situation down to ignorance.[2]

Imposed change, with its basis in a deficit model of teachers and teaching inevitably also carries messages about value. Interestingly, a recently imposed change in England and Wales concerning the provision and funding of in-service teacher education, allowing schools which chose to do so to hold INSET days in pleasant hotels, has raised morale, partly because teachers feel that they are valued enough to have money spent on their comfort.

4. Work Culture

The concept of the 'cultures of teaching' is crucial in any consideration of change because it is through these cultures that change is mediated, interpreted and realized. An emphasis over the years on an individualized, isolationist view of teachers prompted David Hargreaves (1980) to write that neglect of the occupational culture of teachers has led us to underestimate (its) significance as a medium through which many innovations and reforms must pass. Since then various research (e.g. Fullan, 1982; Huberman and Miles, 1984; Invargson and Greenway, 1984; Nias *et al.* 1989; Smith *et al.*, 1986) has indicated how occupational culture determines the way in which change is perceived, experienced and realized in schools.

Within educational institutions, teacher cultures develop. These cultures are the product of the beliefs, values and characteristics of the staff, students and community which combine to make up the shared understandings, the rules and norms which are 'the way we do things here' (Nias, 1988). There may be more than one teacher culture within an institution depending on its history and on the histories, generational experiences, orientations and commitments of individuals and groups of teachers (see Westoby, 1988).

Headteachers, as critical-reality definers, can have an important influence on the culture/s of a school through the sort of management strategies they use and by the values and beliefs their actions encourage (e.g. the sort of people they appoint and promote, the way in which they treat colleagues, the projects they support, etc.). It is perhaps worth noting that headteachers are also subject to professional and life-cycle and generational influences.

Changes which are imposed from outside threaten and can undermine the values and beliefs and the ways of doing things which make up teacher cultures (see Darling-Hammond and Wise, 1985). The result can be that people lose their sense of meaning and direction, their 'framework of reality', their confidence that they know what to do, and consequently they experience confusion and a kind of alienation. Under such conditions their work is likely to suffer and their commitment to decrease. This may be a temporary state until people have made sense of the change and of what it means for them, have developed new routines and have built up a new corpus of beliefs, expectations and values (i.e. gone through a process of 'acculturation') (see Rudduck, 1976; 1977), or it may be more long term. (Even 'successful' change takes time.) Of course, different groups within the institution will perceive and experience the change in different ways and it is the balance of these different groups' beliefs and values which is crucial for the institution as a whole.

Having said this, the schools' culture, or cultures, 'can successfully resist and redefine educational innovations' (Sarason, 1971; see also Whitty, 1985:148). This often, if not always, happens, at least to some degree (see, for example, Sikes, 1987).

The Case of The Experienced Teachers[3]

Having looked at teachers as people, teachers' aims and purposes, work context and conditions, and work culture, I now want to put these areas together and consider the case of 'experienced' teachers who have been and are being affected by imposed change.

I have chosen to focus on 'experienced teachers', that is teachers now in their late 30s, early 40s, because they constitute the largest teacher age-group in Britain (DES, 1986) and in North America (Stats Canada, 1985; US Department of Education, 1987) (as well as in many other countries: see OECD, 1989).

This 'greying' of the teaching force (as OECD, 1989:21, describes it) is due to a variety of factors, chiefly increased teacher recruitment during the 1960s and early 1970s in order to cope with population expansion. In itself, and at the present time, it cannot be considered as a negative phenomenon—teachers are ageing, not aged—but it is significant by sheer force of number.

What does imposed change mean for experienced teachers? It depends on their ideologies and philosophies, their life experiences, their aims and purposes, the contexts and conditions in which they work, and the form and content of the cultures within their schools. Teachers differ. Their careers will have differed depending on their own ambition, the opportunities they encountered, their sex, ethnic group, subject area, and the phase of education they work in. Their perceptions and experiences of imposed change will also vary depending on their philosophies and ideologies and, most importantly, on what the changes actually mean for them. They do, however, have certain experiences in common because they are all of a similar age and they share many historical and generational experiences.

Life-cycle research suggests that between the approximate ages of 37 to 45 people experience a phase which can be at least as traumatic as adolescence. This is because it is during this phase that it usually becomes apparent if the work, begun in the twenties and thirties, of establishing occupational career, family and a personal identity has been successful (see Sikes, Measor and Woods, 1985:50). The phase involves self-reappraisal, and searching for ways of expressing, fulfilling and satisfying oneself in the future. It can mean a re-ordering of priorities and new starts in various areas of life. Imposed changes experienced at this time can be particularly significant because they can either be seen to offer new opportunities or as a criticism and denial of what one has done so far.

By this age, whether or not they occupy formal positions of responsibility and authority—and a large proportion of the men will be in middle management posts—teachers are usually 'established'. They have some seniority by virtue of their age and they can, therefore, have a considerable influence on younger, junior teachers, and upon teacher cultures and the ethos/atmosphere of the school. This is, obviously, particularly true when, as is often the case, they form the largest group in the school. The strategies such teachers adopt, and the adaptations they make when faced with imposed change are, therefore, potentially very influential. Some of these strategies and adaptations will now be considered. (They are not necessarily exclusive to experienced teachers—but they may set a pattern for younger staff to follow.)

Carrying On as Before

When changes are introduced older teachers who have a longer term perspective often claim to 'have seen it all before'. They point to the way in which educational fashions come and go: 'We've gone full circle', and 'If you wait long enough you end up swimming with the tide again', are typical comments. Such remarks suggest that these teachers have strategically or ostensibly complied (cf. Lacey, 1977) or have carried on as before when faced with imposed change.

Carrying on as if nothing had happened is, indeed, perhaps one of the most common responses to most forms of change. There is plenty of evidence from various (quantitative and qualitative) evaluations and research projects to support this supposition (e.g. Barker-Lunn, 1970; Sharp and Green, 1972; Sikes, 1984; Troyna, 1985; Wolcott, 1977). Sometimes what teachers say suggests that changes have taken place but in reality the gap between rhetoric and practice is wide. It may be that the more experienced teachers are, the more experienced and adept they become at constructing 'screens made up of "instrumentalist" vocabularies to protect continuing "expressive" practices' (Dale, 1988:58). Even when changes are legally enforced it may be possible to go through the motions and present an appearance of change without any real change taking place, although this becomes increasingly difficult when monitoring and assessment are involved as they tend increasingly to be.

Cliques, Factions and Enclaves

When changes are introduced schools frequently become split into factions. Those who are opposed to the change may join together and form cliques which may be 'grumbling cliques'. This can result in 'old guard', defenders of the faith or reactionaries depending on your point of view, versus 'new' up-to-date people who hope to benefit or who have benefited in some way. Such divisions are exacerbated if there are incomers brought in directly because of the change (see Riseborough, 1981; Sikes, 1984). The 'old' guard tend to be older, experienced and influential people, though this is not axiomatic (Mac An Ghaill, 1988), which tends to mean that there are implications for the socialization of new, particularly young and inexperienced, staff.

In the case of imposed interventions which directly and overtly involve part as opposed to the whole of a school staff there may be what Saunders (1986a) describes as an 'enclave effect'. An enclave involves

> a set of practices, expressed in a policy text, which are inserted or which intervene in an established set of practices...from which they may be clearly distinguished and be, in some cases, oppositional. A feature of an innovation enclave is that it is accompanied by strong rhetoric which allies participants and distinguishes them from non-participants or outsiders.

Enclaves, therefore, threaten existing cultures. (See also Saunders, 1986b.)

Leaving

If imposed changes affect all state-maintained schools, the option of leaving and moving elsewhere is obviously not viable—unless, that is, the teacher is prepared to move into the independent sector. Some teachers may choose to leave teaching entirely and to start a new career. This is more difficult for experienced teachers who have made considerable personal investments in teaching, not least in terms of time, and who also tend to have financial and familial commitments.

Career Entrepreneurs

Imposed change frequently involves new career opportunities and promotion prospects (Huberman and Miles, 1984:51). New and different jobs may be created in the classroom, in management and administration. Since these jobs are new there may be no 'obvious' contenders and where this is the case the field is open to entrepreneurial individuals.

In teaching, career 'entrepreneurs' tend to be teachers in junior and lower-scale middle-management posts. They frequently work in marginal, low status areas (e.g. PE, craft). Generally they are under 45 and male. The explanations offered for this are that such teachers are not heavily committed to a particular career path; their commitment to advancing their career is strong and they have an eye to the main chance. (This is not to say that they are not committed to the development their new job will involve them in.) Women may be at a disadvantage because entrepreneurial behaviour is not traditionally feminine so an entrepreneurial attitude or the strategies associated with it may not come easily to them. Having said that, experienced women teachers whose families are no longer as dependent upon them sometimes decide that now is the time to pursue their career and consequently may be on the look out for opportunities.

Imposed changes may affect and alter the status of different areas within a school and some teachers may find themselves being promoted simply by virtue of being 'in the right place at the right time'. Such elevations are not always welcome, particularly if they change the nature of the job. There is of course the corollary that some areas are 'demoted' and the prospects of teachers working in them are therefore depressed.

General Resistance and Sabotage

Experienced teachers who have been teaching for some years will have developed ways of doing things which they have found to work for them in their situations. Consequently they may be reluctant to abandon tried and tested methods for new ones which they may be afraid will fail. With regard to technological changes some people may be 'afraid' of using new equipment, they may doubt their ability to learn how to use it. (There is some evidence which suggests that women may be more apprehensive than men, and that this is particularly true in the case of 'older' women (Kathy Sylva, personal communication)).

Huberman (1988) found that older teachers were not only more resistant to change, they were also less likely to believe that it would work. In making this assessment they were drawing on their experience and their observation of previous changes. This age-related trend is obviously significant given the ageing workforce.

Extensive, wide-ranging knowledge which comes from observation and experience of different situations and circumstances is an important influence on the 'success' of change. Evaluations of the Technical and Vocational Education Intiatives (TVEI) in Britain indicate that, in many cases, curriculum development and the development of experiential and active teaching and learning styles were carried by older staff who were in a position to draw on their experience. Younger staff may well have been enthusiastic and committed to change but they often lacked the skill and expertise which was necessary if they were to realize their intentions.

Teachers can overtly or covertly set out to sabotage imposed change by doing things wrong or by refusing to cooperate. Active sabotage requires commitment because it can result in difficult working conditions and can mean that students 'suffer'.

Shifting the Balance

Teachers who are no longer satisfied with their jobs following imposed change may decide to shift the balance or weight which they give to their work in the context of their lives as a whole. In other words they reduce the importance they attach to work and put more time, effort and energy into their families or into a particular interest or an alternative, supplementary career. There is a tendency for teachers to do this in their 40s in any case, so disaffection resulting from changes may just accelerate the process.

Grasping the Opportunity

Imposed change may, of course, offer some teachers the opportunity to be the sort of teacher and do the sorts of things they want to be and do. Others who did not initially see the change in a positive light, may find benefits, or even a solution to particular problems (Ball, 1981; Troyna, 1985) and consequently re-define their ideologies and philosophies in a way which makes sense of the change. For example, with regard to the introduction of compulsory in-service training in England, Holly *et al.* (1987) found that some teachers did not see the need for INSET and were initially hostile. On the basis of their positive experience, however, their view changed from seeing INSET as an unnecessary and time-wasting extra to seeing it as an essential right.

Conclusion

Fullan writes that, 'change can either aggravate the teachers' problems or provide a glimmer of hope' (1982:112). The same change can do both of these things for different teachers within the same institution depending on the perceived nature, extent and significance of the change and what is affected. Imposed change can solve some teachers' and schools' problems (Ball, 1981; Ozga and Lawn, 1988:333; Troyna, 1985:213) and if this is the case it is more likely to be supported. The situation is, however, usually not this straightforward insofar as there tend to be a number of aspects to most imposed changes and teachers may be in agreement with some but not others. The result of this may be that teachers take an exchange/bargain view; in other words they trade the 'positives' for the 'negatives'.

Ultimately, imposition generally implies criticism. This inevitably colours teachers' perceptions and consequent responses. Much depends on what the change means for teachers' ideologies and philosophies, for the kind of teacher they want to be and be seen as being, for their objective and subjective career aspirations, and for what they are required to do in their job.

Imposed change carries official authority which challenges professional experience, judgement and expertise. This challenge is likely to be viewed with greater disfavour by older teachers who have some experientially-based confidence that they are the ones best qualified to make professional decisions. While this is not axiomatic it does need to be borne in mind to a greater degree than it has tended to be by those imposing and those charged with managing change since the cooperation of experienced, senior teachers is particularly important and necessary for success.

Research shows that within the relative privacy of their classrooms and schools teachers are able to resist even legally imposed changes if they so wish (Hargreaves, D., 1980). Ensuring absolute conformity requires extensive inspectorial provision or a radical alteration to the way in which schools are organized; requirements which are both expensive and difficult to implement.

The imposition of change can lead to low morale, dissatisfaction and reduced commitment. If schools and teachers do face changes not of their own devising, one way forward is for managers to take an active, participative, democratic approach to the management of that change. They need to find out and to understand what the change means for individuals and for the institution and then develop, implement and evaluate strategies which take account of these differential meanings (i.e. take a praxis-based approach, Fullan, 1989). Such an approach, while taking up a considerable amount of time and requiring commitment, would ensure that the expertise and strengths of teachers of different ages and generations would be used, and differential age and generational-related needs and orientations accommodated. It would also give teachers some sense of control and of 'ownership' which may help to make their experience of the change more positive. In any case, the evidence suggests that teachers interpet and give changes meanings which make sense for them, they make changes their own as far as this is possible. Formalizing the interpretation may lead to more collegially satisfactory results. As the OECD (1979:20) states:

> So long as teachers are increasingly required to provide their pupils with an understanding of the concepts of responsibility and autonomy, it is difficult to see why they should be denied the opportunity of assuming their own responsibilities in this area and of effectively participating in the management of their schools and in the debate about general developments affecting the education system.

Imposed change can mean that teachers find themselves in a job which is quite different to that which they originally chose. It is sad to hear teachers coming up to retirement who say that they have enjoyed and had a good career up to now but that recently a plethora of imposed changes, changes in student and public attitudes to teachers and schooling have soured their experience of the job. Remarks of this kind are common and they do not bode well for the development of the quality of schooling via 'improved' teacher effectiveness.

Change is necessary if we are to move forward; and imposed change is also necessary if equality of opportunity and entitlement are valued. Accepting that there will always be those who are opposed to change, those in the position of implementing and imposing it should: (a) consult with practitioners and find out what the change actually means for as many teachers as possible, taking different types and size of school into consideration; (b) be sensitive to the personal as well as the professional needs and interests of the teachers who will be required to carry out the change; (c) resource changes at an adequate and appropriate level; (d) make adequate provision for in-service education and provide continuing support; and (e) treat teachers as autonomous and capable professionals and have trust in their ability.

Teachers are important and this simple truth must be recognized, and sooner rather than later. The closing quote from the OECD (1989:chapter 1) seems particularly appropriate:

> It has taken time since the difficulties and pessimism of the 1970s and early 1980s for the perception to be widely shared that the success of educational reforms, no matter how well they are conceived in principle, will be only fortuitous if the teachers who are actually responsible are not made an explicit and pivotal plank of those reforms. An uncommitted and poorly motivated teaching body will have disastrous effects for even the best of intentions for change. Teachers lie at the heart of the educational process. The greater the importance attached to education as a whole—whether for cultural transmission, for social cohesion and justice, or for the human resource development so critical in modern, technology-based economies—the higher is the priority that must be accorded to the teachers responsible for that education.

Acknowledgments

I would like to thank Barry Troyna, Andy Hargreaves and Michael Fullan for their constructive and helpful comments on earlier drafts of this paper.

Notes

1 Paulston (1976) differentiates between 'innovation' and 'reform' as types of change. He views 'innovation' as relatively isolated technical or programmatic alterations or as low-level change; whereas 'reform' is seen as a normative national and broad structural change. In practice such neat categorization is rarely possible, but it is useful to distinguish changes in terms of scope and legal authority.

2 For instance, a British teacher who was expected to implement the National Curriculum with a reception class of 37 in a room only really large enough for 20 said she believed that if only the administrators came from County Hall they would immediately be bound to recognize the difficulties and would do something to ease the situation.

3 The data on which this paper is based have been collected in the course of various research and evaluation projects. The chief sources are: (1) research into secondary school teachers' perceptions and experiences of teaching as a career in a contracting secondary school system. The study involved over 1,100 teachers working in 31 schools throughout England and Wales (Sikes, 1986); (2) a project which used life-history methodology to investigate secondary school teachers' experiences of teaching as a career (see Sikes, Measor and Woods, 1985); (3) TVEI (Technical and Vocational Education Initiative) evaluation. The TVEI is a major project sponsored and funded by what was the Manpower Services Commission, now the Training Agency. Ultimately the majority of (state) secondary schools in Britain are expected to be involved in the scheme. In brief, TVEI aims explicitly to link the curriculum to 'the work of work' and to encourage experiential, active approaches to teaching and learning. For further details see Dale, *et al.*, 1989 and Gleeson, 1987; and (4) collaborative 'action research' work with primary school teachers.

References

APPLE, M. (1981) 'Curriculum Form and the Logic of Technical Control', *Economic and Industrial Democracy*, 2, 3.

APPLE, M. (1987) 'Mandating Computers: The Impact of the New Technology on the Labour Process, Students and Teachers' in WALKER, S. and BARTON, L. (Eds.) *Changing Policies, Changing Teachers: New Directions for Schooling?*, Milton Keynes, Open University.

BALL, S. (1981) *Beachside Comprehensive: A Case Study of Secondary Schooling*, Cambridge, Cambridge University Press.

BALL, S. and GOODSON, I. (Eds.) (1985) *Teachers' Lives and Careers*, Lewes, Falmer.

BARKER-LUNN, J.C. (1970) *Streaming in the Primary School*, Slough, NFER.

BEYNON, J. (1985) 'Institutional change and career histories in a comprehensive school', in BALL, S. and GOODSON, I. (Eds.) *Teachers' Lives and Careers*, Lewes, Falmer.

BROADFOOT, P. and OSBOURNE, M. with GILLY, M. and PAILLET, A. (1988) 'What professional responsibility means to teachers: National contexts and classroom constraints', *British Journal of Sociology of Education*, 9, 3, pp. 265–87.

BUTT, R., RAYMONDE, D., McCUE, G. and YAMAGISHI, L. (1986) 'Individual and collective interpretations of teacher biographies', Paper presented at AERA, San Francisco.

CROW, N.J. (1987a) 'Preservice teachers' biography: A case study', Paper presented at AERA, Washington, DC.

CROW, N.J. (1987b) 'A review of the literature on preservice teachers' biographies', Paper presented at Californian Research Association, San Jose.

DALE, R. (1977) *The Structural Context of Teaching*, Milton Keynes, Open University.

DALE, R. (1988) 'Implications for progressivism of recent changes in the control and direction of education policy', in GREEN, A. (Ed.) *Progress and Inequality in Comprehensive Education*, London, Routledge, pp. 39–62.

DALE, R. *et al.* (1989) 'TVEI: A policy hybrid?' in HARGREAVES, A. and REYNOLDS, D. (Eds.) *Education Policies: Controversies and Critiques*, Lewes, Falmer.

DARLING-HAMMOND, L. and WISE, A. (1985) 'Beyond standardization: state standards and school improvement' in *Elementary School Journal, 85*, 3, pp. 315–36.

DENSCOMBE, M. (1982) 'The hidden pedagogy and its implications for teacher training' in *British Journal of Sociology of Education*, 3, pp. 249–65.

DENSCOMBE, M. (1985) *Classroom Control: A Sociological Perspective*, London, Croom Helm.

DES (1983) *Teaching Quality*, London, HMSO.

DES Education statistics for the United Kingdom: 1986 Edition, London, HMSO.

FULLAN, M. (1982) *The Meaning of Educational Change*, Toronto, OISE Press.

FULLAN, M. (1989) 'Implementing educational change: What we know', World Bank Seminar on *Planning for the Implementation of Educational Change*.

GLEESON, D. (Ed.) (1987) *TVEI and Secondary Education: A Critical Appraisal*, Milton Keynes, Open University.

GRAY, H.L. (1980) *Management In Education*, Driffield, Nafferton Books.

GRAY, H.L. (1988) 'A perspective on organizational theory', in WESTOBY, A. (Ed.) *Culture and Power in Educational Organisations*, Milton Keynes, Open University.

HARGREAVES, A. (1988) 'Cultures of teaching in HARGREAVES, A. and FULLAN, M. (Eds.) *Understanding Teacher Development*, London, Cassell.

HARGREAVES, A. (in press) 'Cultures of teaching in HARGREAVES, A. and FULLAN, M. (Eds.) *Understanding Teacher Development*, London, Cassell.

HARGREAVES, A. and DAWE, R. (1989) 'Coaching as unreflective practice: Contrived collegiality or collaborative culture?', Paper presented at AERA, San Francisco.

HARGREAVES, D. (1980) 'The occupational culture of teachers', in WOODS, P. (Ed.), *Teacher Strategies: Explorations in the Sociology of the School*, London, Croom Helm.

HATTON, E. (1988) 'Teachers' work as bricolage: Implications for teacher education', in *British Journal of Sociology of Education*, 9, 3, pp. 337–57.

HOLLY, P., JAMES, T. and YOUNG, (1987) *The Experience of TRIST: Practioners' Views of INSET and Recommendations for the Future*, London, MSC.

HOYLE, E. (1972) *Problems of Curriculum Innovation: 1* (Unit 13), Milton Keynes, Open University.

HUBERMAN, M. (1988) 'Teacher Careers and School Improvement', in *Journal of Curriculum Studies, 20*, 2, pp. 119–32.

HUBERMAN, M. and MILES, M. (1984) *Innovation Up Close: How School Improvement Works*, New York, Plenum.

INVARGSON, L. and GREENWAY, P. (1984) 'Portrayal of teacher development', in *Australian Journal of Education*, 28, 1, pp. 45–65.

KNOWLES, J. (1988) 'Models for understanding preservice and beginning teachers' biographies: Illustrations from case studies'. Paper presented at AERA, New Orleans.

LACEY, C. (1977) *The Socialization of Teachers*, London, Methuen.

LAWN, M. and OZGA, J. (1981) 'The educational worker? A reassessment of teachers', in WALKER, S. and BARTON, L. (Eds.) *Changing Policies, Changing Teachers: New Directions for Schooling?*, Milton Keynes, Open University.

LEVIN, H. (1976) 'Educational reform; Its meaning', in CARNOY, M. and LEVIN, H. (Eds.) *The Limits of Educational Reform*, New York, McKay.

LEVINSON, D., DARROW, C., KLEIN, G., LEVINSON, M. and McKEE, B. (1978) *The Seasons of a Man's Life*, New York, Alfred A. Knopf.

LORTIE, D. (1975) *Schoolteacher: A Sociological Study*, Chicago, University of Chicago Press.

MAC AN GHAILL, M. (1988) *Young, Gifted and Black*, Milton Keynes, Open University.

MARDLE, G. and WALKER, M. (1980) 'Strategies and structure: Some critical notes on teacher socialization', in WOODS, P. (Ed.) *Teacher Strategies: Explorations in the Sociology of the School*, London, Croom Helm.

MILLER, J.P., TAYLOR, G. and WALDER, K. (1982) *Teachers in Transition: Study of an Aging Teaching Force*, Ontario, OISE, Occasional Series 44.

NIAS, J. (1984) 'The definition and maintenance of self in primary teaching', in *British Journal of Sociology of Education*, 5, 3, pp. 167–80.

NIAS, J. (1988) 'Creating a collaborative culture', Paper presented at the conference on Histories and Ethnographies of Teaching as Work, St Hilda's College, Oxford.

NIAS, J. (1989) *Primary Teachers Talking: A Study of Teaching as Work*, London, Routledge.

NIAS, J., SOUTHWORTH, G. and YEOMANS, R. (1989) *Staff Relationships in the Primary School: A Study of Organizational Cultures*, London, Cassell.

OECD (1979) *Teacher Policies in a New Context*, Document on free distribution, Paris.

OECD (1985) OECD Ministers Discuss Education in Modern Society, (press communiqué issued 21/11/84).

OECD (1989) *The Condition of Teaching: General Report*, Restricted Draft, Paris.

OZGA, J. and LAWN, M. (1988) 'Interpreting the labour process of teaching', in *British Journal of Sociology of Education*, 9, 3, pp. 323–6.

PAULSTON, R.G. (1976) *Conflicting Theories of Social and Educational Change: A Typological Review*, Pittsburgh University Centre for International Study.

PETERSON, W. (1964) 'Age, teachers' role and the institutional setting' in BIDDLE, B. and ELENA, W. (Eds.) *Contemporary Research on Teacher Effectiveness*, New York, Holt Rinehart.

POPPLETON, P. (1988) 'Teacher professional satisfaction', in *Cambridge Journal of Education*, 1, pp. 5–16.

RISEBOROUGH, G. (1981) 'Teacher careers and comprehensive schooling; A sociological study', in *Sociology*, 15, 3, pp. 352–81.

RISEBOROUGH, G. (1986) '"Know-alls", "whizz-kids", "dead wood" and the crisis of schooling', Paper presented at BERA, University of Bristol.

RUDDUCK, J. (1976) 'Dissemination as acculturation research', in *SSRC Newsletter*, *23*, November.

RUDDUCK, J. (1977) 'Dissemination as encounter of cultures', *Research Intelligence*, *3*, pp. 3–5.

SACHS, J. and SMITH, R. (1988) 'Constructing teacher culture', in *British Journal of Sociology of Education*, *4*, pp. 423–36.

SARASON, S. (1971) *The Culture of the School and the Problem of Change*, Boston, Allyn and Bacon.

SAUNDERS, M. (1986a) 'Managing the enclave—teachers outside TVEI', in McCABE, C. (Ed.) *The Organization of the Early Years of the Technical and Vocational Education Initiative*, Clevedon, Multilingual Matters.

SAUNDERS, M. (1986b) 'The innovation enclave: Unintended effects of TVEI implementation', in *TVEI Working Papers No. 1*, CARE, University of East Anglia.

SHARP, R. and GREEN, A. (1972) *Education and Social Control*, London, Routledge and Kegan Paul.

SIKES, P.J. (1984) 'Teacher careers in the comprehensive school', in BALL, S. (Ed.), *Comprehensive Schooling: A Reader*, Lewes, Falmer.

SIKES, P.J. (1986) 'The mid-career teacher: Adaptation and motivation in a contracting secondary school system', Unpublished Ph.D. thesis, University of Leeds.

SIKES, P.J. (1987) 'Teachers and the MSC', in WALKER, S. and BARTON, L. (Eds.) *Changing Policies, Changing Teachers: New Directions for Schooling?* Milton Keynes, Open University.

SIKES, P.J. (1988a) '1968 is a long time ago: A humanities faculty revisited', Paper presented at BERA, University of East Anglia.

SIKES, P.J. (1988b) '1968 and teachers' careers: A faculty culture'. Paper presented at conference on Histories and Ethnographies of Teaching as Work, St Hilda's College, Oxford.

SIKES, P.J., MEASOR, L. and WOODS, P. (1985) *Teacher Careers: Crises and Continuities*, Lewes, Falmer.

SMITH, L., KLEINE, P., PRUNTY, J. and DWYER, D. (1986) *Educational Innovators: Then and Now*, Lewes, Falmer.

STATS CANADA (1985) *Salaries and Qualifications of Teachers in Public Elementary and Secondary Schools 1983–84*, Ottawa.

TIPTON, F. (1988) 'Educational Organizations as Workplaces', in OZGA, J. (Ed.) *School Work: Approaches to the Labour Process of Teaching*, Milton Keynes, Open University.

TROYNA, B. (1985) 'The great divide: Policies and practices in multi-cultural education', in *British Journal of Sociology of Education*, *6*, 2, pp. 209–24.

US DEPARTMENT OF EDUCATION (1987) *The Digest of Educational Statistics: 1987 Edition*, Washington, DC, National Center for Educational Statistics.

WALKER, S. and BARTON, L. (Eds.) (1987) *Changing Policies, Changing Teachers: New Directions for Schooling?* Milton Keynes, Open University.

WESTOBY, A. (Ed.) (1988) *Culture and Power in Educational Organizations*, Milton Keynes, Open University.

WHITTY, G. (1985) *Sociology and School Knowledge*, London, Methuen.

WISE, A. (1977) *Why educational policies often fail: The hyperrationalization hypothesis*', in *Curriculum Studies*, *9*, 1, pp. 43–57.

WOLCOTT, H. (1977) *Teachers vs Technocrats*, Eugene Center for Educational Policy and Management, University of Oregon.

ZEICHNER, K. and GRANT, C. (1981) 'Biography and social structure in the socialization of student teachers: A re-examination of the pupil control ideologies of student teachers', in *Journal of Education for Teaching*, 7, pp. 298–314.

Chapter 4

The Nature of Collegiality in Teacher Development: The Case of Clinical Supervision

Peter P. Grimmett and E. Patricia Crehan

Introduction

Ever since Little's (1981) classic study of six schools highlighting positive norms and conditions in the workplace, the term 'collegiality' has acquired something of a mystique. Despite this, Little (1987) argues that, by working closely with colleagues, teachers derive instructional range, depth, and flexibility. The structures of collaborative group-work enable teachers to attempt curricular-instructional innovations that they would probably not have tried as individuals. For example, teachers may undertake interclass visitation and observation or they may study classroom-related issues together. But it is not merely the team work that creates the willingness to try new things— it is the joint action that flows from the group's purposes and obligations as they shape the shared task and its outcomes.

In addition to these benefits, teachers derive influence from their ranks; they also derive respect from others, such as administrators, pupils, and parents. These benefits, like the ones mentioned above, accrue from work conditions which foster collegiality. 'The more public an enterprise teaching becomes, the more it both requires and supports collective scrutiny' (Little, 1987:496). This collective scrutiny breeds influence and respect among teachers. The highest levels of reciprocal influence reported by teachers in studies conducted by Meyer, Cohen, Brunetti, Molnar, and Lueders-Salmon (1971) at Stanford were reserved for schools in which teachers were both routinely visible to one another and routinely and intensively involved in teams. It would appear, then, that a combination of visibility (planning for teaching and actual classroom instruction is carried out in the presence of other teachers), shared responsibility, and widespread interaction heightens the influence of teachers on one another and on the school as a whole.

Little (1987) also suggests that teachers derive career rewards and daily satisfaction from conditions of collegiality. Working with colleagues helps teachers to shape their perspectives on their daily work. It also enables them to reduce what Lortie (1975:134) referred to as 'the endemic uncertainties of teaching', which typically deny teachers a sense of success. Little (1987) describes this specific benefit in the following way:

> Instead of grasping for the single dramatic event or the special achievements of a few children as the main source of pride, teachers [enjoying conditions of collegiality] are more able to detect and celebrate a pattern of accomplishments within and across classrooms. (p. 497)

Professional recognition, professional involvement, and professional influence become rewards that keep teachers career-oriented and help them establish a high sense of efficacy.

Writing two years later, Little (1989) admits that she and others have contributed to the growing mystique surrounding collegiality:

> Advocates have imbued it with a sense of virtue—the expectation that any interaction that breaks the isolation of teachers will contribute in some fashion to the knowledge, skill, judgement, or commitment that individuals bring to their work, and will enhance the collective capacity of groups or institutions. Researchers have ascribed benefits to teacher collaboration; among them student achievement in inner city schools, teacher morale in times of stress, support for innovation, and an easing of the 'reality shock', visited upon beginning teachers. (p. 1)

Yet, eight years after her ground-breaking study, Little (1989) is also forced to conclude that much of the traditional school culture has superimposed itself on the collegial practices which seemed to hold so much promise:

> The conditions of individualism, presentism, and conservatism persist, nourished in part by the very forms of 'collegiality' that enthusiasts admire for their ability to penetrate the walls of privacy. The various forms of teacher exchange that pass as 'collegiality' comprise fundamentally different conceptions of teachers' professional relations. 'Weak' and 'strong' versions of collegial relations plausibly produce or sustain quite different conditions of teacher performance and commitment. Patterns of interaction that support mutual assistance or routine sharing may account well for maintaining a certain level of workforce stability, teacher satisfaction, and a performance 'floor'; they seem less likely, however, to account for high rates of innova-

tion or for high levels of collective commitment to specific curricular or instructional policies. They seem less likely to force teachers' collective confrontation with the school's fundamental purposes or with the implications of the pattern of practices that have accumulated over time. (p. 30)

Why is this the case? Why has something of such promise turned out to have such desultory effects?

The last decade has witnessed a significant trend towards the centralization of bureaucratic control. Fullan and Connelly (1987) maintain that there has been a tightening of administrative surveillance over both curriculum content and pedagogical process in the school systems of most western societies. Hargreaves (1989a) suggests that these developments are driven by powerful social forces amounting to fundamental crises of legitimation, belief, motivation, and purpose. These crises have continually assailed the economically destabilized societies of the western world (and are now beginning to ravage the eastern bloc). One consequence of this state of affairs is the 'peculiar paradox that teachers are apparently being urged to collaborate *more*, just at the moment when there is less for them to collaborate *about* (Hargreaves and Dawe, 1989:3, emphasis in original). Teachers may therefore engage in a contrived form of collegiality which 'may be little more than a quick, slick administrative surrogate for more genuinely collaborative teacher cultures' (Hargreaves and Dawe, 1989:25). Such examples of collegial practices have been instituted without building the professional culture that Lieberman (1989) holds to be so essential to fostering interdependent collaboration in schools. In other words, attempts at initiating collaboration have reproduced the artifacts, i.e. collegial practices of the school cultures studied by Little in 1981, without nurturing the underlying beliefs, values, and norms that make up the sustaining culture. In so doing, collegial practices have been grafted on to existing school cultures with the result that the processes of collaboration appear to be contrived and their effects subverted.

This chapter examines the nature of collegiality and teacher development in the case of clinical supervision. It begins with an examination of school culture and the culture of collaboration or professional interdependence. It contrasts this with a different culture, notably the one sustaining contrived collegiality. The case of clinical supervision is then examined in light of this contrast to determine the relationship between different types of collegiality and teacher development.

School Culture

'Culture is not itself visible, but is made visible only through its representation' (Van Maanen, 1988:3). Culture is constructed reality.

It is known by its representation. It consists of the beliefs, values, and norms which govern 'what is of worth to this group and how the members should think, feel, and behave' (Sergiovanni, 1984:9). These constructs are portrayed in an interpretive way by persons who study them in rigorous fieldwork. For ethnographers and sociologists, the purpose is to understand them, although Goodson's (1989:14) reference to 'the ideal that to understand may be to begin to undermine' serves as a useful corollary. At the school level, the representation of culture is important for the derivation of meaning and shared assumptions:

> The more understood, accepted, and cohesive the culture of the school, the better able it [the school] is to move in concert toward ideals it holds and objectives it wishes to pursue. (Sergiovanni, 1984:9)

School culture can be said to be influenced by teacher sub-cultures framed by personal biographies, ontological perspectives, and career experiences (see Hargreaves, 1986:137ff.) and by the occupational culture of teaching (see Waller, 1932; Jackson, 1968; Lortie, 1975) which represents attributes of the teaching profession as a whole. Leadership at the school level becomes an exercise in 'building a professional culture' (Lieberman, 1989) wherein considerable attention is paid to the informal, subtle and symbolic aspects of school life. As Greenfield (1984) puts it, 'the task of leadership is to create the moral order that binds them...and the people around them' (p.159). This is not to suggest that school cultures can be manipulated by leaders towards their own political ends, for 'cultures are not made; they are born and grow' (Cooper, 1989:46). Rather, it is to emphasize that culture-building is essentially the infusion of value into the regular enterprise:

> The art of the creative leader is the art of institution building, the reworking of human and technological materials to fashion an organism that embodies new and enduring values...To institutionalize is to infuse with value beyond the technical requirements of the task at hand. The prizing of social machinery beyond its technical role is largely a reflection of the unique way it fulfils personal or group needs. Whenever individuals become attached to an organization or a way of doing things as persons rather than as technicians, the result is a prizing of the device for its own sake. From the standpoint of the committed person, the organization is changed from an expendable tool into a valued source of personal satisfaction...The institutional leader, then, is *primarily an expert in the promotion and protection of values*. (Selznick, 1957:17, emphasis in original)

Culture is important, then, because it represents the values which bind people together. Put differently, it depicts the framework of beliefs which provides a normative basis for action and ultimately holds teachers professionally accountable for the many tasks involved in educating students. Since schools function more like 'organized anarchies' (Cohen, March, and Olson, 1972) and the educational programme itself is 'loosely coupled' (Weick, 1982), the culture of the school becomes an important and influential determinant of how teaching and learning take place. Weick (1982) suggests that the culture is the 'glue' which holds loosely coupled systems together: '[Teachers'] action becomes richer, more confident, and more satisfying when it is linked with important underlying themes, values and movements' (p. 675). But school cultures do not always permit the positive linking that Weick describes. That is because Weick is essentially portraying a strong culture, and school cultures can also be cult-like, weak, and stifling.

Different Characterizations of Cultures

Strong school cultures[1] are built deliberately around tightly structured beliefs, values, and norms within a loosely coupled organizational structure (Peters and Waterman, 1982; Sergiovanni, 1984). By contrast, schools which have cultures framed around tightly structured beliefs, values, and norms within a tightly coupled organizational structure appear to be *cult-like*. An example of this type of culture can be drawn from the work of Cohen (1983) who claims that many so-called 'effective' schools are not loosely coupled organizationally at all. What he is suggesting is that these schools have tended to rely on tight organizational control to hold teachers accountable rather than on the beliefs and values which constitute their shared assumptions and normative basis for action. This approach tends to force people into a cohesive group but in a manner which creates a non-rational kind of commitment to the school culture. As Sergiovanni puts it, 'As bonding grows, one is apt to "think" less and "feel" more about work and commitments to school' (p. 13).

It is also possible for schools to have a typically loosely coupled organizational structure accompanied by a loosely structured framework of beliefs, values and norms. Such schools could be characterized as having *weak* cultures and would not even appear to be, in Cohen, March, and Olson's (1972) terms, 'organized anarchies'. The laissez-faire, liberal-romantic flavour of such schools can be equated with 'ineffectiveness' in that levels of teacher satisfaction and student learning are generally quite low. When such schools tighten up the organizational control but not the framework of beliefs, values, and norms, the culture becomes a *stifling* one, analogous to a prison or other forms of incarceration.

Figure 4.1:   *Exemplars of Beliefs, Values, and Norms Found in a* Typical *Culture of Schools*

Exemplar 1

Belief: 'I must be able to cut the mustard'
Value: It is important to succeed without help
Norm: Self-sufficiency, individualism

Exemplar 2

Belief: 'I should not intrude into another teacher's classroom'
Value: Teachers' privacy is to be respected
Norm: Reticence, isolationism

Exemplar 3

Belief: 'Teachers' needs are practical, not theoretical; any abstractions are irrelevant'
Value: Knowledge/skills that are relevant and useful
Norm: Scepticism, potential resistance to externally-imposed innovation

Of these four characterizations, only the first two are typically found in schools. That is because most schools do have a tightly structured framework of beliefs, values, and norms accompanied by a loose (or occasionally tight) organizational coupling. Why, then, can the majority of schools not be characterized as possessing strong cultures? Because there is another factor that these characterizations do not take into account, namely, the nature of the beliefs and values which together constitute the basis for normative action. And it is this factor which differentiates a culture of collaborative interdependence from a culture of contrived collegiality when educational change takes place. To establish this claim, we will look first at the beliefs, values, and norms which characterize a typical school culture and contrast them with the beliefs, values, and norms which characterize a strong culture of collaborative interdependence and an overlay of the typical on the collaborative resulting in a culture of contrived collegiality.

A Typical Culture of Schools

This characterization of a typical culture of schools[2] draws heavily on work portraying the occupational culture of teaching (see Waller, 1932; Jackson, 1968; Lortie, 1975) and conditions of the workplace (see Lieberman and Miller, 1984; Chism, 1985). Figure 4.1 demonstrates the beliefs, values, and norms most typically associated with school cultures. This typification is, by definition, not comprehensive; obvious exceptions exist.[3] However, the effects of early socialization into teaching have tended to reinforce these beliefs, values, and norms in many teachers.

Most teachers generally learn their role the hard way—by experience (Lieberman and Miller, 1984). Faced with a situation which is fraught with dilemmas arising from basic concerns about adequacy, beginning teachers tend to operate on the belief that they must be able 'to cut the mustard'. In other words, they must prove their classroom competence to others and, primarily, to themselves. This situation is not atypical of any new major undertaking in either personal or professional life but the cellular organization of schools tends to make such teachers value the importance of proving themselves without any help from others. The success that is valued, then, occurs when teachers can stand on their own two feet, as it were, as a result of *their* efforts and not anyone else's. In a very real sense, this transcending of survival concerns is essential to classroom-teaching effectiveness. But it is the belief that one must do it *alone* and the value placed thereon that fosters norms of self-sufficiency and individualism. When teachers act in self-sufficient and individualistic ways, they are less likely to engage in the kind of powerful collegial discourse that accompanies educational change.

The cellular organization of schools also shapes the ways in which teachers relate to one another professionally (Bird and Little, 1986; Chism, 1985). Teachers tend to believe that they should not *intrude* into one another's classrooms. The word 'intrude' is important here because it suggests a lack of willingness or readiness on the part of the teacher being observed to have another professional in the classroom. Such control over one's workplace is essential to any professional endeavour but the value accompanying this belief frequently confounds teachers' needs for professional autonomy with their idiosyncratic wish for privacy. In other words, teacher autonomy is not regarded as something to be exercised in a context of 'rich professional dialogue about a plethora of challenging educational alternatives' (Goodlad, 1984:186); rather, it is seen as a surrogate for teacher seclusion and secrecy. This preference for privacy over responsible autonomy breeds norms of reticence and isolationism. When teachers are reticent to provide feedback to one another and prefer to act as 'gatekeepers' to their isolated 'kingdoms' rather than as professional colleagues, the prospects for positive educational change are reduced.

Schools of this ilk tend to embody what Doyle and Ponder (1977) have termed the 'practicality ethic'. That is, teachers become interested in educational change only when the proposed innovation is congruent with their existing practice, when the cost in terms of time and effort is minimal, and when the innovatory practices are seen to serve a utilitarian purpose. Consequently, teachers believe that their instructional needs are practical, not theoretical, and that any abstractions or theoretical formulations are therefore irrelevant (Lieberman and Miller, 1984). Knowledge and skills which are deemed useful and relevant to classroom practice are valued over the kind of knowledge and skills which teachers find abstruse and label 'theoretical'. Or, as Lieberman and Miller (1984) suggest, teachers label proposed changes 'theoretical' when they do not understand their practical relevance.

Such a state of affairs breeds norms of scepticism and potential resist-ance to externally-imposed innovation. When teachers are unduly sceptical of and resistant to externally-imposed change, innovation is less likely to take place than when such scepticism is replaced by sensitive understanding.

Typically, the beliefs, values, and norms operative in such school cultures are tightly structured and the organization around the educa-tional programme is loosely coupled. Why, then, do these typical cultures[4] not represent strong ones? Because, as mentioned previous-ly, it is the nature of beliefs, values, and norms in addition to the 'tight and loose' formulation which determines whether a school culture is, or is not, strong.

A Strong School Culture: Interdependent Collegiality

This characterization of a strong school culture draws heavily on the ground-breaking study of Little (1981) and the work of Weick (1982). As such, it is a portrayal of a culture of *interdependent collegiality*. Figure 4.2 displays two exemplars of the beliefs, values, and norms found in the schools studied by Little (1981) and documents the essential difference between a *typical* and a *strong* school culture. The difference lies not in the 'tight and loose' formulation, but in the fact that the beliefs, values, and norms that are tightly structured have a highly specific professional focus.

Teachers in the schools studied by Little (1981) believed that talking about teaching and observing it builds up 'shared referents for a shared language of teaching...adequate to the complexity of teaching, capable of distinguishing one practice and its virtue from another' (p. 12). The value in this is that focused talk about teaching embedded in a shared language is preferred over the imprecise and undifferentiated talk emanating from idiosyncratic and individualistic perceptions of classroom reality. Such openness to observing, to being observed, and to discussing observed classroom practice tends to break down isolationist barriers and promote the norm of collegial interdependence. Complementing Little is Weick's (1982) 'tight-loose' formulation. When teachers are held accountable by tightly structured beliefs and values sustaining the norm of collegial interdependence, the organizational structure in which collegial conditions develop can be loose. In other words, the administrative hierarchy can invest in teachers the power required to make collegiality happen:

> Highly successful leaders practise the principle of power in-vestment: they distribute power among others in an effort to get more power in return. But their view of power investment is sophisticated: they know it is not power over people and events that counts but, rather, power over accomplishments

Peter P. Grimmett and E. Patricia Crehan

Figure 4.2:   Exemplars of Beliefs, Values, and Norms Found in a Strong Interdependent
Collegiality

Exemplar 1

TIGHT
Belief: Talking about and observing teaching builds up shared referents adequate
to the complexity of teaching
Value: Shared referents are preferred over idiosyncratic perceptions
Norm: Collegial interdependence

LOOSE   Organizational structure for how collegial conditions occur

Exemplar 2

TIGHT
Belief: Learning accrues from the active pursuit of the demonstration and risk-
taking that teaching provides
Value: Taking risks is preferred over the stagnation resulting from isolationist,
avoidance tendencies
Norm: Experimentation

LOOSE   Organizational structure for how experimentation takes place

and over the achievement of organizational purposes. They understand that teachers need to be empowered to act—to be given the necessary responsibility that releases their potential and makes their actions and decisions count. (Sergiovanni, 1987:121)

A further belief operative in the schools studied by Little (1981) was that learning accrues from the active pursuit of the demonstration and risk-taking features that teaching provides. The value here is that the taking of risks is to be preferred over the stagnation resulting from the isolationist, avoidance tendencies exhibited by teachers in typical school cultures. Such openness to learning through the active pursuit of risk-taking promotes the norm of experimentation. When teachers are given to experimentation because of the beliefs and values that support such normative action, the organizational structure in which experimentation develops can be loose. In other words, the administration has no need to organize teachers for experimentation when they believe in and value risk-taking; rather, it needs to reinforce the beliefs and values that sustain such a norm and facilitate teacher enactment by supporting the organizational conditions initiated by such keen professionals. Strong cultures in schools, then, are framed around tightly structured *professionally oriented* beliefs and values, which constitute the basis for normative action, within an appropriately loose bureaucratic structure.

Such cultures are frequently associated with collaborative action research wherein teachers function as researchers. Oja and Pine (1987) note how collaborative action research involves teachers in temporary systems in which they handle different roles and functions while engaged in a sustained, deliberate process of inquiry generating general programmatic knowledge. Elliott (1988) postulates a developmental progression in teachers who act as researchers from basic concerns of adequacy to professional attempts at initiating fundamental change in curriculum and instruction. The logical sequence of his argument (pp. 47ff.) is that: teachers engaging in collegial interdependence and experimentation increase their ability to tolerate losses in self-esteem; teachers able to tolerate losses in self-esteem become more open to feedback from students and other colleagues; teachers' openness to feedback enables them to give others access to their classroom problems; giving others access to their classroom problems helps teachers to become self-monitoring; self-monitoring teachers are more likely to bring about fundamental changes in classroom practice.

A strong school culture, then, is one which sustains those collaborative practices which lead teachers to raise fundamental questions about the nature of teaching and student learning. In short, it represents the intellectual ferment within which ideas for educational change can flourish and expand. Why, then, given the merits of *interdependent collegiality* does it exist so rarely in schools? Because such a culture, as Little (1986) points out, runs right against the grain of all the pressures and constraints that make up the teachers' workplace, leading Hargreaves (1989b) to conclude that the preferred culture of teaching is not compatible with the prevailing context of teachers' work. Moreover, in the trend towards greater centralization of control over the curricular-instructional programme, school reformers have attempted to implement collegial practices without regard for the necessary beliefs, values, and norms which combine to sustain professional interdependence. As a consequence, features of the typical culture found in schools have been superimposed on the innovative collegial practices to establish a culture of contrived collegiality.

A Culture of Contrived Collegiality

Hargreaves (1989b) has described contrived collegiality as being:

> characterized by a set of formal, specific bureaucratic procedures to increase the attention being given to joint teacher planning and consultation. It can be seen in initiatives such as peer coaching, mentor teaching, joint planning in specially provided rooms, formally scheduled meetings and clear job descriptions and training programmes for those in consultative roles. These sorts of initatives are administrative contrivances designed to get collegiality going in schools where little has existed before. They are meant to encourage greater association among teachers; to foster more sharing, learning and improvement of skills and expertise. Contrived collegiality is also meant to assist the successful implementation of new approaches and techniques from the outside into a more responsive and supportive school culture. (p. 19)

Figure 4.3: *Exemplars of Beliefs, Values, and Norms Found in a 'Typical' Culture of Contrived Collegiality*

Exemplar 1

TIGHT
- *Belief:* Talking about and observing teaching is necessary to satisfy requirements of bureaucratic hierarchy or innovation
- *Value:* Fitting in, not being critical, doing what must be done constitute preferred actions
- *Norm:* Collaborative pretence

LOOSE   Organizational structure exploited for 'impression management'

Exemplar 2

TIGHT
- *Belief:* Teaching provides opportunities for demonstration and risk-taking which are threatening
- *Value:* Job security and professional comfort (conflict)
- *Norm:* False experimentation

LOOSE   Organizational structure exploited by 'going through motions'

In other words, the emphasis is placed on fulfilling the form of collegiality without regard for the spirit or underlying assumptions of interdependence.[5] It is as if it has become mandatory that practitioners collaborate voluntarily. Indeed, as Figure 4.3 demonstrates, contrived collegiality consists of practitioners engaging in actions similar to those documented by Little (1981) but on the basis of radically different beliefs and values. The practice of talk about teaching does not represent the public outworking of the belief that such talk builds up a shared language, but that talk with other practitioners about classroom teaching is deemed necessary to satisfy the requirements of the bureaucratic hierarchy and/or those of the innovation under experiment. The value assumption behind such talk is that attempting to satisfy such requirements is preferred in formal organizations over practitioners engaging in a perceptive critique of the purposes and processes inherent in the required actions. The practice of observing and being observed is not based on the belief that such actions contextualize talk about teaching but that the observation process is either a necessary evil or a co-requisite of responsible professionalism. Consequently, educators would, at one level, speak in favour of such a practice while, at a deeper level, tend to resent such intrusion into their instructional 'kingdoms'. The value assumption behind their engaging in observation lies in the preference for being regarded as a professional who does what must be done over merely 'doing one's own thing'. These beliefs and values breed a norm of 'collaborative pretence' whereby teachers tend, wittingly or unwittingly, to conceal their real motivation for acting as they do. In the process, they engage in much sophistry and, not infrequently, self-deception. Although the above beliefs and values are tightly structured as a normative basis for action, the organizational structure is nonetheless loose; and it is this looseness that teachers, governed by the norm of collaborative pretence, exploit for purposes of 'impression management'. When teachers act in these ways, there is both surface support for and deep-seated rejection of educational change. In essence, the practices of the typical school culture have been replaced, but not the deep-rooted beliefs and values that constitute the basis for the norms of self-sufficiency, isolationism, and scepticism.

Just as the overlay of the typical school culture on collegial practices results in a norm of collaborative pretence, so the beliefs and values sustaining the norm of experimentation in interdependent collegiality are also subject to the more dominant features of the typical school culture. The belief operative in interdependent collegiality— that teaching provides opportunities for learning through demonstration and risk-taking—is supplemented with the individualistic view that such learning is threatening. This individualistic belief puts teachers in a value conflict between their job security and professional comfort. On the one hand, the grafting of collaboration by administrative requirement makes them fear for their job security if they do not comply; on the other hand, their own professional comfort zones are violated when they do comply. Such a value conflict fosters a norm of false experimentation. Teachers experiencing this acute value conflict go to great lengths to make it appear as if they are entering into collegiality while at the same time neutralizing any risks they take to make them felicitous and fail-safe. The loose organizational structure generally accompanying these tightly structured beliefs, values, and norms is exploited by teachers 'going through the motions' and paying lip-service to the norm of experimentation. Teachers acting in this manner generally thwart the purposes of educational change.

But they do not always set out deliberately to frustrate educational change. Rather, they realize that they, and not administrators, ultimately have students' educational benefit at heart and they then act as gatekeepers to safeguard stability in the classroom:

> In professional settings, when teachers are moved to share, it is usually because they are *proud of something they have done with the children*. No amount of posturing about new roles and responsibilities can even begin to approach that powerful motivation to be professional. By the same token, the greatest fear and frustration teachers have is not the denial of professional opportunity (though this is of value), but the concern engendered when they feel powerless to resist the actions of other authorities who do not exist in relationship to children and whose decisions teachers may view as potentially damaging to children. In this case, teachers, often regardless of professional sophistication, perform a protective role...When teachers are trapped between what their judgement tells them should be done and what is actually done, and when they see

no recourse, they become alienated and disaffected. (Cooper, 1989:51–2, emphasis in original)

Teachers view collegial practices in a similar fashion. When they sense that the proposed changes in roles have less to do with how students learn and more to do with how the administrative hierarchy's educational leadership role is perceived, teachers rely on their own individualistic understanding of students as a way of protecting the learning environment. When they see that they have no recourse but to 'do' collegiality, teachers become disaffected. It is this disaffection which makes the collegiality contrived.

Contrived collegiality can be characterized, then, as the overlay of a typical set of school cultural beliefs and values on the administratively required practices of interdependent collegiality. Compared with the risk-taking, generative, and fertile nature of interdependent collegiality, contrived collegiality appears to represent a safe and sterile ethos which, far from nurturing a bracing and professionally efficacious dialogue among teachers, potentially breeds a sense of disenchantment and associated impotence with attempts to eschew cellular isolationism. The essential difference between the two cultures lies not in their formulation (in Weick's terminology, both are tight-loose) but in the nature of the beliefs and values which constitute the basis for normative action.

Since clinical supervision is a conception of instructional supervision which emphasizes collegiality, evidence of both the interdependent and contrived cultures is likely to be found in attempts to foster teacher development through this approach. The case of clinical supervision will be examined to ascertain the way in which both cultures are at work in the process and also to determine the relationship between each of the two cultures and teacher development.

The Case of Clinical Supervision

Clinical supervision was originally conceived at the Harvard–Newton summer school as a means of fostering teacher development through discussion, observation and analysis of teaching 'in the clinic of the classroom' (Cogan, 1973:ix). The emphasis was on 'colleagueship' (Cogan, 1973:63) between teacher and clinical supervisor, bound together in a 'relationship that teaches' (Goldhammer, 1969:365) by the common purpose of enhancing student learning.

Three decades later, the claim that clinical supervision can foster teacher development through collegial conditions remains a moot one. Indeed, Smyth (1989) argues that clinical supervision has, over the last twenty years or more, essentially lost its collaborative emphasis and has been harnessed into a sophisticated mechanism of teacher inspection and surveillance. He documents how this cooption occurred historically through the progressive alignment of clinical supervision with the conservative educational reform movement in schools. Smyth's contention is that, unless and until clinical supervision takes on a 'critical' perspective which problematizes teaching and confronts the social, historical, and political agenda expressed therein, the collaborative intent of Goldhammer (1969) and Cogan (1973) will not be restored and teachers will remain unable to gain control over their classroom world and work.

The major authors writing about clinical supervision (Cogan, 1973; Goldhammer, Anderson and Krajewski, 1980; Mosher and Purpel, 1972) would claim that the beliefs, values and norms which constitute interdependent collegiality are operative when principals and teachers or teachers and teachers work together in the clinical approach to instructional supervision. The purpose of this emphasis on interdependent collegiality is 'the development of a professionally responsible teacher who is analytical of his [sic] own performance, open to help from others, and withal self-directing' (Cogan, 1973:12). This collegial relationship between supervisor and teacher does not imply similar and equal professional competencies. Rather, clinical supervision draws its strength from the heterogeneity nurtured in the association of dissimilar and unequal competencies:

> In clinical supervision the interaction of similar competencies at equal levels is generally less productive than the interaction of unequal levels of competence and dissimilar competences. Such productive heterogeneity may be observed when the clinical supervisor, highly competent in observation, the analysis of teaching, and the process connected with the cycle of supervision, works with a teacher who is more competent in knowledge of the curriculum, his [sic] students, their learning characteristics and transient and persistent problems, and the school sub-societies to which they belong. (Cogan, 1973:68)

As a consequence, principals and teachers or teachers and teachers working together in clinical supervision can, theoretically, engage in talking about teaching, observing classroom practice, planning and preparing materials together, and generally teaching one another the practice of teaching. These conditions of interdependent collegiality are associated by Little (1987) with teacher development. But Hargreaves and Dawe (1989) maintain that supervision (including the clinical approach) is incompatible with healthy collegial relations because it consists of 'hierarchical relations embedded in bureaucratically-driven systems' (p. 25). In their view, clinical supervision amounts to a form of contrived collegiality and rarely, if ever, can foster the conditions associated with interdependent collegiality.

What, then, is the nature of collegial conditions in clinical supervision when one professional functions in the role of supervisor? Is the culture inevitably one of contrived collegiality in which little or no teacher development occurs or can interdependent collegiality emerge in a manner that enables teachers to transform their classroom experience?

A close examination of case studies developed by Grimmett and Crehan (1988) would suggest two distinctively different types of contrived collegiality, namely collegiality that is *administratively imposed* and that which is *organizationally induced*. The administratively imposed type of contrived collegiality consists of 'top-down' attempts to manipulate directly the practices and behaviours of teachers as professional educators. The organizationally-induced type of contrived collegiality is characterized by 'top-down' attempts at fostering 'bottom-up' problem-solving approaches to school improvement through careful manipulation, not of teachers' practices and behaviours, but of the environment within which teachers live and work and have their professional being. As such, it constitutes a deliberate attempt on the part of administrators to influence indirectly teachers' professional practices and behaviours. Administratively imposed collegiality, by contrast, is more 'cult-like' in its attempt to influence teachers directly towards acting collaboratively.

Administratively Imposed Collegiality

The case of Audrey, working in a clinical supervision relationship with her principal Brian, illustrates the nature of the collegial culture when certain practices are administratively imposed.

Audrey has a total of fifteen years of teaching experience. She has taught in her present school, with her present principal, for four years. Prior to working with her current principal, Audrey had received two 'less than satisfactory' evaluation reports and had, at one point in time, been placed on extended medical leave. Although these events had occurred more than five years previously in a different school with a different principal, they had nevertheless scarred her sense of professional confidence and teacher efficacy, leaving her somewhat negatively predisposed towards instructional supervision. They also constituted one of the reasons why Brian, as principal, had to supervise Audrey's teaching.

Brian has a total of eleven years of experience as an administrator. He is viewed by his peers as an instructional leader, having had a provincial profile during the days when he worked with the local teachers' federation in the planning and implementation of modules designed to assist classroom teachers' professional development. Since becoming a principal, he has found that his apparent difficulty in finding time for classroom observation and conferencing has been exacerbated by the escalating demands on his time from central office, the community, and the daily routine of school life.

Brian's natural propensity in dealing with teachers was towards collegiality. He held a tremendous respect for their professional autonomy and would go to great lengths in his conferencing to avoid giving the impression of intruding into the teacher's workspace. Nevertheless, the situation of Audrey presented him with a challenge. He was required to supervise her yet he also wished to act with her as a professional colleague. His chosen course of action was to inform her that he would be supervising her classroom teaching along clinical lines. Whether Audrey naturally would have wanted this kind of relationship or not was superseded by the constraints of her particular situation—supervision was required and she had to comply. Brian, in turn, felt that using the collegial approach of the clinical model would, to some extent, ameliorate the evaluative aspects of the administrative requirement. He also doubted, however, that Audrey would willingly enter into a clinical supervisory relationship. Hence, in his inimitable low-key style, Brian laid the activity on.

Not surprisingly, the conferences conducted by Brian and Audrey about the latter's observed classroom teaching did not proceed smoothly. Audrey had complied with the request for a supervisory relationship but she proved to be no 'shrinking violet' when it came to defending her instructional practices. Possibly because of her negative experience with previous supervisors, she neither offered a critique of her own teaching, nor did she agree with Brian's feedback. Rather, she indulged in instances of disparaging the students' behaviour and justifying her own. Brian attempted to pinpoint her lack of adequate group management and consequent loss of instructional time in the lesson but Audrey would have none of it. In her view, the principal understood neither the instructional context nor the curriculum content.

Such resistance provokes conflict. Conflict can be viewed either as an opportunity to explore the issues of divergence or as a source of subversion. Over time in the conferencing process, Brian became convinced that Audrey's 'denial of reality', as he termed it, was subverting the collegial purposes of clinical supervision. He consequently began to act on this assumption and became oblivious to those occasional moments when Audrey displayed a willingness to consider that her behaviour, and not merely the students', had contributed to the loss of valuable instructional time. These moments could have represented the genesis of a restructuring of some aspects of her teaching but they were lost in Brian's determined attempts to emphasize, if not cudgel, the points that Audrey should note. Indeed, he became preoccupied with refraining the lesson for her at a time when she was possibly open to exploring different alternatives for the specific problem of group management he was addressing. Whereas Audrey wanted to discuss the problem of distributing and collecting lesson materials, Brian was proposing a solution. But it was his solution and not hers; Audrey interpreted what was happening as a further instance of the administration imposing its ideas on teachers powerless to critique them.

Audrey's resistance and self-justifying behaviour in the conferences with Brian, combined with the circumstances surrounding the initiation of such a supervisory relationship, had produced a situation full of conflict. Brian began to assume that this conflict was potentially subverting the collegial purposes to clinical supervision whereby the teacher analyzes his or her own classroom instruction. He consequently began to make decisions for both of them which were essentially in accordance with the original political purposes of the administrative requirement that Audrey's teaching be supervised. Audrey also interpreted the events in this way and therefore listened to what was proposed without agreeing or disagreeing. Thus, the conflict that existed between the two was never explored; rather, it was initially denied and suppressed, and ultimately ignored.

Figure 4.4 documents the beliefs, values, and norms which operate in such an *administratively imposed* form of contrived collegiality. It is characterized by the belief that the effects of the typical school culture are so dominant that teachers will not willingly enter into collaboration with other teachers and/or administrators. Consequently, teacher commitment to collaboration is viewed as coming *after* engagement in activities structured for that purpose. The value then is placed on extrinsic motivation. Educational change is brought about by administrative 'strong-arming [which] can, and often does, lower users' initial commitment' (Huberman and Crandall, 1983:65). The resistance associated with this process, however, does not prevent central office staffs from pressuring teachers into action through 'enforced, stabilized use' (Huberman, 1983:24). This, in turn, breeds the norm of unilateral imposition. When collegial practices, such as clinical supervision or peer coaching, are imposed in this way, teachers feel that it is 'mandatory that they volunteer for the programme' (Grimmett, 1987:20). In the case of administratively imposed collegiality, it is not merely the beliefs, values, and norms that are tightly structured; rather, the nature of the very beliefs and values which constitute the normative basis for action is such that the organizational structure is also tight. The tight-tight formulation gives this form of contrived collegiality a 'cult-like' ethos which ultimately leads to unresolved conflict and an impasse between teachers and the administration.

The presence of conflict is, however, endemic to all forms of collegiality. What distinguishes one form from another are the beliefs and values accompanying such conflict. In *administratively imposed collegiality*, the belief at work is that conflict potentially leads to a subversion of the purposes of working collaboratively. What is valued, then, are decisions that are made in accordance with the original (and often political) purposes for which the administration imposed collegial practices. As a consequence, conflict is not explored as a potential for transforming teachers' understanding of the task around which

Figure 4.4: *Exemplars of Beliefs, Values, and Norms Found in Administratively Imposed Collegiality*

Exemplar 1

TIGHT
- *Belief:* Teacher commitment to collaboration comes after engaging in activities structured for that purpose
- *Value:* Extrinsic motivators
- *Norm:* Unilateral imposition: teachers mandated to work together

TIGHT Organizational structure

Exemplar 2

TIGHT
- *Belief:* Conflict leads to subversion of collaborative purposes
- *Value:* Decisions made in accordance with political purposes of administration
- *Norm:* Conflict denied, suppressed, ignored

TIGHT Organizational structure

collegial practices are operating; rather, the tight organizational structure combines with the tightly structured beliefs, values, and norms to bring about the denial, suppression and ignoring of conflict when teachers and/or administrators function together in collegial settings. Whereas administratively imposed collegiality has a 'cult-like' oppressiveness to it, *organizationally induced collegiality* is characterized by a more typical 'tight-loose' formulation of its culture.

Organizationally Induced Collegiality

The case of Barry,[6] working in a clinical supervision relationship with his principal Margaret, illustrates the nature of the collegial culture when certain practices are organizationally induced.

Barry has a total of twenty years of teaching experience of which the most recent two have been at the intermediate level (grades 4–7). His prior experience includes sixteen years at the secondary level (grades 8–12) and two as a district consultant. Barry has taught in his present school for two years, both of them with his current principal. During the course of these two years, Barry engaged in five supervisory cycles with Margaret and they worked collaboratively in the study of classroom management for at least six months. Margaret, the principal, has a total of eight years of experience as an administrator, three of which were as an elementary school vice-principal and five years as an elementary principal in her current school. All eight years were spent in her present district.

Unlikely Audrey, Barry's previous experience of clinical supervision had been relatively positive. He held the view that engaging in collegial discourse about teaching with another professional (even an administrator) was ultimately beneficial to his classroom practice and student learning. Margaret, as principal, conceived of her role in clinical supervision as facilitating teaching development. She felt strongly that teacher development could not be facilitated when administrators used 'strong-arming' tactics. Consequently, when she approached Barry about a supervisory relationship in his first year in the school, she was open to the prospect of his turning her down. Barry was equally capable of saying 'no' if he felt particularly uncomfortable about or unduly pressured into a supervisory arrangement. Having been a district consultant and enjoying a reputation as a very experienced and creative teacher, Barry had little to lose by declining Margaret's invitation. But he did consider that he could gain professionally by entering into a clinical supervisory relationship with her. Moreover, he sensed that the longer they engaged in clinical supervision the more he would appreciate the professional development aspect of the relationship.

Just as Margaret extended freedom of choice to Barry to decide whether or not to engage in clinical supervision, she also demonstrated in the conferences her belief that teachers should be given choices. Her role as clinical supervisor, then, was to help Barry clarify the consequences of his instructional choices as they related to student learning. To do this, she engendered an atmosphere of supportiveness: she made frequent use of a 'we' strategy to identify her own teaching with that of Barry's; she also presented data to him in a neutral manner and always used positive statements as precursors to raising an instructional concern. Not only did she hold a deep sense of respect for teachers' professional autonomy, but also evidenced in the conferences an ability to transcend her own instructional leanings to accommodate Barry's preferences as classroom teacher.

At the same time, she did not deny her own goals for the school's instructional programme. She regarded clinical supervision as a process which stimulated a mutual negotiation of classroom reality as well as one which respected the teacher's instructional autonomy. She had her agenda for the conferences and Barry had his. Both realized that the negotiation inherent in the process could potentially spill over into conflict but neither one saw that as abnormal. On the contrary, Margaret felt that Barry had to be exposed to a total school perspective and Barry, in turn, made sure that Margaret interpreted the events of his classroom within the context of the learning needs of the students and of himself as teacher. Grimmett and Crehan (1990) report two episodes from this case which evidence this potential conflict. In the first episode, the principal's agenda prevailed to the extent that the purpose of using clinical supervision to develop Barry's teaching was disrupted. In the second episode, however, the negotiation that took place represented considerable adaptation by both parties with the result that Barry began to appreciate his teaching in a fresh and transforming way. The decisions made in this episode of the conference truly reflected the original purpose towards which Margaret and Barry had initiated a clinical supervision relationship.

Figure 4.5: *Exemplars of Beliefs, Values, and Norms Found in Organizationally Induced Collegiality*

Exemplar 1

TIGHT

> *Belief:* Teacher commitment to collaboration possible *before* and *during* activities structured for that purpose
> *Value:* Intrinsic motivators
> *Norm:* Fashioning of environment for collaboration

LOOSE   Organizational structure

Exemplar 2

TIGHT

> *Belief:* Conflict a source of frustration and perplexity potentially capable of disrupting or transforming project's purposes
> *Value:* Decisions made in accordance with project's purposes
> *Norm:* Conflict seen as normal aspect of collaboration

LOOSE   Organizational structure

The negotiation of divergent views and conflict was therefore a normal aspect of their working together.

Because the principal asked the teacher to enter into a clinical supervision experience with her, the collegiality is contrived. But the fact is that she did not impose her wishes on the teacher suggests that it does not equate to administratively imposed collegiality; rather, the administrator induced it organizationally. Figure 4.5 documents the beliefs, values, and norms which operate in such an *organizationally induced* form of contrived collegiality. It is characterized by the belief that teachers can willingly enter into collegial practices and that the very act of engaging in collaboration reinforces their original commitment. Commitment to collegiality, therefore, can precede and be strengthened by engagement in activities structured for the purpose of collaboration. Such a belief places tremendous value on teachers' intrinsic motivation. No teachers are expected to enter into collegial practices grudgingly. This, in turn, breeds the norm of environmental fashioning. The context within which teachers work and make instructional decisions is cultivated to encourage practitioners to choose collaboration over isolation. Whereas administrators make choices which influence the workplace environment of teaching, the ultimate choices about collaboration, both before and during the process, are made by teachers. Unlike *administratively imposed collegiality*, this form of contrived collegiality is not 'cult-like' in its effects; rather, it has a typical 'tight-loose' formulation. Because of the nature of the tightly structured beliefs and values constituting the basis for normative action, the organizational structure is loose.

When conflict occurs, it is viewed, not as a source of subversion, but as a point of frustration and perplexity potentially capable of disrupting or transforming the purposes of the collegial practices. Such a belief does not value decisions which are made in accordance with the political purposes of the administration's agenda in instituting collegiality; it prefers those which are made in accordance with the task around which teachers have chosen to collaborate. Conflict, then, is viewed as a normal aspect of collaboration when teachers engage in the mutual negotiation of purpose and task. As mentioned above, the beliefs, values, and norms of such an organizationally induced culture are tightly structured and the bureaucratic control is loose. It represents not a *strong* but a *typical* culture in that the beliefs and values constituting the basis for normative action have not yet evolved into the highly-focused professional orientation characteristic of interdependent collegiality. Yet, when these beliefs, values, and norms take on a professional focus, the prognosis for educational change appears to be good. This evolving into cultures which support or constrain innovative practices, suggesting that *organizationally induced collegiality* plays a pivotal role in the implementation of educational change.

The Pivotal Nature of Organizationally Induced Collegiality

If the purpose of educational change is to foster teacher development through collegiality, then one cannot expect to institute a culture of interdependent collegiality overnight. One has to start somewhere.[7] Any attempt at initiating collegiality is inevitably contrived. But the thesis of this chapter is that there are two forms of contrived collegiality and that the organizationally induced form is essentially pivotal by nature. A further examination of the case of Barry suggests that, under certain conditions and circumstances, organizationally induced collegiality can evolve into a truly interdependent culture in which the teacher reflectively transforms his classroom experience.

The Case of Barry Reivisited

Grimmett and Crehan (1990) document two episodes in this case which contain instances of Barry seemingly on the verge of engaging in the reflective transformation of his classroom practice. Yet their analysis shows that this process was consummated in only one of the two episodes. The first episode revolved around Barry's naming of the instructional problem as engaging the uninvolved pupils who formed a class within a class. This problem was essentially refocused by the principal around the theme of teacher proximity to pupils, a theme which had emerged in their previous conferences. In other words, she saw Barry's instructional dilemma in terms of the pupils' physical location in the classroom rather than in terms of their possible difficulty in grasping conceptually what was being presented. The consequence was that her suggestion about changing the position of the overhead projector constituted a reframing of the instructional context according to the principal's definition of the problem and not the teacher's. Inasmuch as the principal's refocusing did not constitute a deliberate overriding of an indomitable teacher but was more the product of a keenly supportive and respectful mind which failed to grasp the deeper significance of the teacher's problem, this case was different from the 'private cold war' metaphor that Blumberg (1980) used to characterize typical instructional supervision practices. It was also different in the sense that the principal's suggestion was offered as a tentative hypothesis to be tested out in action, whereas typical principals would, according to Leithwood and Montgomery (1982), attempt to impose their suggestion as a solution to the problem which they themselves had named. Although teacher development did not occur, the culture of organizationally induced collegiality appeared nevertheless to remain in place.

The second episode proved to be very different from the first. The teacher named the problem as dealing with end–of–lesson activities in an educationally sound manner. Barry suggested that his difficulties came about because the pupils had worked hard for too long a period of time. Margaret chose to explore what he typically does in situations in which such a break-down occurs up to ten minutes before the end of the lesson. Barry responded that, if it occurred with less than five minutes remaining, he effected closure. If, however, it happened with more than five minutes remaining in the lesson, then he admitted to being sometimes bereft of ideas and asked the principal for advice. Margaret empathized with the predicament Barry had described (she used the 'we' strategy here) but also added that this kind of dilemma was a normal one and that teachers needed to plan some short activities which could productively fill the remaining minutes. The principal's empathetic exploration of Barry's predicament enabled him to admit that, in such situations, he frequently did not know what to do. In so doing, Barry was naming the ways of filling the remaining minutes of a lesson when the planned material had been exhausted. The principal accepted this as the problem and began to share how she always used to read poetry to pupils when she felt they had reached their saturation point. This provided a change of pace for the pupils but still fulfilled the teacher's mandate to be educating them. The principal's reporting of how she had tackled a situation similar to the dilemma that he had described immediately fired Barry's interest, for he saw, perhaps for the first time, that such back-up activities did not necessarily constitute busy work.

This fresh appreciation by Barry of the potentially educative purpose of end–of–lesson additional activities is a noteworthy instance of the generative quality of reflective transformation. The principal's shared experience has facilitated a reconstruction of his prevailing view of back-up activities such that it has led to a new understanding of their educational significance. Having reframed the context within which he thought of such activities, Barry then experienced a further enriching instance of reflective transformation. He suddenly realized that he could have read something else out of the newspaper material he had used in the third and final segment of the lesson. In so doing, he was seeing his end-of-lesson classroom teaching as a version of his principal's. Her reported actions had served as a metaphor which prompted him to reframe his own teaching in a highly creative yet exploratory way. He did not *transfer* the principal's reported activity, i.e. poetry, to the context of his teaching; rather, he *transformed* both the activity (from reading poetry to reading a newspaper article) and his teaching context (from dead-time or busy-work to educationally significant work) in the process.

Four factors working together would seem to account for this double portion of teacher development through reflective transformation. First, the teacher himself named the problem which was explored in the conference. Second, the principal did not appear, in this instance, to have an agenda of her own and consequently accepted and explored the problem identified by the teacher. Third, the teacher felt secure enough in the supportive atmosphere engendered by the principal to take a professional risk in admitting a shortcoming and asking for assistance. Fourth, the principal's empathetic sharing of how she tackled the problem enabled the teacher to reconstruct his view of back-up activities and reframe the context of the lesson in which he had originally experienced the problem.

These two episodes demonstrate how an organizationally induced form of contrived collegiality can both frustrate and lead to teacher development through the reflective transformation of classroom experience. In the first episode, the teacher's naming of the problem was, either wittingly or unwittingly, not accepted by the principal and the subsequent reframing of the instructional context was therefore not owned by the teacher. As a consequence, the reflective transformation of classroom experience did not occur and the culture remained as an organizationally induced form of contrived collegiality. In the second episode, however, the teacher's articulation of the problem was accepted and he, not the principal, reframed the context in which the problem could be addressed. In this episode, the culture evolved into an interdependent form of collegiality in which mutual negotiation, interpersonal support and challenge, and ultimately teacher development occurred.

A Different Evolution: The Case of Helen

The case of Helen,[8] working in a clinical supervision relationship with her principal Hugh, illustrates how organizationally induced collegiality can evolve, not into a culture of interdependence, but into an administratively imposed form of contrived collegiality.

Helen has seventeen years teaching experience, all of which have been at the intermediate level (grades 4–7). This was her first year in her present school with her present principal. Hugh was also in his first year at his present school and this was his first principalship. He has a total of four years experience as an administrator, three of which were as an elementary school vice-principal.

The Hugh-Helen supervisory relationship had been initiated in a similar manner to the Margaret-Barry dyad. Hugh had approached Helen about a clinical supervision experience but had left the final decision up to her. Helen was a very experienced and quietly self-assured teacher who entered into the experience because she felt she could learn from it. Both seemed comfortable with the possibility of conflict and negotiation and both held a deep respect for the other as a professional. At the outset then, their clinical supervision relationship was a further instance of organizationally induced collegiality. But it did not stay that way for long. Unlike Margaret, Hugh appeared unable to present accurate classroom data in a neutral manner to Helen. He began to apologize for his lack of preparation for conferences, attributing blame for the situation to his overcrowded administrative schedule. At a time when Helen began to articulate a specific instructional dilemma, Hugh's attention was resolutely focused on keeping to the pre-conference agreement which, he argued, precluded a discussion of the teacher's concern. The principal's socialization as a clinical supervisor had alerted him to the requirement of not digressing from the pre-conference agreement during the post-conference discussion. Such a requirement was originally designed to protect the teacher from the possibility of the principal bringing up a hidden agenda. It was not designed to prevent the teacher from refocusing the post-conference discussion. Hugh's limited construal of the purpose of the pre-conference agreement led him to dismiss Helen's identification of her use of time as an instructional concern. For Helen, it seemed that her sense of authority had been violated and that conference decisions would now be made, not in accordance with her developmental needs, but in accordance with the principal's political purposes in engaging in clinical supervision. Hugh had viewed the perplexity arising from Helen's concern as potentially disruptive to the purposes of clinical supervision and chose, therefore, not to explore it but to suppress it and ultimately to ignore it. Helen, in turn, felt subtle pressure to comply rather than to negotiate and began to alert herself to the dependency-inducing cues she perceived Hugh to be emitting.

What, then, determines the direction in which organizationally induced collegiality evolves? Figure 4.6 diagrams the pivotal nature of organizationally induced collegiality and suggests two determinant factors in its evolution. When organizationally induced collegiality is initiated with practitioners who are very experienced in terms of the number of years spent teaching and who have a well-grounded pro-

Figure 4.6:   The Pivotal Nature of Organizationally Induced Collegiality

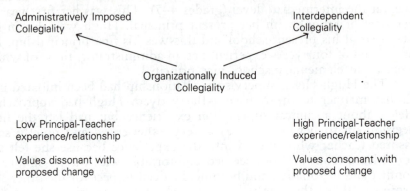

Administratively Imposed
Collegiality

Interdependent
Collegiality

Organizationally Induced
Collegiality

Low Principal-Teacher
experience/relationship

High Principal-Teacher
experience/relationship

Values dissonant with
proposed change

Values consonant with
proposed change

fessional relationship, it leans in the direction of collaboration. When the beliefs and values of such practitioners are consonant with the proposed change (in the case of clinical supervision, with the supportively rigorous analysis of classroom teaching), then its evolution towards a culture of interdependent collegiality is greatly enhanced. However, when collegiality is organizationally induced among practitioners who are less experienced and whose relationships are not well-grounded, the potential for it to become administratively imposed is increased. When the beliefs and values of the practitioners involved in the project are, or through unanticipated circumstances become, dissonant with the proposed change, then organizationally induced collegiality evolves into collegiality by administrative fiat. The outcomes of the latter form of contrived collegiality are teacher resistance, deception, and compliance; the outcomes of interdependent collegiality are teacher development, the reflective transformation of classroom practice, and the enhancement of pupil learning.

The cases of Barry and Helen demonstrate that teacher development through the reflective transformation of classroom experience associates with interdependent, as distinct from contrived, collegiality. They further confirm the validity of Hargreaves' (1989b) view that contrived collegiality can serve as a precursor to a culture of collaboration. What the cases also reveal is that there are two forms of contrived collegiality and that the organizationally induced form represents a preliminary phase of either interdependent or administratively imposed collegiality. They suggest that organizationally induced collegiality pivots towards collaborative interdependence when, within the context of well-grounded professional relationships, the values of the project are consonant with those of the practitioners involved. Moreover, when professional relationships are not well-grounded and the value match is a dissonant one, organizationally induced collegiality is likely to pivot in the direction of collegiality by administrative fiat.

Concluding Note

The culture of interdependent collegiality occurs all too rarely in schools. When it does occur, teacher development is left with one nagging question: under what circumstances and conditions do such strong school cultures develop? We have suggested that all attempts at initiating collegiality are, to some extent, contrived in their genesis. But we have also suggested that the organizationally induced form of contrived collegiality plays a pivotal role in the implementation of educational change. It is our hope that the distinction articulated between organizationally induced and administratively imposed collegiality will enable practitioners and researchers alike to understand how to begin to address the aforementioned question. We also hope that our description of the pivotal nature of organizationally induced collegiality will stimulate further rigorous study of how school cultures of collaborative interdependence come into being.

Acknowledgments

The case studies cited in this chapter were funded by the Social Sciences and Humanities Research Council of Canada (Grants #410-85-0339 and #410-86-2014). The authors gratefully acknowledge that this work could not have been carried out without this funding. The opinions expressed in this paper do not necessarily reflect the policy, position, or endorsement of SSHRCC. The authors also acknowledge the contributions of Maryl Stewart, Bruce McGillivray and Cindy Drossos to the data collection, data analysis and manuscript preparation aspects of the study respectively.

Notes

1   As with Hargreaves, A. (1989b), these characterizations are less concerned with the *content* of culture than they are with its *form* and the beliefs, values, and norms that associate with particular patterns of organizational relationships found between and among teachers in school settings.
2   Feiman-Nemser and Floden (1986) argue that the assumption of cultural uniformity is untenable. They point to differences in age, experience, social background, gender, subject matter, and other factors to make a case for cultural diversity. However, writers on both sides of the Atlantic (Hargreaves, D., 1983; Waller, 1932; Sarason, 1982; Lortie, 1975) all point to the existence of a pervasive culture of individualism, presentism, and conservatism among teachers. Hargreaves, A. (1989b), in a perceptive critique of Feiman-Nemser and Floden's review, posits that they have confused the various subcultures that teaching sustains with the more generic and pervasive culture of the occupation as a whole. Indeed, he suggests that this confusion is

exacerbated by their apparent lack of classification and explanation with the result that the reader remains unclear about the factors that create and sustain the diverse cultures they describe.

3 One obvious exception is John Elliott, so closely associated with the 'teachers as researcher' movement. In a somewhat autobiographical beginning to his 1988 AERA address, he documents how his first years of teaching were characterized by a powerful curriculum discourse which inevitably encouraged collegial challenge and support:

> There [in the staffroom] over coffee we sat during breaks discussing and debating our attempts to bring about change with colleagues who regarded our ideas with some scepticism. The quality of this curriculum discourse was an experience which has influenced all my subsequent thinking and action...I learned as a teacher that theories were implicit in all practices, and that theorizing consisted of articulating those 'tacit theories' and subjecting them to critique in free and open professional discourse. I also learned that high quality professional discourse depends upon the willingness of everyone involved to tolerate a diversity of views and practices. (Elliott, 1988:4)

4 Hargreaves (1989b), describes two broad types of typical cultures found in schools, namely, fragmented individualism and Balkanization. Fragmented individualism essentially isolates teachers from their colleagues and ties them irrepressibly to the immediacy of classroom life. It represents the 'seedbed' to pedagogical conservatism. Balkanization finds teachers working in competing territorial groups which bestow identity and provide bases for the pursuit of power, status, and resources. Both cultures deny teachers the opportunity of collaborating in details of classroom practice, thereby precluding the possibility of fundamental educational change.

5 Hargreaves (1989b) explicates three reservations about the over-hasty adoption of contrived collegiality in school systems. First, contrived collegiality cannot legislate a collaborative culture into existence, nor can it provide an 'instant' substitute for a culture that requires much time and care to develop. Second, it may sometimes affront the dignity of teachers by failing to recognize existing collaborative conditions, and, in the process, actually discourage collegial relations by making them more administratively cumbersome. Third, contrived collegiality can lead to a proliferation of unwanted meetings, causing teachers to suffer from administrative overload and crowding out the informal camaraderie that represents a vital interpersonal foundation of any collaborative culture.

6 A more detailed examination of this case exploring the relationship between collegial conditions and teacher reflection is to be found in Grimmett and Crehan (1990). The full version of the case of Barry is to be found in Grimmett and Crehan (1988).

7 Hargreaves (1989b) acknowledges that contrived collegiality can be a useful preliminary phase in the move towards more enduring collaborative relationships among teachers but he does not comment on how this happens; nor does he articulate the possibility that contrived collegiality may have more than one form.

8 Although referred to in Grimmett and Crehan (1988), the full version of this case is found in Tyler (1989). In a sensitive comparison of the cases of Barry

and Helen, Tyler generated an insightful, explanatory framework for mapping the development of two experienced teachers under clinical supervision conditions.

References

BIRD, T. and LITTLE, J.W. (1986) 'How schools organize the teaching occupation', in *The Elementary School Journal, 86*, 4, pp. 493–511.

BLUMBERG, A. (1980) *Supervisors and Teachers: A Private Cold War*, 2nd edn., Berkeley, McCutchan.

CHISM, N. (1985) *The Place of Peer Interaction in Teacher Development: Findings From a Case Study*, Paper presented at the annual meeting of the American Educational Research Association, Chicago, Illinois.

COGAN, M. (1973) *Clinical Supervision*, Boston, Houghton Mifflin.

COHEN, M. (1983) 'Instructional management and social conditions in effective schools', in ODDEN, A. and WEBB, L.D. (Eds.), *School Finance and School Improvement: Linkages in the 1980s*, Yearbook of the American Educational Finance Association, 1983, Washington, DC, AEFA.

COHEN, M.D., MARCH, J.G. and OLSON, J. (1972) 'A garbage can model of organizational choice', in *Administrative Science Quarterly, 17*, 1, pp. 1–25.

COOPER, M. (1989) 'Whose culture is it, anyway', in LIEBERMAN, A. (Ed.), *Building A Professional Culture In Schools*, New York, Teachers College Press, pp. 45–54.

DOYLE, W. and PONDER, G. (1977) 'The practicality ethic in teacher decision-making', *Interchange, 8*, 3, pp. 1–12.

ELLIOTT, J. (1988) 'Teachers As Researchers: Implications For Supervision and Teacher Education', Paper presented at the annual meeting of the American Educational Research Association.

FEIMAN-NEMSER, S. and FLODEN, R.E. (1986), 'The cultures of teaching', in WITTROCK, M.C. (Ed.), *Handbook of Research on Teaching*, 3rd edn., New York, Macmillan.

FULLAN, M.G. and CONNELLY, F.M. (1987) *Teacher Education in Ontario*, Toronto, Ontario Ministry of Education.

GOLDHAMMER, R. (1969) *Clinical Supervision: Special Methods for the Supervision of Teachers*, New York, Holt, Rinehart and Winston.

GOLDHAMMER, R., ANDERSON, R. and KRAJEWSKI, R. (1980) *Clinical Supervision: Special Methods for the Supervision of Teachers*, 2nd edn., New York, Holt, Rinehart and Winston.

GOODLAD, J.I. (1984) *A Place Called School*, New York, McGraw-Hill.

GOODSON, I.F. (1989) 'Critical introduction: Understanding/undermining hierarchy and hegemony', in HARGREAVES, A., *Curriculum and Assessment Reform*, Milton Keynes, Open University Press.

GREENFIELD, T.B. (1984) 'Leaders and schools: Wilfulness and non–natural order in organization', in SERGIOVANNI, T.J. and CORBALLY, J.E. (Eds.), *Leadership and Organizations Culture*, Urbana-Champaign, University of Illinois Press.

GRIMMETT, P.P. (1987) 'The role of district supervisors in the implementation of peer coaching', *Journal of Curriculum and Supervision, 3*, 1, pp. 3–28.

GRIMMETT, P.P. and GREHAN, E.P. (1988) *A Study of the Effects of Supervisors' Intervention on Teachers' Classroom Management Performance*, Final report to the

Social Sciences and Humanities Research Council of Canada, Grants 410-85-0339 and 410-86-2014.

GRIMMETT, P.P. and CREHAN, E.P. (1990) 'Barry: A case study of teacher reflection in clinical supervision', in *Journal of Curriculum and Supervision, 5,* 3, pp. 214–35.

HARGREAVES, A. (1986) *Two Cultures of Teaching: The Case of Middle Schools,* Philadelphia, The Falmer Press.

HARGREAVES, A. (1989a) *Curriculum and Assessment Reform,* Milton Keynes, Open University Press.

HARGREAVES, A. (1989b) 'Contrived collegiality and the culture of Teaching', Paper presented at the annual meeting of the Canadian Society for the Study of Education, Quebec City.

HARGREAVES, A. and DAWE, R. (1989) 'Coaching as unreflective practice: Contrived collegiality or collaborative culture?', Paper presented at the annual meeting of the American Educational Research Association, San Francisco.

HARGREAVES, D. (1983) 'The occupational culture of teachers', in WOODS, P. (Ed.), *Teacher Strategies,* London, UK, Croom Helm.

HUBERMAN, M. (1983) 'School improvement strategies that work: Some scenarios', in *Educational Leadership, 41,* 3, pp. 23–7.

HUBERMAN, M. and CRANDALL, D. (1983) 'People, policies, and practices: Examining the chain of social improvement' in *Implications for Action, A Study of Dissemination Efforts Supporting School Improvement, IX,* Andover, Mass., The Network.

JACKSON, P.W. (1968) *Life In Classrooms,* New York, Holt, Rinehart and Winston.

LEITHWOOD, K.A. and MONTGOMERY, D.J. (1982) 'The role of the elementary school principal in program improvement', *Review of Educational Research, 52,* 3, pp. 309–39.

LIEBERMAN, A. (1989) *Building A Professional Culture In Schools,* New York, Teachers College Press.

LIEBERMAN, A. and MILLER, L. (1984) *Teachers, Their World, and Their Work,* Alexandria, VA, ASCD.

LITTLE, J.W. (1981) 'The power of organizational setting: School norms and staff development', Paper presented at the annual meeting of the American Educational Research Association, Los Angeles, CA.

LITTLE, J.W. (1986) 'Seductive images and organizational realities in professional development', *Teachers' College Record, 86,* 1, pp. 84–102.

LITTLE, J.W. (1987) 'Teachers as colleagues', in KOEHLER, V.R. (Ed.), *Educators' Handbook: A Research Perspective,* New York, Longman, pp. 491–518.

LITTLE, J.W. (1989) 'The persistence of privacy: Autonomy and initiative in teachers' professional relations', Paper presented at the annual meeting of the American Educational Research Association, San Francisco.

LORTIE, D.C. (1975) *Schoolteacher: A Sociological Study,* Chicago, University of Chicago Press.

MEYER, J., COHEN, E., BURNETTI, F., MOLNAR, S. and LUEDERS-SALMON, E. (1971) *The Impact of the Open-space School upon Teacher Influence and Autonomy: The Effects of an Organizational Innovation,* Technical Report No. 21, Centre for the Research and Development in Teaching, Stanford.

MOSHER, R. and PURPEL, D. (1972) Supervision: *The Reluctant Profession,* Boston, Houghton Mifflin.

OJA, S.M. and PINE, G.J. (1987) 'Collaborative action research', *Peabody Journal of Education, 64,* 1, pp. 96–115.

PETERS, T.J. and WATERMAN, R.H. (1982) *In Search of Excellence*, New York, Harper and Row.

SARASON, S. (1982) *The Culture of the School and the Problem of Change*, 2nd edn., Boston, Allyn and Bacon.

SELZNICK, P. (1957) *Leadership and Administration: A Sociological Interpretation*, New York, Harper and Row.

SERGIOVANNI, T.J. (1984) 'Leadership and excellence in schooling' in *Educational Leadership*, 42, 5, pp. 4–13.

SERGIOVANNI, T.J. (1987) 'The theoretical basis for cultural leadership', in SHEIVE, L.T. and SCHOENHEIT, M.B. (Eds.) *Leadership: Examining the Options*, Alexandria, VA, Association for Supervision and Curriculum Development, pp. 116–29.

SMYTH, J. (1989) 'Problematizing teaching through a "critical" perspective on clinical supervision', Paper presented at the annual meeting of the American Educational Research Association, San Francisco.

TYLER, J.P. (1989) *Supervisory Conferences From the Teachers' Perspective; A Comparative Analysis of Teachers' Interactive Responses in Two Different Dyads*, MA Thesis, University of British Columbia.

VAN MAANEN, J. (1988) *Tales of the Field: On Writing Ethnography*, Chicago, University of Chicago Press.

WALLER, W. (1932) *The Sociology of Teaching*, New York, Russell and Russell.

WEICK, K.E. (1982) 'Administering education in loosely coupled schools', *Phi Delta Kappan*, 27, 2, pp. 673–6.

Chapter 5

The Principal's Role in Teacher Development

Kenneth A. Leithwood

A leader's vision is 'the grain of sand in the oyster not the pearl'. (Murphy, 1988, p. 650)

Principals vary widely in how they conceive of their role. These variations are evident in the four different focuses identified in research on principals' styles or patterns of practice (Blumberg and Greenfield, 1980; Hall *et al.*, 1984; Leithwood and Montgomery, 1986; Salley *et al.*, 1978), which comprise: an administration or plant manager focus; an interpersonal relations or climate focus; a programme focus; and a student development focus. The first two patterns function primarily to maintain the school and appear to capture the practices of the majority of principals, at present (e.g. Morris *et al.*, 1982; Trider and Leithwood 1988). The latter two patterns are less common and appear to be relatively effective in improving the school's contribution to student outcomes valued in most North American schools. These two patterns also correspond to what is usually meant by the term 'instructional leadership'.

Between 1975 and 1988, at least sixty-five original empirical studies in the English language have provided evidence for the claim that instructional leadership is an achievable expectation for principals (Leithwood, 1988). These studies, as a whole, also provide detailed descriptions of what such leadership looks like in practice. Despite such evidence, some principals and researchers (e.g. Gersten *et al.*, 1982; Rallis and Highsmith 1986) continue to dispute the viability of an instructional leadership role for the principal, including teacher development, which is arguably the most central function of instructional leadership. Even principals who acknowledge their responsibility to foster teacher development often claim that it is not a function they feel capable of performing well.

* Reprinted with permission. Association for Supervisory and Curriculum Development from B. Joyce (Ed.) *Changing School Culture Through Staff Development*, ASCD, 1990.

To a significant degree, these feelings of inadequacy have two roots: and unclear image of what teacher development looks like, and uncertainty about just how a principal might help foster such development, given the usual job demands. This Chapter attempts to shed light on each of these matters. The first section draws on evidence from three distinct areas of research to build a multidimensional description of teacher development. This description is offered to principals as an aid in reflecting upon, and possibly making more explicit and robust, their own views of such development. The second section of the Chapter provides guidelines that principals may find useful in shaping their efforts to help teachers develop.

Dimensions and Stages of Teacher Development

Figure 5.1 summarizes three dimensions of teacher development that principals can influence: development of professional expertise, psychological development, and career-cycle development. Each of these dimensions reflect quite different lines of inquiry about teacher development.

Development of Professional Expertise

The dimension of teacher development with the most obvious consequences for classroom, school, and district improvement is identified in Figure 5.1 as 'Development of Professional Expertise'. It is through such expertise that teachers contribute directly to the growth of students (amount learned, range of outcomes achieved, and ranges of students who benefit from instruction). Six stages of development are included in this dimension. Stage 1–4 are concerned with teachers' classroom responsibilities; Stages 5 and 6 explicitly address the out-of-classroom and out-of-school roles of the 'mature' teacher. Each of the stages—beyond the first—includes expertise acquired in previous stages. Furthermore, it seems likely that the seeds of expertise in higher stages will begin to develop quite early, given appropriate, formative experiences. Hence, this conception of growth does not imply restricting teacher experiences only to those that will prepare them for their next stage of development. Some preparation for Stage 6 practices might well begin during a teacher's initial entry into the role.

Figure 5.2 illustrates in more detail aspects of professional expertise likely to be a part of each of the six stages. While others might describe the aspect of expertise in each of these stages differently, there is at least good warrant for the substance of Figure 5.2. Stages 1–4 are based on an image of effective classroom instruction as requiring a large repertoire of instructional techniques; such a repertoire is

Figure 5.1: *Interrelated Dimensions of Teacher Development*

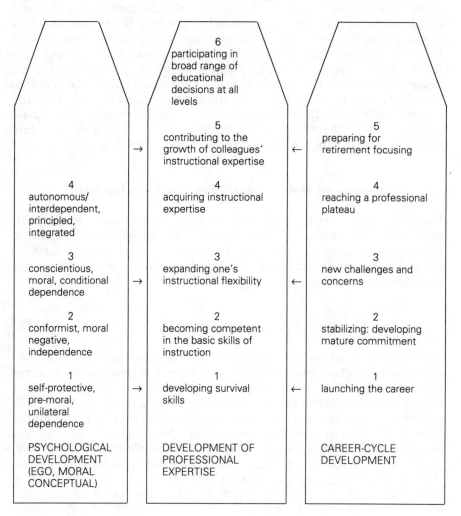

6
participating in
broad range of
educational
decisions at all
levels

5
contributing to the
growth of colleagues'
instructional expertise

5
preparing for
retirement focusing

4
autonomous/
interdependent,
principled,
integrated

4
acquiring instructional
expertise

4
reaching a professional
plateau

3
conscientious,
moral, conditional
dependence

3
expanding one's
instructional flexibility

3
new challenges and
concerns

2
conformist, moral
negative,
independence

2
becoming competent
in the basic skills of
instruction

2
stabilizing: developing
mature commitment

1
self-protective,
pre-moral,
unilateral
dependence

1
developing survival
skills

1
launching the career

PSYCHOLOGICAL
DEVELOPMENT
(EGO, MORAL
CONCEPTUAL)

DEVELOPMENT OF
PROFESSIONAL
EXPERTISE

CAREER-CYCLE
DEVELOPMENT

reflected, for example, in Joyce and Weil's (1986) twenty-three models of teaching, organized into four 'families' or categories. Expertise, in these terms, increases as teachers acquire greater skill in the application of a given teaching model and as an increasing number of such models are mastered. Teaching, however, involves more than the unthinking application of such models, although 'automaticity' is an important characteristic of expertise in most areas of human endeavour. Along with Joyce and Weil (1986), Darling-Hammond *et al.* (1983), Bacharach *et al.* (1987), Shavelson (1973; 1976), and others point out that deciding which model or technique to apply in a

Figure 5.2: *Development of Competence in the 'Technology' of Educational Practice*

1. Developing survival skills	• Partially developed classroom-management skills • Knowledge about and limited skill in use of several teaching models • No conscious reflection on choice of model • Student assessment is primarily summative and carried out, using limited techniques, in response to external demands (e.g. reporting to parents); may be poor link between the focus of assessment and instructional goal
2. Becoming competent in the basic skills of instruction	• Well-developed classroom-management skills • Well-developed skill in use of several teaching models • Habitual application through trial and error, of certain teaching models for particular parts of curriculum • Student assessment begins to reflect formative purposes, although techniques are not well suited to such purposes; focus of assessment linked to instructional goals easiest to measure
3. Expanding one's instructional flexibility	• Automatized classroom-management skills • Growing awareness of need for and existence of other teaching models and initial efforts to expand repertoire and experiment with application of new models • Choice of teaching model from expanded repertoire influenced most by interest in providing variety to maintain student interest • Student assessment carried out for both formative and summative purposes; repertoire of techniques is beginning to match purposes; focus of assessment covers significant range of instructional goals
4. Acquiring instructional expertise	• Classroom management integrated with programme; little attention required to classroom management as an independent issue • Skill in application of a broad repertoire of teaching models
5. Contributing to the growth of colleagues' instructional expertise	• Has high levels of expertise in classroom instructional performance • Reflective about own competence and choices and the fundamental beliefs and values on which they are based • Able to assist other teachers in acquiring instructional expertise through either planned learning experiences, such as mentoring, or more formal experiences, such as in-service education and coaching programmes
6. Participating in a broad array of educational decisions at all levels of the education system	• Is committed to the goal of school improvement • Accepts responsibility for fostering that goal through any legitimate opportunity • Able to exercise leadership, both formal and informal, with groups of adults inside and outside the school • Has a broad framework from which to understand the relationship among decisions at many different levels in the education system • Is well informed about policies at many different levels in the education system

particular situation is central to instructional expertise. As teachers develop, their choice of models is based on increasingly defensible criteria (e.g. instructional objectives v. need for variety) and diagnosis of the instructional needs of students.

While the notion of teacher-as-decision-maker appropriately recognizes the contingent nature of the classroom tasks routinely faced by teachers, it is not sufficiently comprehensive to encompass those unanticipated, non-routine, 'swampy' problems encountered in the classroom from time to time. Schon (1983) depicts the way in which experienced professionals in many domains think about and eventually resolve such problems. This involves a process of reflecting *in* action as well as a process of reflecting *on* action in which the unique attributes of the setting are carefully weighed and the professional's repertoire is adapted in response to such uniqueness.

Stages 5 and 6 acknowledge the roles of teachers in school improvement and educational decisions beyond the classroom and school. While such roles are by no means new, they have received greater attention recently. Peer coaching (Brandt, 1987; Garmston, 1987) and mentoring (Gray and Gray, 1985; Wagner, 1985) strategies, for example, assume those aspects of expertise identified in Stage 5, as do many of the recent career-ladder programmes that place teachers in the role of evaluators (e.g. Peterson and Mitchell, 1985). Stage 6 conceptualizes the mature teacher as one who plays a formal or informal leadership role, in a variety of contexts both inside and outside the classroom and school. Teachers, according to this view, share in the responsibility for most decisions that directly or indirectly touch on students' experiences. Such a view is consistent with recent proposals for reshaping teacher education (e.g. Fullan and Connelly, 1990) and for empowering teachers (e.g. Maeroff, 1988) in the process.

Psychological Development

As outlined in Figure 5.1, 'psychological development' is a synthesis of three distinct and independently substantial strands of psychological stage theory: Loevinger's (1966) seven-stage theory of ego development, Kohlberg's (1970) six-stage theory of moral development, and Hunt and associates (1966) four-stage theory of conceptual development. These three strands of psychological development are both conceptually and empirically related (Sullivan, McCullough and Stager, 1970). The synthesis provided by Figure 5.1 is for heuristic purposes. It is a rough approximation of how the three strands might intersect in real time.

Generally, ego development occurs as a person strives to master, to integrate and otherwise make sense of experience. Greater ego maturity is associated with a more complex and better differentiated understanding of one's self in relation to others. Moral development occurs as the basis on which one's views of rightness and goodness shift from a basis of personal preference toward a basis of universal ethical principles. Finally, conceptual development occurs as one moves toward greater differentiation and integration of concepts—the growth from concrete toward more abstract thought processes.

Viewing the three strands of psychological development together, as in Figure 5.1, provides descriptions of teachers in various stages of growth. A 'Stage 1' teacher has an overly simplistic view of the world and a tendency to see choices as black or white. Such a teacher believes strongly in rules and roles, views authority as the highest good and sees most questions as having one answer. Stage 1 teachers discourage divergent thinking and reward conformity and rote learning (Oja, 1979). Their classrooms are highly teacher-directed.

Stage 2 teachers (conformists) are especially susceptible to the expectations of others. Their wish is to be like their peers, and they may hold stereotyped, distrustful views of those 'outside' their immediate group. The classrooms of conformist teachers are what we think of as 'conventional'. Rules are quite explicit and students are expected to adhere to such rules without much regard for individual differences or contingencies that might justify exceptions to the rules.

At the third stage of psychological development (conscientious), teachers have become much more self-aware and have developed an appreciation for multiple possibilities in situations (e.g. multiple explanations for student behaviour). Rules are internalized and applied with an appreciation for the need for exceptions to the rules, given the circumstances. Teachers at this stage are future-oriented and achievement-oriented. Their classrooms are the product of rational planning and a concern for good interpersonal communication.

At the highest stages of psychological development, teachers are inner-directed but appreciate the interdependent nature of relationships in a social setting such as a classroom. In addition, according to Oja and Pine (1981), these teachers have achieved more of a synthesis in their classrooms between an emphasis on achievement and an interpersonal orientation, and are not only able to view a situation from multiple perspectives but are also able to synthesize such perspectives. Teachers at the highest stage understand the reasons behind rules and so can be wiser in their application: they maintain a broad perspective and are able to cope with inner conflicts as well as conflicting needs and duties. The classrooms of these teachers are controlled in collaboration with students, and the emphasis is on meaningful learning, creativity and flexibility. Being more cognitively complex themselves, teachers at this stage encourage more complex functioning in their students (Hunt, 1966; Oja, 1979).

Career-Cycle Development

The dimension called 'career-cycle development' in Figure 5.1 views teachers' careers from a life-cycle perspective. Five stages of development have been derived primarily from recent research by Huberman (1988) and Sikes, Measor, and Woods (1985); the latter work adopted Levinson *et al.*'s (1978) conceptualization of life development as a framework. Huberman and Sikes *et al.* carried out their research with secondary school teachers in Switzerland and Great Britain, respectively. Nevertheless, their results appear to be sufficiently similar and consistent with other research (e.g. Ball and Goodson, 1985) to warrant tentative generalization to other contexts and teaching assignments in the modified form described in Figure 5.1. Our main interest in teachers' career-cycle development is how it interacts with the development of professional expertise; more particularly, we want to know what career experiences, at each stage, seem likely to foster or detract from the development of professional expertise.

Stage 1, 'launching the career', encompasses up to the first several years of the teacher's classroom responsibilities. Sikes *et al.* (1985) suggest that most teachers at this stage experience a 'reality shock in coming to grips with problems of disciplining and motivating students'—as well as some degree of culture shock, the amount depending on the values and perspectives of staff in their school. Nevertheless, Huberman's (1988) data suggest that experiences at this stage are perceived by some teachers as 'easy' and by others as 'painful'. Conditions giving rise to perceptions of easy beginnings include positive relationships with students, 'manageable' students, a sense of instructional mastery and initial enthusiasm. Painful beginnings are associated with role overload, anxiety, difficult pupils, heavy time investment, close monitoring and feelings of isolation in the school. For those who experience such pain, there may be a protracted period of trial and error in an effort to cope with such problems.

'Stabilizing', the second career-cycle stage, often coincides with receiving a permanent contract and making a deliberate commitment to the profession. This stage is characterized by feeling at ease in the classroom, mastery of a basic repertoire of instructional techniques, and being able to select appropriate methods and materials in light of student abilities and interests. Furthermore, at this stage teachers act more independently, are less intimidated by supervisors, and feel reasonably well integrated into a group of peers. Some teachers at this stage begin to seek greater responsibility through promotion or participation in change efforts.

The stage following stabilization may take several forms. In the main, teachers at this stage tend to be between the ages of 30 and 40. As Sikes *et al.* (1985) point out, their experience is substantial by this point, as is their physical and intellectual energy. For some teachers, such energy is channelled into intense professional effort. Huberman's

(1988) study identified a category of teachers at this stage who actively diversify their classroom methods, seek out novel practices and often look outside their own classrooms for professional stimulation. Another group of teachers at this stage focused their efforts on seeking promotion to administrative roles or appointment to key district or state-wide projects. Yet a third group of teachers, also identified by Sikes *et al.* (1985), reduced their professional commitments. Members of this group sometimes experienced difficult classes and achieved poor results with their students. Building an alternative career was an option pursued by many teachers in this group.

Sikes *et al.* (1985) estimate the fourth stage, 'reaching a professional plateau', to occur between the ages of approximately 40 and 50–55. This is a traumatic period for many teachers who, at this stage, are reappraising their successes in all facets of their lives. Their own sense of mortality is accentuated by continually being surrounded by young students and by having, as colleagues, young teachers who may be the same age as their own children. Responses to this stage appear to be of two sorts. One group of teachers stop striving for promotion and simply enjoy teaching. These teachers may become the backbone of the school, the guardians of its traditions. They may enjoy a renewed commitment to school improvement. A second group, however, stagnates. They may become bitter, cynical, and unlikely to be interested in further professional growth.

Depending to a large extent on which of these two responses is adopted at Stage 4, teachers in the final stage, 'preparing for retirement', may behave in quite different ways. Huberman's (1988) study identified three different patterns of behaviour, each of which involved some type of contraction of professional activity and interest. One pattern of behaviour, 'positive focusing', involved an interest in specializing in what one does best. Such specialization might target a grade level, a subject, or a group of students. Teachers adopting this pattern, as Sikes *et al.* (1985) also found, are concerned centrally with pupil learning, their most compatible peers, and an increasing pursuit of outside interests. A second pattern of behaviour, 'defensive focusing', has similar features to the first; however, teachers exhibit a less optimistic and generous attitude toward their past experiences with change, their students, and their colleagues. Finally, Huberman (1988) labels a third pattern of practice 'disenchantment'. People adopting this pattern are bitter about past experiences with change and the administrators associated with them. They are tired and may become a source of frustration for younger staff.

Guidelines for Principals in Fostering Teacher Development

An explicit, defensible conception of teacher development provides a foundation upon which principals, acting as instructional leaders, can formulate their own approach to teacher development. In this section, four broad guidelines for building this approach are suggested. These guidelines stress the importance of attending to all three dimensions of teacher development and creating school cultures and structures hospitable to such development. Based on assumptions about teachers as adult learners actively involved in bringing meaning to their work, the guidelines stress the importance of understanding teachers' own views of their world. Finally, the guidelines argue that the most helpful teacher development strategies available to principals are to be found among their normal responses to their work environment.

Guideline 1: Treat the Teacher As a Whole Person

As Figure 5.2 indicates, growth in professional expertise consists of teachers expanding their instructional repertoires, responding more flexibly to classroom circumstances, and taking responsibility for the welfare and growth, not only of students, but also of their professional colleagues. Although the acquisition of knowledge and skill concerning instruction, as well as other educational matters, is an obviously necessary condition for such growth, it is not sufficient. That is, the practice of instructional flexibility depends on at least being able to weigh a variety of alternatives. Many instructional strategies also require the teacher to relinquish exclusive control over classroom activities and to trust students to be task-oriented on their own or in groups. This suggests that prerequisite to acquiring instructional expertise (Stage 4 of the professional expertise dimension) is growth to at least the middle stages of the psychological development dimension, as depicted in Figure 5.1. Similarly, practices associated with professional expertise at Stages 5 and 6 appear to depend on the ability to synthesize alternatives, mutuality in interpersonal relations, the ability to cope with conflicting needs and duties, and other attributes of functioning at the highest level of psychological development. Indeed, failure to attend to the interdependence of professional expertise and stages of psychological development offers an additional explanation for lack of application in the classroom of skills acquired through training. To this point, the most compelling explanation for this 'transfer' problem has been limited to the unique and often overwhelming demands placed on teachers' application of newly acquired skills by their particular classroom contexts (Joyce and Showers, 1980).

Typically, staff development efforts (whether by principals or others) do not acknowledge the interdependence of psychological and professional development. While this may be due to ignorance or oversight in some cases, it may also be due to the commonly held view that psychological development is completed by adulthood. That such a view is unwarranted is clear from evidence reported by Harvey

(1970) that a large proportion of teachers in his sample were at the lowest level of conceptual development. Oja's (1981) review of similar evidence suggests that teachers typically stabilize in the middle stages of psychological development.

So far, our attention has been limited to the relationship between psychological development and the development of expertise. What of career-cycle development? The development of professional expertise seems to have an important relationship with such development. There is, for example, an obvious link between the challenges facing a teacher in the first three stages of his or her career-cycle and the expertise to be acquired in the first four stages of development of professional expertise. Indeed, interventions designed to promote the development of such professional expertise seem likely to ensure positive career-cycle development.

Principals have an opportunity to prevent painful beginnings. They are preventable through such interventions as realistic classroom assignments in combination with ongoing assistance in the development of classroom management skills, provision of a supportive mentor close at hand, and the avoidance of heavy-handed supervision practices. On the other hand, failure to provide opportunities for the development of professional expertise may well lead to professional disaffection when teachers are seeking new challenges and have new concerns. Providing opportunities to master an expanded, flexible repertoire of instruction techniques seems an effective way of ensuring that teachers experience a sense of professional self-fulfillment during this third stage in their career-cycle.

A direct relationship appears also to exist between the career-cycle stage 'reaching a professional plateau' and Stages 5 and 6 in the development of professional expertise. A significant part of the explanation for teachers perceiving themselves to be at a plateau is the failure, in many shcools and school systems, to permit teachers greater scope to know and relate to multiple classrooms—to see and work with other teachers and their classrooms. Such challenges respond to the teacher's readiness to accept more responsibility and allow the school and school system to benefit from their accumulated expertise. Teachers who have experienced such challenges seem likely to enter their final career-cycle stage either still in an expansionary frame of mind or at least as 'positive focusers', to use Huberman's (1988) term.

In brief, then, principals should be sensitive to all three development dimensions and seek to help teachers develop these dimensions in a parallel, interdependent fashion.

Guideline 2: Establish a School Culture Based on Norms Of Technical Collaboration and Professional Inquiry

The reason teachers often appear to stabilize in the middle stages of psychological development is inadequate stimulation, not an innate shortcoming (Sprinthall and Theis-Sprinthall, 1983). Such is the case with professional expertise as well. Evidence suggests that the typical school culture and its organizational structures may be responsible, in part, for stifling teacher development (for this discussion, 'culture' includes the underlying assumption, norm, beliefs, and values that guide behaviour).

Typical school cultures are characterized by informal norms of autonomy and isolation for teachers (Lortie, 1973), as well as entrenched routines and regularities (Lieberman and Miller, 1986; Sarason, 1971). Indeed, some aspects of these cultures have been dubbed sacred (Corbett, Fireston and Rossman, 1987) and, as a result, are highly resistant to change. Teachers' individual, personal beliefs about the needs of students are far stronger influences on their classroom practices than other potential influences—for example, the views of their peers or principals, or prescriptions contained in curriculum policies (Leithwood, Ross and Montgomery, 1982). Such autonomy and isolation limits the stimulation for further development to what is possible through private and unguided reflections on what one reads and experiences outside the classroom and one's own informal classroom experiments. It is unlikely that such stimulation will create the sort of dissonance or challenge to one's ways of thinking that appears necessary to foster movement from one stage of psychological development to another. Nor would such stimulation provide the conditions, outlined, for example, by Joyce and Showers (1980), for the successful application of new instructional skills to one's classroom. Little (1981; 1985), on the other hand, found that staff development efforts were most successful where a norm of collegiality and experimentation existed.

Principals' teacher-development strategies seem most likely to be successful within a school culture in which teachers are encouraged consciously to reflect on their own practices (Oberg and Field, 1986), to share ideas about their instruction, and try out new techniques in the classroom. Principals need to develop norms of reflection through the substance of their own communication with teachers and the example of their own teaching. Principals also need to take specific actions to foster norms of collaboration. As Rosenholtz points out, 'Norms of collaboration don't simply just happen. They do not spring spontaneously out of teachers' mutual respect and concern for each other' (1989:44). Rosenholtz identifies four conditions that influence the extent to which teachers are likely to engage technical collaboration: teachers' certainty about their own instructional competence, and hence, self-esteem; shared teaching goals; involvement in the school's technical decisions; and team-teaching opportunities that create the need to plan and carry out instruction with colleagues.

This guideline suggests, in sum, that principals look below the surface features of their schools—at how teachers are treated and what beliefs, norms, and values they share—and redesign their schools as learning environments for teachers as well as for students.

Guideline 3: Carefully Diagnose the Starting Points for Teacher Development

Teachers are not passive recipients of principals' strategies 'to develop them'. Adopting the view of contemporary cognitive psychology (e.g. Calfee, 1981; Schuell, 1986), particularly as it has been applied to research on teacher thinking (e.g. Clark and Peterson, 1986), teachers actively strive to accomplish implicit or explicit goals they hold to be personally important in their work. For example, when teachers judge a new form of instruction introduced to them by their principal as potentially helpful in accomplishing such goals, they attempt to understand and assess that new form of instruction. The primary resources used by teachers to develop such understanding are what they already know (as contained in their long term memory). Understanding develops as matches are made between the new form of instruction and what they already know (e.g. 'Oh! "Direct Instruction" means the traditional instruction I was taught in teachers' college'); as existing knowledge structures are modified to accommodate novel aspects of the new form of instruction (e.g. 'Ah! "Cooperative Learning" just means grouping with different rules than I have used'); and as links are established among previously unconnected pieces of information in the teacher's memory (e.g. 'I think "mastery learning" is a combination of what I call behavioural objectives, criterion-referenced testing, and remedial teaching'). These brief examples make clear that successful development strategies build on a careful diagnosis of the relevant knowledge already possessed by teachers. Such strategies will assist teachers to identify relevant aspects of what they already know and to use that knowledge as an instrument for giving meaning to new practices which they may wish to understand and use better.

The formal mechanism most obviously available to principals for carrying out this diagnosis is teacher evaluation. Virtually all principals spend considerable time doing it. Nevertheless, such evaluation as it is normally practised rarely results in useful diagnostic information and generally appears to have little influence on teacher development (Lawton *et al.*, 1986).

Recent research has provided some useful clues for how principals can redesign their approaches to teacher evaluation so as to be a more effective 'needs assessment front end' for teacher development (e.g. Stiggins and Duke, 1988). For example, such evaluation needs to be based on criteria or goals that both principals and teachers agree are relevant to teacher development. Multiple forms of data should be collected as a more powerful means of accurately reflecting teachers' practices and needs. Regular observation of classroom practice with considerable time in the classroom is an important part of such data collection. The formality, frequency and length of evaluation should be adapted to individual teachers' characteristics and needs. Rosenholtz (1989) found that teacher evaluation with features such as these was one of four organizational factors contributing directly to teacher learning opportunities in the school (the other factors were school goal setting, shared values, and collaboration).

In sum, this guideline reminds principals that development is an incremental process that builds on teachers' existing stock of attitudes, knowledge, and skill: they are at the same time the objects of and instruments for development.

Guideline 4: Recast Routine Administrative Activities into Powerful Teacher Development Strategies

Many principals remain sceptical about the contribution that they can make to teacher development because they believe that the strategies required would place unrealistic demands on them. They believe that such strategies would include, for example, detailed planning of in-service programmes, creation of large amounts of teacher release time for participation in such programmes, and perhaps acting themselves as in-service instructors. It is not usually the lack of know-how that causes principals the most despair in the face of such strategies. Rather, it is the lack of congruence between the demands such formal strategies place on principals' work and the real demands of that work. The point of this guideline is to argue that such a view of teacher development strategies is essentially misguided. As Pfieffer suggests, 'Teachers don't need superman—Clark Kent or Lois Lane will do just fine (1986)'. Indeed, the more informal strategies available to principals in their normal responses to the demands of the job can be much more effective in fostering teacher development than such formal, hard-to-implement strategies. Effective principals have learned this lesson well.

What are the 'real' demands faced by principals in their work? We know, for example, that principals' activities are typically characterized by brevity, fragmentation, and variety (Bradeson, 1986; Davies, 1987; Gally, 1986; Martin and Willower, 1981; Willower and Kmetz, 1982). Rarely, it seems, do principals spend more than ten minutes at a time on a single task, and they make about 150 different decisions in the course of an average day. Communication of one sort or other is the primary goal of most principals' activities. Almost three-quarters of such activities are interpersonal and take place with only one other person: over half involve face-to-face contact. Principals' work environments also require high levels of spontaneity: the largest single expenditure of a principal's time is reported to be unanticipated meetings.

Although most principals experience the demands just described, recent research suggests at least one compelling source of difference in the responses of 'highly effective' as compared with 'typical' principals (Leithwood and Montgomery, 1986). What is different is the amount of consistency that principals are able to bring to their activities and decisions. Typical or less effective principals approach them in a relatively piecemeal fashion: for example, decisions about budget, discipline, timetabling, reporting, and staffing all may be based on different criteria. As a consequence, the overall effects of these decisions may work at cross purposes.

In contrast, highly effective principals base their decisions and actions on a relatively consistent set of criteria. They 'can articulate direct and remote links between their actions and the instructional system' (Bossert, 1988). As a result, the effects of the many, seemingly trivial, unrelated, and often unanticipated decisions made by these principals eventually add up to something. Their impact accumulates in a way that consistently fosters school improvement. And what is the glue that holds together the myriad decisions of highly effective principals? It is the goals they and their staffs have developed for their schools and a sense of what their schools need to look like and to do in order to accomplish those goals. Such a clear, detailed vision (incorporating a conception of teacher development) and its systematic daily use appear to be absent among less effective principals (Stevens, 1986).

This opportunistic but clearly directed approach by highly effective principals to their work, as a whole, manifests itself in the strategies they use for teacher development. Such principals do not attempt to deny the fragmented, interpersonal and spontaneous demands of the job (as would be required by a formal, in-service training approach to teacher development). On the contrary, they adapt and build on strategies that are part of their normal responses to their work demands. McEvoy's (1987) results illustrate, more specifically, the types of subtle, sometimes opportunistic teacher development strategies used by effective principals. In this study, twelve elementary and intermediate principals were observed using six strategies: informing teachers of professional opportunities; disseminating professional and curriculum materials to teachers with personal follow-up and discussion; focusing teachers' attention, through meetings and informal contacts, on a specific theme in order to expand the concepts and practices teachers considered; soliciting teachers' opinions about their own classroom activities as well as school and classroom issues, thereby contributing to a sense of collegiality among staff; encouraging teachers' experimenting with innovative practices and supporting their efforts; and recognizing, sometimes publicly, the achievements of individual teachers.

Examples of other teacher development strategies used by effective principals are provided in Leithwood and Montgomery's literature reviews (1982; 1986). These strategies included: working alongside individual teachers in their classes to resolve problems or implement changes; helping staff gain access to outside resources; and helping teachers arrange to observe other teachers in other schools. Even relatively 'impersonal' strategies normally available to principals may be designed in such a way as to foster teacher development. Hannay and Chism (1988), for example, found that teacher transfers could become an effective means for fostering such development when the transfer prompted teachers to re-examine their practices.

Wilson and Firestone (1987) refer to most of the strategies that have been mentioned as 'linkage strategies' and show how principals' fostering of both bureaucratic and cultural linkages can lead to teacher development. Bureacratic linkages (such as creating more free time for teachers) can affect how teachers interact with each other. Cultural linkages (such as introducing more consistency into school communications) work on the consciousness of teachers 'by clarifying what they do and defining their commitment to the task'.

Effective principals, in sum, use the energy and momentum created naturally by the demands of their work for purposes of teacher development. They have redefined the problem as the solution.

Conclusion

Gideonese has suggested that the teaching profession is 'undergoing revolutionary transformation' (1988),—although many of us are too close to see it. That transformation appears to begin from a perception of teaching as a routine job conducted with craft-like knowledge in isolation from other adults in a hierarchical status structure. The new perception of teaching views it as a non-routine activity drawing on a reliable body of technical knowledge and conducted in collaboration with other professional colleagues. Awareness of this transformation has been fostered by recent effective schools research and proposals included among second-wave reforms in the US (Bacharach, 1988).

Nevertheless, we need to devote much more attention to how this newly perceived image of the teacher can be realized. This Chapter has outlined plausible stages through which teachers are likely to grow as they acquire the attributes associated with a collaborative professional image of the role. Some general strategies principals might use in fostering such teacher growth also have been proposed. These principal strategies, however, only touch the surface of a problem which requires much further thought. The implications are clear for the role of the principal in creating an image of teaching as a collaborative professional enterprise. Only when we have clearly conceptualized, coherent images of both teacher and principal roles and how they develop will we realize the combined contribution toward student learning of those in both roles. Much of the knowledge required for this task is already in hand. Although more knowledge will be helpful, using what we already know constitutes a crucial and immediate challenge.

References

BACHARACH, S.B. (1988) 'Four themes of reform: An editorial essay', *Educational Administration Quarterly*, *24*, 4, pp. 484–96.

BACHARACH, S.B., CONLEY, S.C. and SHEDD, J.B. (1987) 'A career developmental framework for evaluating teachers as decision-makers', *Journal of Personnel Evaluation in Education*, *1*, pp. 181–94.

BALL, S. and GOODSON, I. (Eds.) (1985) *Teachers' Lives and Careers*, Lewes, Falmer Press.

BOSSERT, S.T. (1988) 'School effects', in BOVAN, N. (Ed.) *Handbook of Research on Educational Administration*, New York, Longman.

BRADESON, P.V. (1986) 'Principally speaking: An analysis of the interpersonal communications of school principals'. Paper presented at the annual meeting of the American Educational Research Association, San Francisco.

BRANDT, R.S. (1987) 'On teachers coaching teachers: A conversation with Bruce Joyce', *Educational Leadership*, *44*, 5, pp. 12–17.

CALFEE, R. (1981) 'Cognitive psychology and educational practice', *Review of Educational Research*, *56*, 4, pp. 411–36.

CLARK, C.M. and PETERSON, P.L. (1986) 'Teachers' thought processes', in WITTROCK, M.C. (Ed.) *Handbook of Research on Teaching*, 3rd edn., New York, Macmillan.

CORBETT, H.D., FIRESTONE, W.A. and ROSSMAN, G.B. (1987) 'Resistance to planned change and the sacred in school cultures', *Educational Administration Quarterly*, *33*, 4, pp. 36–59.

DARLING-HAMMOND, L., WISE, A.E. and PEASE, S.R. (1983) 'Teacher evaluation in the organizational context: A review of the literature', *Review of Educational Research*, *53*, 3, pp. 285–328.

DAVIES, L. (1987) 'The role of the primary head', *Educational Management and Administration*, *15*, pp. 43–7.

FULLAN, M. and CONNELLY, M. (1990) *Teacher Education of Ontario: Current Practice and Options for the Future*, Ontario Ministry of Education.

GALLY, J. (1986) 'The structure of administrative behavior'. Paper presented at the Annual Meeting of the American Educational Research Association, San Francisco.

GARMSTON, R. (1987) 'How administrators support peer coaching', *Educational Leadership*, *44*, 5, pp. 18–28.

GIDEONESE, H.D. (1988) 'Practitioner oriented inquiry for teachers: Meaning, justification and implication for school structure', Journal of Currciulum and Supervision, *4*, 1, pp. 65–77.

GRAY, W.A. and GRAY, M.M. (1985) 'Synthesis of research on mentoring teachers', *Educational Leadership*, *43*, 3, pp. 37–43.

HANNAY, L. and CHISM, N. (1988) 'The potential of teacher transfer in fostering professional development', *Journal of Curriculum and Supervision*, *3*, 2, pp. 122–35.

HARVEY, O.J. (1970) 'Beliefs and behavior: Some implications for education', *The Science Teacher, 37*, pp. 10–14.

HUBERMAN, M. (1988) 'Teacher careers and school inprovement', *Journal of Curriculum Studies, 20*, 2, pp. 119–32.

HUNT, D. (1966) 'A conceptual systems change model and its application to education', in HARVEY, O.J. (Ed.) *Experience, Structure and Adaptability*, New York, Springer-Verlag.

JOYCE, B. and SHOWERS, B. (1980) 'Improving in-service training: The message of research', *Educational Leadership, 37*, pp. 379–85.

JOYCE, B. and WEIL, M. (1980) Models of Teaching, 2nd edn. Englewood-Cliffs, N.J., Prentice-Hall.

KOHLBERG, L. (1970) *Moral Development*, New York, Holt, Rinehart & Winston.

LAWTON, S.B., HICKCOX, E.S., LEITHWOOD, K.A. and MUSELLA, D.F. (1986) *Development and Use of Performance Appraisal of Certified Education Staff in Ontario School Broad*, Toronto, Ministry of Education.

LEITHWOOD, K.A. (1988) *Description and Assessment of a Program for the Certification of Principals*, Toronto, Ministry of Education, Ontario.

LEITHWOOD, K.A. and MONTGOMERY, D.J. (1982) 'The role of elementary school principals in program improvement', *Review of Educational Research, 52*, 3, pp. 309–39.

LEITHWOOD, K.A. and MONTGOMERY, D.J. (1986) *Improving Principal Effectiveness: The Principal Profile*, Toronto, OISE Press.

LEITHWOOD, K.A., ROSS, J. and MONTGOMERY, D.J. (1982) 'An investigation of teachers' curriculum decision making', in LEITHWOOD, K.A. (Ed.) *Studies in Curriculum Decision Making*, Toronto, OISE Press.

LEVINSON, D.J. *et al.* (1978) *The Seasons of a Man's Life*, New York, Knopf.

LIEBERMAN, A. and MILLER, L. (1986) 'School improvement: themes and variations', in LIEBERMAN, A. (Ed.) *Rethinking School Improvement*, New York, Teachers College Press.

LITTLE, J.W. (1982) 'Norms of collegiality and experimentation: Workplace conditions of school success', *American Educational Research Journal, 19*, 3, pp. 325–40.

LITTLE, J.W. (1985) 'Teachers as teacher advisors: The delicacy of collegial leadership', *Educational Leadership, 43*, 3, pp. 34–6.

LOEVINGER, J. (1966) 'The meaning and measurement of ego development' *Amercian Psychologist, 21*, pp. 195–206.

MAEROFF, G.I. (1988) 'A blueprint for empowering teachers', in *Phi Delta Kappan, 69*, 7, pp. 472–77.

MARTIN, W.J. and WILLOWER, D.J. (1981) 'The managerial behavior of high school principals' *Educational Administration Quarterly, 17*, 1, pp. 69–90.

McEVOY, B. (1987) 'Everyday acts: How principals influence development of their staff', *Educational Leadership, 44*, 5, pp. 73–7.

MURPHY, J.T. (1988) 'The unheroic side of leadership: Notes from the swamp', *Phi Delta Kappan*, May, pp. 654–9.

OBERG, A. and FIELD, R. (1986) 'Teacher development through reflection on practice', Paper based on presentations to the Annual Meeting of the American Educational Research Association, San Francisco.

OJA, S. (1979) 'A cognitive-structural approach to adult ego, moral and conceptual development through in-service education'. Paper presented to the Annual Meeting of the American Educational Research Association, April.

OJA, S.N. and PINE, G.J. (1981) 'Toward a theory of staff development: Some questions about change'. Paper presented at the Annual Meeting of the American Educational Research Association, Los Angeles.

PETERSON, K. and MITCHELL, A. (1985) 'Teacher-controlled evaluation in a career ladder program', *Educational Leadership*, *43*, 3, pp. 44–9.

PFIEFFER, R.S. (1986) 'Enabling teacher effectiveness: Teachers' perspectives on instructional management'. Paper presented at the Annual Meeting of the American Educational Research Association, San Francisco.

ROSENHOLTZ, S. (1989) *Teachers' Workplace*, White Plains, NY, Longman Inc.

SALLEY, C., McPHERSON, R.B. and BAEHR, M.E. (1978) 'What principals do: An occupational analysis', in ERICKSON, D. and RELLER, T. (Eds.) *The Principal in Metropolitan Schools*, Berkeley, McCutchan Pub.

SARASON, S. (1971) *The Culture of the School and the Problem of Change*, Boston, Allyn and Bacon.

SCHON, D.A. (1983) *The Reflective Practitioner*, New York, Basic Books.

SCHUELL, T.J. (1986) 'Cognitive conceptions of learning', *Review of Educational Research*, *56*, 4, pp. 411–36.

SHAVELSON, R.J. (1973) 'What is the basic teaching skill?' *Journal of Teacher Education*, *14*, pp. 144–51.

SHAVELSON, R.J. (1976) 'Teachers' decision making', in GAGE, N.L. (Ed.) *The Psychology of Teaching Methods*, Seventy-fifth Yearbook of the National Society for the Study of Education, Chicago, University of Chicago Press.

SIKES, P.J., MEASOR, L. and WOODS, P. (1985) *Teacher Careers: Crises and Continuities*, Lewes, Falmer.

SPRINTHALL, N.A. and THEIS-SPRINTHALL, L. (1983) 'The teacher as an adult learner: A cognitive developmental view', in GRIFFIN, G.A. (Ed.) *Staff Development*, Chicago, University of Chicago Press.

STEVENS, W. (1986) 'The Role of Vision in the Life of Elementary School Principals'. Unpublished doctoral dissertation, University of Southern California.

STIGGINS, R. and DUKE, D. (1988) *The Case for Commitment to Teacher Growth*, Albany, State University of New York Press.

SULLIVAN, E.V., McCULLOUGH, G. and STAGER, M. (1970) 'A developmental study of the relationship between conceptual, ego and moral development', *Child Development*, *41*, pp. 399–411.

WAGNER, L.A. (1985) 'Ambiguities and possibilities in California's Mentor Teacher Program', *Educational Leadership*, *43*, 3, pp. 23–9.

WILLOWER, D.J. and KMETZ, J.T. (1982) 'The managerial behavior of elementary school principals'. Paper presented at the Annual Meeting of the American Educational Research Association, New York.

WILSON, B. and FIRESTONE, W.A. (1987) 'The principal and instruction: Combining bureaucratic and cultural linkages', *Educational Leadership*, pp. 18–23.

Chapter 6

Teacher Growth in the Effective School

Louise Stoll

Teachers, school administrators and board personnel are all involved in the search for excellence. 'How can we improve our schools?' is a frequently posed question. Researchers in the effective schools movement have identified characteristics that are associated with enhanced student outcomes, particularly achievement. Schools, however, still need to deal with the practicalities of how to translate this knowledge into realistic implementation strategies. Lezotte (1989) reflects: '[T]he effective schools research provided a vision of a more desirable place for schools to be, but gave little insight as to how best to make the journey to that place'.

Three problems are highlighted by Lezotte. First, districts with little understanding of how to implement these research findings have mandated, through a 'top-down' approach, that schools should become more effective. Second, many principals have felt burdened with the responsibility that it is their duty to make their schools more effective, while they lack confidence in their ability to be change agents. Third, many teachers have viewed this process as an implication that they are inadequate.

It is only when school effectiveness research is merged with what is known about school improvement, planned change and staff development, that schools and teachers can be empowered and supported in their growth towards effectiveness. Attempts to blend these areas occur to a much greater extent in North America than in Britain (Stoll and Fink, 1988a; Reynolds, 1989). In Britain, although sophisticated school effectiveness research has been carried out, its findings have had a limited impact on local education authorities. In contrast, in Canada there is an active desire on the part of school boards to make use of findings from research studies undertaken elsewhere. For this reason, having been a member of a team that carried out a large-scale school effectiveness study in England, I find myself working with the Halton Board of Education, a school board of eighty-three schools and 43,000 students, outside Toronto, to implement the findings. In this paper, therefore, I wish to draw greater links between school effectiveness research and school improvement efforts, and discuss the opportunities offered by both for teacher development.

Self-chosen and self-directed teacher development has considerable benefits. Teachers are not just empty vessels waiting to be filled with the knowledge of staff developers. Without the development of particular skills and group processes however, some teachers, especially those who are inexperienced, might have some difficulty in finding a focus for their own professional development. At a teacher development conference I once spoke with a first-year teacher who mused: 'I'm still trying to work out what a teacher is...My long-range plan is to be a teacher'. In teacher development workshops, Barrie Bennett, consultant to The Learning Consortium, a cooperative venture between the University of Toronto Faculty of Education and four Ontario school boards, also describes his early months in teaching: 'I looked into my bag of skills and I pulled out anger.' There is a message in these comments for teacher developers. Even though the stimulation of reflective activity is very important and needs to be encouraged, there is always more we can learn from others with regard to teaching skills. A recently introduced mentoring programme in the Halton Board has highlighted this. Workshops for first-year teachers and their mentors have focused on particular teaching skills and strategies and classroom management techniques. Evaluations have shown that the mentor teachers are as enthusiastic as their first-year teacher partners about this in-service experience. In this paper, I will argue that teacher growth in the effective school depends upon a balance of approaches to teacher development.

To provide a context for this topic, I will first describe the key findings of a major British school effectiveness study in which I participated, highlighting implications for teacher growth. I will then discuss the relationship between this type of research and school improvement, with a focus upon the attempt of one Canadian school board to link these two areas. Finally, the major teacher development and training issues of this project will be outlined.

School Effectiveness

In the late 1960s and early 1970s, social scientists, such as Coleman *et al.* (1966) and Jencks *et al.* (1972), delivered a depressing message to teachers: that schools were far less influential on students' development than their home background. For those in education, these words did not ring true. Although it is not disputed that an economically advantaged family contrasts dramatically with a disadvantaged one, it is also true that schools vary a great deal. Over the last ten years, researchers (Brookover *et al.*, 1979; Edmonds, 1979; Goodlad, 1979) have challenged the view that the effects schools have are only trivial. Their conclusion is clear; schools *do* make an important difference to the achievement of students.

An extensive longitudinal study of school effectiveness, the Junior School Project, took place in London, England, where we followed 2000 pupils throughout their junior schooling (Grades 2 to 5) in fifty schools randomly selected, but representative of the schools in Inner London (Mortimore *et al.*, 1988). The Project shared some common features with the *Fifteen Thousand Hours* study of secondary schooling (Rutter *et al.*, 1979), but took into account criticisms of the methodology of that earlier study. Multilevel statistical models were used to explain differences between schools in terms of data measured at different levels, such as the individual child, the class and the school.

The Project differed from the North American school effectiveness research in several significant ways. First, school effects were examined on a much broader range of pupil outcomes than the basic skills focus of the American studies. Pupils' progress and attainment were followed in reading, written mathematics, practical mathematics and writing and their attainment was also assessed in speaking skills. Furthermore, their development was monitored in terms of attitudes, behaviour, self-concept and attendance. Our belief was that a good school is one in which a broad range of student outcomes are positive. Consequently, through an examination of a wide selection of outcomes, a fairer assessment of the general effectiveness of schools could be obtained.

Because the study was longitudinal, it was possible to study progress as well as attainment. Only by studying progress could proper account be taken of the very different levels of skills possessed by children at the start of their junior schooling.

Information was also collected for each pupil on a range of background factors, including parental occupation, sex, ethnic background and one-parent family status. Full account of these was taken before examining schools' effects on their pupils. Even when this was done, however, it was found that the school made a very important contribution to pupils' progress and development. In fact, the school was much more important than background in determining the progress of pupils. For reading it was four times more important than background characteristics, and for mathematics and writing, ten times more important.

For each of the schools, the size of their effects on each of the measures of educational outcomes was calculated. The differences between the most and the least effective schools were striking. Taking reading as one example, the most effective school improved a pupil's attainment by an average of 15 raw points above that predicted by the child's attainment at entry to junior school and by background factors. But in the least effective school, each child's attainment was, on average, 10 points lower than predicted. This compares with an overall average reading score for pupils of 54 points. There was, therefore, a 25 point difference between the most and least effective schools for reading in the average attainment of their pupils at the end of the study. This was the effect of the school.

The effects of schools on the progress of different groups of pupils, by age, race, sex and social class were also compared. Generally, schools which were effective in promoting the progress of one group were also effective for other groups, and those which were less effective for one group were also less effective for others. An effective school tended to be effective for all its pupils, irrespective of their sex, social class or race.

Having established that schools do make an important difference to pupils' progress and development, the next task was to identify the ways in which the more effective schools differed from those which were less effective.

What Makes a School Effective?

Certain 'given' features made it easier to create an effective school. These were aspects over which schools and teachers have little direct control, such as class size and school size. These 'given' characteristics, however, only contribute to effectiveness. They do not, by themselves, ensure it. It is the characteristics within the control of the headteacher (principal) and teachers that are crucial. These are the characteristics that can be changed and which can provide a framework for school improvement efforts.

Key Characteristics of Effective Schools

We identified twelve key characteristics of effective schools. They are outlined below. The first four characteristics focus more generally on the whole school, whereas the middle six and aspects of the last two are directly related to the teacher in the classroom. All, however, have implications for teacher development.

1. Purposeful leadership of the staff by the headteacher. Headteachers in effective schools were actively involved in the school's work, without exerting total control. Thus, for example, they participated in curriculum discussions and influenced the content of guidelines, without completely determining curriculum policies. They also requested that teachers keep records and discussed these with teachers. Effective headteachers were not afraid to influence teaching strategies where necessary, but knew when there was no need to intervene. Teacher development was also a feature of their role. These heads encouraged teachers to become involved in professional development activities, particularly where these met the needs of the school.

2. Involvement of the deputy headteacher (vice principal). The findings showed that deputy headteachers can play a major role in school effectiveness. Where headteachers shared and delegated some of their responsibilities, benefits to pupils occurred. Frequent absence of the deputy, in contrast, was detrimental to pupils' progress.

The role of deputy head is often one of responsibility for the day-to-day management of the school. The majority of the deputy heads in our Project also perceived themselves, and were viewed by others, as providing a vital link between the head and the rest of the staff. Many, despite participation in management courses, felt unprepared for the role they had assumed, having been selected primarily because of their excellent teaching skills. School boards have begun to address this concern. For example, this year, my own board has offered an orientation programme for shortlisted vice principals. Training is given in supervision skills and conflict resolution, as well as an introduction to the organization of different services within the board. New vice principals will also spend two days in the school in which they will be posted.

There is a paucity of research on the vice principal, unlike the principal whose role has been extensively examined (Hall *et al.*, 1984; Leithwood and Montgomery, 1986; Adam, 1987). Further research needs to be undertaken on the vice principal's involvement in school improvement, and assessment of current courses for potential administrators is also necessary. The work on mentoring (reviewed by Gray and Gray, 1985) might offer some useful guidance. Just as new teachers are paired up with more experienced colleagues, a support network could be set up within school systems to pair new vice principals with those who have been in the post for a period of time.

3. Involvement of teachers. In successful schools, we found that teachers were involved in curriculum planning and played a major role in developing their own guidelines. It also appeared that schools in which teachers were consulted on issues affecting school policy, as well as those affecting them directly, were more likely to be successful.

In schools where deputy heads were involved in policy decisions, teachers were also more likely to be consulted. Thus, effective elementary schools did not operate a small management team— everyone had their say. Collaboration and shared decision-making are key to successful school improvement efforts, and will be discussed subsequently in more detail.

4. Consistency among teachers. Where all teachers were consistent in their use of guidelines such that work was not repeated, the impact on pupil progress was positive. Again, this demonstrates an emphasis upon a shared belief system and collaboration between teachers to provide a consistent approach to pupils within the school.

5. Structured sessions. Pupils benefited when their school day was given some structure. In effective classes, the broad outline of pupils' work was organized by the teacher, who ensured that there was always plenty for them to do. More progress was made when pupils were not given unlimited responsibility for planning their own daily programme of work, but were taught the skills necessary to manage areas of study independently. In general, therefore, the more successful teachers organized a framework within which pupils could work, and yet encouraged them to work relatively freely and independently within that framework. Children, however, vary in their motivation and require differing degrees of support. The implication for student and beginning teachers in particular, is that the provision of structure and appropriate support for children while they are learning is vital.

6. Intellectually challenging teaching. It is little surprise that the quality of teaching was found to have an influence on pupils' progress and development. The findings clearly demonstrated that in those classes where pupils were stimulated and challenged, progress was greatest. How did teachers in those classes challenge their pupils? First, they made greater use of higher-order questions and statements, explaining and discussing work in more detail and encouraging pupils to make reasoned or imaginative responses to their work and to focus on creative problem-solving.

Additionally, the classrooms of effective teachers were brighter and more interesting. A stimulating context had been created by these teachers who communicated their own interest and enthusiasm to the pupils. These teachers rarely intervened with instructions and directions, yet pupils knew what to do and could work without close supervision. Essentially, the message conveyed by effective teachers was one of high expectations: 'I believe in you. I know you can do this, and you know that I know you can do this.'

Unfortunately, the expectations of all teachers were not equally high. Some teachers expected less of particular groups of children within their classrooms. The pupils most at risk of teachers' low expectations were younger children within the class and those from blue collar backgrounds, homes where parents were unemployed, or one-parent families where the parent at home, usually the mother, was not employed.

Many of the influences on teachers' expectations are subtle, and expectations are transmitted in both direct and intangible ways. Where they differ for groups of pupils, as described above, they perpetuate differences in achievement and self-image that are deeply unfair. Thus, one implication for all teachers must be the need to focus carefully on classroom practice and to challenge the existence of such differential expectations.

The findings of this research clearly illustrate that children's performance can and does change over time. Given an effective school and teacher, children make greater progress, which leads to greater capability. Their confidence is also enhanced. Children's ability, therefore, can grow in an effective school.

7. *Work-centred environment.*   We discovered a busy, action–oriented atmosphere in the effective classrooms. Where teachers focused more on discussions of the content of work and on giving pupils feedback, and less on routine issues of classroom management, pupils' progress was enhanced. Children in these classes appeared to enjoy their work more and to be keen to commence new tasks. Although the more effective classrooms were by no means silent places, the noise level and amount of movement were reasonable and both were generally work-related.

For student teachers, new teachers and also many with experience, one of the most difficult tasks is to create a classroom environment which supports and fosters purposeful activity. Several writers have described ways in which skilled teachers manage the classroom so as to avoid disruption and encourage an effective learning atmosphere (Kounin, 1970; Marland, 1975; Dreikurs *et al.*, 1982). A work-centred environment may appear, to a visitor, to be simple maintenance of natural order. It will, however, have taken skilful training on the part of the teacher.

Bennett and Rolheiser-Bennett's (1988) model of 'What makes teaching go?' emphasizes classroom management as one of four interrelated cogs in the world of teaching. It is, undoubtedly, the most vital cog for the inexperienced teacher, for without skills in classroom management, all other strategies and techniques may be rendered useless.

8. *Limited focus within sessions.*   Learning was also facilitated when teachers concentrated on one or, perhaps, two subject areas within a session. When three or more activities took place within one classroom at any particular time, teachers' attention was more likely to be fragmented and they concentrated more on managing pupils and on discipline, and less on the work itself. Clearly, in attempting to organize many different learning experiences within one classroom, teachers were often unable to cope with the range of demands on them and consequently found it hard to ensure that learning in each separate area was progressing satisfactorily.

A focus on one subject area, however, does not imply that all pupils should do the same work. This was not an effective strategy. On the contrary, different approaches were effective for different aspects of teaching. The successful teachers varied their techniques and geared the level of work to pupils' needs.

9. *Maximum communication between teachers and students.*   It was evident that pupils gained from having a lot of communciation with the

teacher. The majority of teachers in the project devoted most of their attention to speaking with individuals. During the course of the day, however, each pupil only had an average of eleven individual contacts with the teacher. Given that some children demanded, and received, more teacher attention than the average, others necessarily received less. By speaking to the whole class, or to groups, teachers increased the overall number of contacts with children. Group work was seen relatively rarely, although its benefits have been expounded by other researchers (Johnson *et al.*, 1984). In particular, however, higher-order communications occurred more frequently when the teacher talked to the whole class.

This is not an advocation of traditional class teaching, where the teacher stands in front of the class and lectures all day. The findings did not show this approach to be beneficial for pupils. In fact, from the research, there was no evidence of identifiable teaching styles. Teaching is far too complex to categorize teachers in this way. Nonetheless, the results point to a flexible approach, utilizing a blend of individual, class and group communications, as appropriate. Some popular and effective activities were: class discussions and storytelling, as well as the introduction of a topic to the whole class before sending pupils off to work individually or in groups.

One clear implication of these findings is that teachers should be encouraged to develop a varied repertoire of strategies, and to learn when and how to implement these different approaches. All teachers need to be able to reflect upon and evaluate the effectiveness with which they are communicating with pupils, but this is of particular significance to new teachers and those still in training. Observation and feedback, the study of video-taped lessons and the critical appraisal of teaching practices can be useful forms of support.

10. Record keeping. Keeping records, both related to work progress and personal and social development, was a valuable and effective aspect of teachers' planning and assessment. In British secondary schools, records of achievement and other forms of profiling have been developed to promote a wider recognition of the broad range of students' achievements and abilities beyond academic attainment. Although this initiative has not been without its problems, records of achievement have been a source of motivation to less able students (Broadfoot, Nuttall *et al.*, 1988; Hargreaves, 1989). For schools and teachers interested in developing the 'whole student', whether at elementary or secondary level, a recognition of their strengths in areas other than traditionally measured achievement levels is vital. It is of concern that many of the teachers in our project based their assessments of pupils' ability solely on their written work. Gardner (1983) believes that people possess seven intelligences: linguistic; logical/ mathematical; musical; spatial; bodily kinaesthetic; personal interpersonal; and personal intrapersonal. All are relatively independent, and none of these skills is any more important than the others. Assessments by teachers based on all of these intelligences would provide much fairer and more realistic pictures of children's potential.

11. Parental involvement. An informal 'open-door' policy, parental help in the classrooms and on visits, and the organization of meetings with parents to discuss their children's progress all played a role in the promotion of school effectiveness. Parental involvement in pupils' educational development within the home was also beneficial.

Traditionally, some teachers have not felt comfortable having parents, or indeed any other adults, in the classroom. The climate, however, is changing. School improvement depends, to a large extent, on cooperation, communication and trust between all the partners in a school, including parents. A positive teacher attitude towards parental involvement in the classroom, however, may not in itself be sufficient. Teachers also require the appropriate skills to utilize what may be an untapped resource.

12. Positive climate. Our study provided confirmation that an effective school has a positive atmosphere. Both around the school and within the classroom, less emphasis on criticism and punishment and more on praise and rewarding pupils had a positive impact. The research pointed to the effectiveness of firm but fair classroom management.

In both British studies (Rutter *et al.*, 1979, and Mortimore *et al.*, 1988), however, more criticism was observed than praise. Some teachers in the latter project felt that an overemphasis on praise would devalue it. While this may be true, on the basis of many hours of classroom observation, it is fair to say that there could definitely be an increase in praise in most classroom before 'inflation' becomes too real a possibility.

We also found that positive teacher attitude to their classes and an interest in the children as individuals and not just learners also fostered progress. The organization of trips, visits and lunchtime or after-school clubs further contributed to a positive 'ethos'. The enhancement of pupils' self-concept, therefore, appeared to be an important focus of the effective schools.

It is important to note that the climate in effective schools was not only positive for the pupils. The teachers' working conditions were important. Where teachers had timetabled non-teaching periods for planning, positive effects occurred in pupils' progress and development.

In summary, the twelve key characteristics point to effective schools as being friendly, supportive environments, led by head-teachers who are not afraid to assert their views and yet are able to share management and decision-making with the staff. Teachers within effective schools provide a structured learning situation for their pupils but give them freedom within this framework. By being flexible in their use of whole class and individual contacts, they maximize communication with each pupil. Furthermore, through limiting their focus within a session, teachers' attention is less fragmented, and the opportunities for presenting challenging work to pupils are increased.

Links between School Effectiveness Research and School Improvement

In recent years, it has not been unusual for schools to work through a planning process to set future improvement goals. Priorities are set, often based on gut feeling of what should be changed. Furthermore, traditionally, teachers in many schools have not been closely involved in the decision-making process. This has led to a lack of teacher commitment to these goals and, frequently, no subsequent improvement. If such attempts to improve schools are to be successful, two issues must be addressed:

1. The Knowledge Base of School Effectiveness Research

School improvement efforts need to take into account the findings of school effectiveness research. Although this research itself does not inform practitioners how to create an environment in which implementation is most likely to succeed, it provides information on a fairly cohesive list of teacher behaviours and organizational strategies that have been effective in a range of jurisdictions. The work on successful change efforts gives guidance as to how to incorporate these characteristics of effectiveness into a school improvement programme, and one of the prerequisites of successful educational change is teacher involvement.

2. The Involvement of Teachers

For school improvement to occur, the culture within the school has to be right and this is dependent upon the involvement and commitment of teachers. Fullan (1985) identifies four essential factors for successful school improvement that mirror several of the effective schools characteristics already described: the 'feel' of the leader for the improvement process; a shared value system; a high level of communication and interaction; and collaboration in planning and implementation. In more effective schools, there is an agreement between all the partners in a school community to work together for growth. Furthermore, the responsibility for school and classroom improvement lies with those who work in the school, rather than the adoption of the traditional view that improvement can be imposed from outside (Joyce *et al.*, 1983; Goodlad, 1984). There is, therefore, an intimate link between school improvement and teacher development, as teachers become equal partners in the process of school development.

If school growth depends on collaboration at the individual school level, there is a need for school districts to provide a context within which this can occur, and for teacher developers within these districts to encourage and support teachers through the collaborative study, implementation process and evaluation of school effectiveness projects. An illustration of such support can be seen in the Halton Board of Education's Effective Schools Project.

The Effective Schools Project

Based on what is known about school effectiveness, successful organizations and the change process, an Effective Schools Project was established in the Halton Board. I came to Canada to work with a Task Force to develop a vision of an ideal future state, based on a 'top-down, bottom-up' model of change (Stoll and Fink, 1988b). In other words, what outcomes did we hope for a few years down the road, and how could schools be empowered to take charge of their own development without feeling abandoned?

Within the last year, there has been a major reorganization within the school system. The new Strategic Directions of the Halton Board emphasize the improvement of instruction through a focus on school-based planning. This decentralization will be supported by a substantial increase in the number of consultants who will work closely with schools to meet their expressed in-service needs.

A growth planning process has been designed, and currently schools are beginning to develop their own School Growth Plans. These include their vision of the future and goal setting for a three-year period. A sequential, collaborative process is used (Stoll and Fink, 1989):

1 Assessment of the current state of the school and student outcomes
2 Identification of priorities and a plan of action
3 Implementation of this plan
4 Reassessment of outcomes and evaluation of the plan to see if it has made a positive difference.

The title 'School Growth Plan' is deliberate. The word 'improvement', though commonly used, has certain negative connotations. 'Growth', in contrast, encourages schools to build on previous successes. Starting, therefore, with a focus on their own strengths, staff examine the effective schools characteristics in relation to the particular context of their schools. Their needs assessments also, however, take into account any regional or provincial initiatives that are likely to impact their schools in the near future. It is hoped that student academic data, self-concept assessement results and historical information will be made available to each school in the form of a school profile. This individualized profile will be developed centrally and is intended to provide further information for the needs assessment process. The profile is not being designed in order that it might be used to compare one school with another. It will be a support instrument through which individual schools can examine their own development over time. One of the difficulties with benchmark testing, already mandated in England and being considered in Canada, is that comparisons between schools are based on snapshots of attainment taken at one point in time. These attainment tests take no account of students' background characteristics. It is, therefore, unfair to base comparisons upon such results. As argued earlier, the examination of progress controlling for background influences is a much fairer way to compare schools, and also enables a school to look at its own growth. These considerations will be taken into account when the school profile is developed in Halton.

The ultimate goals of a school are to enhance student achievement and self-concept, developing young people who are motivated, curious and eager to learn, who feel good about themselves, and who will become positive citizens in society. Following the basic premise that achievement and self-concept are promoted in schools where attributes of effectiveness are part of the culture, the school uses the growth-planning process as a vehicle to reach its final goals.

A significant shift has been made by the school board. Greater control has been given to individual schools, and, where possible, resources, staff development and consultancy support will be provided in response to the school's planning process. This places the onus on schools to incorporate within their plans a list of needs, specifically, in the area of teacher development. If, therefore, a group of teachers decide that one area of focus will be cooperative group learning, they may request, for example, general training in this strategy, specific training in cooperative group learning in math, release time to plan sessions collaboratively and to observe each other in the classroom, and help with evaluation of this area of emphasis.

Implications for Teacher Development

What, then, are the major implications for teacher development of Halton's project, and what extra help is necessary to enable teachers to collaborate in a meaningful way to develop and implement School

Growth Plans? Three linked areas of teacher development are high-lighted in this project. They focus on the teacher as a reflective researcher, the teacher as a collaborative partner, and the teacher in ongoing training.

1. Teacher as Reflective Researcher

Many teachers may not actively seek out or be aware of significant research findings on more effective practices. During the course of Halton's project, teachers' access to and consciousness of such findings has been increased. Already, several teachers have begun to reflect on this information as it relates to their own current practice (Schon, 1983). Some have also selected areas for further study as part of their Masters of Education requirements. It has been encouraging to see the desire of many teachers to use research in their classrooms to diagnose areas of need. More could be achieved, however, in this area. Principals could stimulate teachers to examine the characteristics in more detail and allow them time to test out relevant ones within their own classrooms as classroom researchers. In addition, researchers should devote more of their time to collaborative work with teachers to help them design research measures that will enable them to reflect upon their planned curriculum in the light of what actually occurs in the classroom.

The benefits of classroom research have been extolled by other writers (Hopkins, 1985; Good, 1989) who see it as a meaningful professional development activity to enhance teacher practice, as well as engagement in a process of refinement and the creation of autonomy in professional judgement. If such benefits accrue from classroom research, as certainly appears to be the case, then student outcomes will also be enhanced, which is surely the ultimate aim of all educators.

A further opportunity for teacher reflection is offered by the Halton Board through personal goal-setting. There is already a Co-operative Supervision and Evaluation process in place, whereby teachers discuss their goals with their principal or department head. Within this forum, the individual teacher's commitment to the School Growth Plan can be incorporated. There is no intention that any teacher should be forced into participation against their wishes, nor that their commitment to a particular activity will be 'carved in stone'. Nonetheless, it is hoped that most teachers will find it meaningful and stimulating to select an area of professional development related to the Growth Plan.

Although classroom research is more often seen as an opportunity for individual teacher development, it also offers potential for the development of collaborative partnerships. Research support networks could be set up within school boards where teachers could share ideas, formulate strategies, provide feedback, and also formulate joint classroom research projects. Without trying to inhibit an individual teacher's creative independence, there is still much to be said for the adage 'two heads are better than one'. The next implication examines collaboration in teacher development more directly.

2. Teacher as Collaborative Partner

Traditionally, teachers were seen to be autonomous; teachers' classrooms were their castles, and they were not expected to participate in school-level decision-making. The implication of school effectiveness and improvement research is that this is no longer acceptable.

A variety of teacher development activities are required to support School Growth Plans. As the emphasis in schools has shifted to collaborative decision-making, group skills will become increasingly important. Killion (1988) argues that for teachers to work and plan together, and to become increasingly involved in decisions at a school level, staff development is necessary in the areas of shared decision-making, group processing and conflict resolution.

Principals undoubtedly also require in-service training in the same skills, given that for some, at least, to relinquish complete control of the school's reins is likely to cause anxiety, and may be seen as a threat. People in a variety of roles within the system are being trained as process consultants to help facilitate schools through the growth planning process. Several teachers have elected to participate in this intensive in-service experience.

A key group in the implementation of this strategic plan is the consultants, for it is they who must respond to development needs as requested by individual schools. Their input and training in instructional and management techniques, and facilitation skills in this transition year is also crucial.

3. Teacher in Ongoing Training

Collaboration is also a theme that underpins the third area of teacher development; that of ongoing training in teaching skills and strategies. The majority of the schools have selected goals with a focus on instructional techniques, many of which have been identified earlier in this paper as being effective. For the development of specific teaching skills and strategies, as highlighted in effective schools research and elsewhere, theory alone of what appears to be successful has not been found adequate to ensure mastery by teachers of particular techniques. Joyce and Showers (1980) conclude that five fundamental components are necessary for the development of skills and their transfer into regular practice. These are: theory; demonstration; practice; feedback;

and coaching. It is the final part of the equation, the coaching component, that appears to have the most significant impact on teacher development. One of the main reasons for this is that coaching enables feedback, adaptation, and analysis of teaching skills to occur within a climate of companionship (Joyce *et al.*, 1983). Some concern has been expressed that coaching designed to implement specific models of teaching may not give teachers the opportunity to reflect on their appropriateness to certain curriculum areas or school contexts, and that cooperative learning may not suit all teachers (Hargreaves and Dawe, 1989). Robertson (1988) also points out that coaching can promote inequity towards women unless sensitively handled. Goodlad (1984) maintains, however, that successful school improvement can only result if the environment is one in which the collaborative study of teaching occurs, and risk-taking is encouraged in an atmosphere of trust and support. If handled appropriately, this should be the essence of the coaching partnership, such that teachers are able to work together to examine their behaviour, secure in the knowledge that they can take risks and that they are part of a mutual support system.

Currently, another leadership programme in the Halton Board encourages participants to work with a coaching partner, and focuses on techniques which administrators can later use in their schools for teacher development activities. The evaluations have been particularly positive with regard to benefits of working with a coaching partner. Administrators have commented on the opportunity to clarify concepts, share experiences and problem solve together. After three months, one reflected: 'My trust level and respect is at a very high level for my coaching partner and is growing'.

For the assessment of school needs, the first phase of the planning process, it is evident that teachers need support in the form of provision of instruments and help with interpretation of the results. At the second and third stages, planning and implementation, staff development activities are required on how to set goals and maintain momentum during the implementation process. For the final phase, staff development needs include techniques to evaluate student progress and development, and strategies for evaluation of the success of School Growth Plans.

Currently, one of my responsibilities is to work closely with individual teachers, groups and whole schools to help determine their assessment and evaluation needs, and to locate or develop with them instruments that will enable them to answer the questions important to the pursuit of their goals. My role is one of support. It is the teachers who decide upon their focus. If questionnaries or surveys are developed, it is always after discussions with them, and nothing is used until it has been vetted by the teachers concerned. The three areas of reflective research, collaboration and ongoing training are brought together in this activity.

Figure 1 summarizes Halton's cyclical growth-planning process,

Figure 6.1: *School Growth Plans and School Effectiveness*

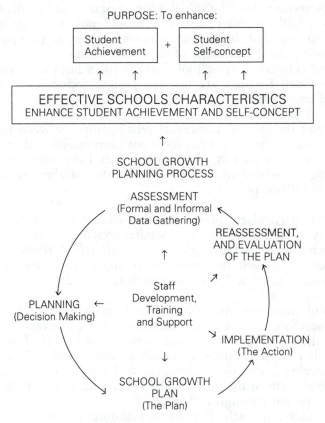

how it is related to the characteristics of effective schools, and the central role of staff development and support in the process.

Despite the development and training required to sustain such plans, the effects can be remarkable. Sparks *et al.* (1985) described the strengths of a staff development programme in which teachers in two schools were involved on planning teams to develop a school plan which was submitted to the rest of the staff for approval. Noted benefits were improvements in knowledge, skills, communication, and participation in decision-making. More significant, perhaps, was the improved staff morale that ensued.

Conclusion

School effectiveness research is complex, and its use for school improvement efforts should not be treated lightly. Research findings on school and teacher effects should be interpreted carefully before being translated into guidelines for practice. Thus, if the frequency of a teacher behaviour, for example the use of praise, and student achievement are positively correlated, this should not be an invitation for teachers to use that behaviour whenever possible (Brophy, 1988). Furthermore, the literal usage of checklists of the identified characteristics of effectiveness by school districts for school evaluation is not desirable. Such findings are not the perfect recipe for success, and further research still needs to be carried out to examine the issue of causality in more detail.

Despite the claims that causal relationships between teacher behaviours and student outcomes have not been established, it cannot be ignored that no matter in what context they have occurred, many of the findings of school and teacher effectiveness studies are similar. As Joyce *et al.* (1983) point out:

> What is particularly pleasing is that different researchers in a variety of studies are reaching similar conclusions about effective schooling, and that these conclusions are reinforced by teachers and administrators who bring to research programmes the critical eyes of experience. (p. 23)

School improvement efforts based on school effectiveness research, therefore, can provoke discussion that encourages teachers to examine their previous experience, values and beliefs. They can also offer teachers opportunities to reflect privately upon their teaching, and to develop instructional, research and group process skills. They foster the growth of the individual teacher and, in particular, encourage development through collegiality.

Essentially, the school growth planning process places the responsibility on teachers to select the goals most relevant to them, after consideration has been given to factors that have been shown to distinguish between more and less effective schools and account taken of their own unique school context. Teachers are, thus, more, rather than less, involved in the establishment of the school's direction and where they, personally, will fit into this plan. If planning and decision-making are going to become increasingly decentralized, teachers will need to be able to work together to reflect on what constitutes quality teaching, and have in their possession a repertoire of techniques, both professional and personal. In this way, they can become empowered, which, in turn will lead to increased involvement and satisfaction. Perhaps even more important is the positive impact that will also result on student outcomes. Thus, essentially, school improvement and teacher development are dependent upon each other. Given a true culture of ongoing learning and collaboration in a school, therefore, and a supportive school system and training network, the benefits to both students and teachers can be far reaching.

References

ADAM, E. (1987) *Steps to success: The principal's role*, Halton Board of Education, unpublished research paper.

BENNETT, B. and ROLHEISER-BENNETT, C. (1988) 'What makes teaching go?', *Supervision for Growth: Developmental Track*, North York Board of Education, Ontario.

BROADFOOT, P., NUTTALL, D. *et al.* (1988) *Records of Achievement—Evaluation of Pilot Schemes*, London, HMSO, Department of Education and Science.

BROOKOVER, W., BEADY, C., FLOOD, P. and SCHWEITZER, J. (1979) *School Systems and School Achievement: Schools Make a Difference*, New York, Praeger.

BROPHY, J. (1988) 'Research on teacher effects: Uses and abuses', *The Elementary School Journal*, 89, 1, pp. 3–21.

COLEMAN, J., CAMPBELL, E., HOBSON, C., McPARTLAND, J., MOOD, A., WEINFIELD, F. and YORK, R. (1966) *Equality of Educational Opportunity*, Washington National Center for Educational Statistics.

DREIKURS, R., GRUNWALD, B. and PEPPER, F. (1982) *Maintaining Sanity in the Classroom: Classroom Management Techniques*, 2nd edn., New York, Harper Row.

EDMONDS, R. (1979) 'Effective schools for the urban poor', *Educational Leadership*, 37, 1, pp. 15–27.

FULLAN, M. (1985) 'Change processes and strategies at the local level', *The Elementary School Journal*, 85, 5, pp. 391–420.

GARDNER, H. (1983) *Frames of Mind*, New York, Basic Books.

GOOD, T. (1989) 'Using classroom and school research to professionalize teaching', Paper presented at the Second International Congress for School Effectiveness, Rotterdam, January.

GOODLAD, J. (1979) *A Study of Schooling*, Indiana, Phi Delta Kappa Inc.

GOODLAD, J. (1984) *A Place Called School: Prospects for the Future*, New York, McGraw-Hill.

GRAY, W. and GRAY, M. (1985) 'Synthesis of research on mentoring beginning teachers', *Educational Leadership*, 43, 3, pp. 37–43.

HALL, G., RUTHERFORD, W., HORD, S. and HULING, L. (1984) 'Effects of three principal styles on school improvement', *Educational Leadership*, 45, 5, pp. 22–31.

HARGREAVES, A. (1989) *Curriculum and Assessment Reform*, Milton Keynes, Open University Press.

HARGREAVES, A. and DAWE, R. (1989) 'Coaching as unreflective practice: Contrived collegiality or collaborative culture?', Paper presented to the American Educational Research Association, San Francisco, March.

HOPKINS, D. (1985) *A Teacher's Guide to Classroom Research*, Milton Keynes, Open University Press.

JENCKS, C., SMITH, M., ACKLAND, H., BANE, M., COHEN, D., GINTIS, H., HEYNS, B. and MICHOLSON, S. (1972) *Inequality: A Reassessment of the Effect of Family and Schooling in America*, New York, Basic Books.

JOHNSON, D., JOHNSON, R., JOHNSON HOLUBEC, E. and ROY, P. (1984) *Circles of Learning*, Alexandria, Virginia, ASCD.

JOYCE, B. and SHOWERS, B. (1980) 'Improving in-service training: The messages from research', *Educational Leadership*, 37, 5, pp. 379–85.

JOYCE, B., HERSH, R. and McKIBBIN, M. (1983) *The Structure of School Improvement*, New York, Longman.

KILLION, J. (1988) 'The reality of implementing school improvement: What we've learned in hindsight may provide foresight to others', Paper presented at the Second International Congress for School Effectiveness, Rotterdam, January 1989.

KOUNIN, J. (1970) *Discipline and Group Management in Classrooms*, New York, Basic Books.

LEITHWOOD, K. and MONTGOMERY, D. (1986) *Improving Principal Effectiveness: The Principal Profile*, Toronto, OISE Press.

LEZOTTE, L. (1989) 'School improvement based on the effective schools research', in GARTNER, A. and KERZNER LIPSKY, D. (Eds.) *Beyond Separate Education: Quality Education for All*, Baltimore, MD, Paul H. Brooks Publishing Co.

MARLAND, M. (1975) *The Craft of the Classroom: A Survival Guide*, London, Heinemann.

MORTIMORE, P., SAMMONS, P., STOLL, L., LEWIS, D. and ECOB, R. (1988) *School Matters: The Junior Years*, Wells, Open Books, and Berkeley University of California Press.

REYNOLDS, D. (1989) 'School effectiveness and improvement in England and Wales', Country Report prepared for the Second International Congress for School Effectiveness, Rotterdam, January.

ROBERTSON, H. (1988) 'Teacher development and sex equity' in HARGREAVES, A. and FULLAN, M. (Eds.) *Understanding Teacher Development*, London, Cassell.

RUTTER, M., MAUGHAN, B., MORTIMORE, P. and OUSTON, J. (1979) *Fifteen Thousand Hours*, Wells Open Books, and Cambridge, MA, University of Harvard Press.

SCHON, D. (1983) *The Reflective Practitioner: How Professionals Think in Action*, New York, Basic Books.

SPARKS, G., NOWAKOWSKI, M., HALL, B., ALEC, R. and IMRICK, J. (1985) 'School improvement through staff development', *Educational Leadership, 42*, 6, pp. 59–62.

STOLL, L. and FINK, D. (1988a) 'Educational change; An international perspective', *International Journal of Educational Management, 2*, 3, pp. 26–31.

STOLL, L. and FINK, D. (1988b) 'An effective schools project: The Halton approach', Paper presented at the First International Congress for School Effectiveness, London, January.

STOLL, L. and FINK, D. (1989) 'Implementing an effective schools project: The Halton approach', Paper presented at the Second International Congress for School Effectiveness, Rotterdam, January.

Chapter 7

School-Based Teacher Development

Marvin F. Wideen

Introduction

At one time in the not too distant past, studies which described efforts to improve schools and schooling were for the most part reports of attempts that failed or in some way fell short. Today that picture is changing. Case descriptions of successful school change now appear regularly. For example, the National Writing Project in the United States and the Young Writers Program in Canada, which involves teachers and students focusing on writing across all subjects, has, according to popular reports, produced dramatic results in improved teaching practice (Goldberg, 1984). Hechinger (1983), writing in the *New York Times*, reported that teachers not only swear by the prog- ramme, but argue that it has changed their entire attitude toward teaching. The encouraging aspect in this and other examples lies in the fac' .hat we can now examine success in school change and try to understand it, rather than, as was so often the case in the 1960s and 1970s, document our failures. A small but growing body of literature is now extant concerning what constitutes success in a school im- provement project (Davis and Thomas, 1989; Fullan, 1985; Little, 1986; Huberman and Miles, 1986).

But, although we do have this knowledge, our understanding of how school improvement comes about still remains limited. As Huberman and Miles (1986) recently put it, 'even though we may know what successful school based innovation looks like, delivering it is another question' (p. 61). In short, we still must address the ques- tions: How do successful school improvement projects come about? How does a school initiate change and build it into its ongoing life?

I argue, in this Chapter, that the answer lies in building an ongoing capacity for continued change within the schools, a capacity which acknowledges the importance of the teacher's role in school change and the importance of the teacher's own development as an

This paper is based on research conducted under a grant from the Social Science and Humanities Research Council and seed grants from Simon Fraser University and the Prince Rupert School District.

ongoing feature of that change. Central to that argument lies teacher development within the context of a school. In the past, teachers were objects to be 'in-serviced'; they were seen as individuals operating without a context. Today, that thinking has changed. We now hear that in good schools, teachers talk to other teachers about instructional matters (Little, 1986). We see reference to phrases such as 'among the consistent findings of research in these and related areas is that teachers play a central role in effective implementation of school change' (Stein and Wang, 1988:171). The National Writing Project, to which I referred earlier, illustrates this bottom-up reform. It began in schools, evolved there, and changed schools and classrooms in the process. Thus, both in rhetoric and practice the centrality of the teacher appears established.

This emphasis on the teacher has led to the concept of teacher development—a concept which recognizes that no major reform in our school system will occur without the front line people who will eventually make it work: the teachers. However, seductive that notion, many questions remain. How does teacher development come about? In what settings does it best occur? How does it relate to school improvement? What motivates teachers to engage in teacher development?

In this Chapter, I examine a case study where a school staff supported by the district created a setting in which teacher development occurred naturally within the setting of a school improvement project. The setting also appeared to produce an ongoing capacity for change and adaptation within the school which enabled the staff to process new information and environmental pressures while maintaining an overall direction to the improvement plan. I first set out the context by describing the school improvement plan as a case study, and then discuss those factors which collectively appeared to create a school ethos which was conducive not only to change within the school, but to teacher development as well. The Chapter ends with some summary implications for teacher development. Before turning to these sections, I briefly describe the methodology used in this study.

I first visited the school in April 1986 at the request of the principal. Convinced that a significant change had occurred in the school, I continued to visit the school on a regular basis until June 1989. My visits aimed at describing the change that had occurred, identifying how the different players involved brought it about, and what factors contributed to its success. Each of the twelve site visits typically consisted of two or three days and involved classroom and staffroom observation and teacher interview. All interviews were recorded and later transcribed for close analysis. The repeated site visits enabled me to interview the teachers and principals on successive occasions. I also interviewed teachers who had left the school, district staff, the superintendent and the director of instruction in the school district, as well as school board members. Each site visit produced samples of student work, documents of various types, and several pages of hand-written field notes. In the Spring of 1989, I worked with a group of teachers over a four-day period to reconstruct the events, changes and influences over the observation period. They also reviewed my perception of the developments within the school.

The factors supporting the change came largely through interviews with key players. During early interviews the participants mentioned several factors that contributed to the change. In subsequent interviews the principal and teachers ranked these in order of importance and commented on them. These perceptions were checked out through a close analysis of the transcribed interviews, my own observations and follow-up interviews.

The Development and Implementation of the School Improvement Plan

The innovation, which began in September 1985, can be traced back to the situation at Oceanside prior to the Fall of that year and also to the experience of the principal and certain teachers new to the staff. Both parents and teachers describe the situation that existed prior to the Fall of 1985 as something akin to a 'little shop of horrors'. Given a choice, parents would send their children elsewhere. Everything had to be done according to the rules set out by the principal. The cupboards which contained the supplies were locked and could only be accessed through the secretary. Teachers kept their distance from each other and from the principal. Language arts were taught using the basal readers.

The arrival of the new principal and staff at Oceanside School in the Fall of 1985 saw the beginning of the innovation that was to be the subject of this case study. The new teachers who came to Oceanside that Fall and the perceptions that they carried with them provided a fertile background for the school improvement project that was to develop. Two of the teachers had taught with the new principal in a nearby village school and came with him to Oceanside. A common desire to interact with each other, to break down the perpetual isolation that they had previously experienced, and to explore possible improvements in education linked the three. Only four of the original teachers remained. The new mix of teachers now seemed to include a significant number who were interested in discussing teaching approaches and philosophies, in developing common units, and in comparing notes with one another. This became an important factor in shaping a new ethos that would develop in the school.

While the principal and teachers became the driving force behind the changes occurring in the school, in-service workshops and conferences attended by the staff influenced changes as well. These are illustrated in Figure 7.1 for the first year of the project. Across the top appear a series of rectangles intended to depict events or happenings. The bottom of the figure includes a series of triangle shapes depicting influences which come in the form of workshops, conferences or visitors. Through the centre appear oval shapes which depict changes. The connecting lines are links, with arrows showing direction. Some events had more influence on changes than others. For example, to the left of Figure 7.1 we see two items which preceded the opening of school: the administrative retreat and a reading workshop. The emergence of the changes that became the subject of this case study had roots in both. On other occasions, change happening in the school influenced events.

It became apparent from preparing this flow of events, changes and influences over the four-year period that the school improvement project was not one innovation, but many. Also, a surprising number of happenings occurred that could potentially influence work in the school. Further, the in-service activity occurring was huge and often quite unconnected.

The principal, Ron, traces his own thinking back to the administrative retreat which included the administrators in the district and school board members. They discussed fairly general issues of school improvement. At that meeting language development emerged as one of the main goals of the district. Despite this overall direction, schools were free to focus on other areas should they choose to. The other event having considerable influence on the principal was a language arts workshop, shown in Figure 7.1, attended by Ron and two teachers at Oceanside.

At the opening of school in September the initial event was a staff discussion of school goals. The principal describes the beginnings in this way:

> when I came to Oceanside, we went through the same kind of process, a kind of needs assessment, and it was not an ultra-formal pencil and paper kind of analytical process. It was based on a lot of talk and getting to know one another in a short period of time. We did not say to ourselves, 'the district direction is in language development. We had better come up with something in that area.' We just looked at what our needs were and what our experiences had been. And it turned out that a lot of people were concerned about language development.

The 'same kind of process' referred to by the principal involved the discussion he had encountered at the district level during the retreat with administrators. The other point of significance in this comment by the principal involves his emphasis on a 'lot of talk'. That norm, which involved talk about teaching, established early that

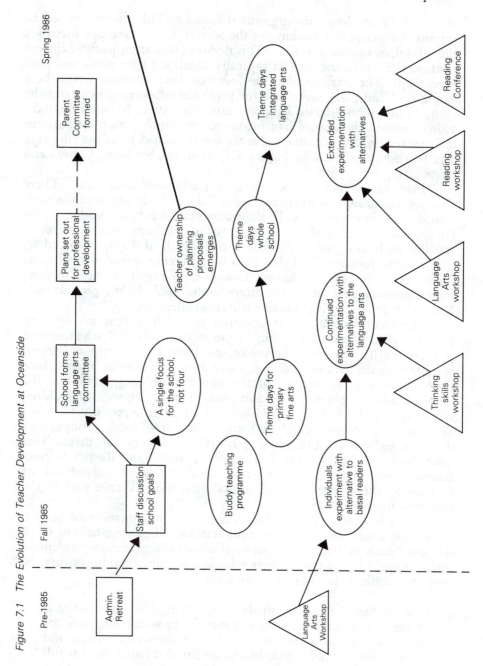

Figure 7.1 The Evolution of Teacher Development at Oceanside

year, was in evidence throughout the study. This discussion led to certain changes in the thinking of the school, i.e. to take one focus for the school, as opposed to four. This decision was an important change because schools in the district typically identified four goals and pursued them. The staff decided the focus on language arts would be a single goal and plans were laid for professional development and the forming of a school-based language arts committee. Meanwhile, individuals within the school had begun to experiment with alternatives to basal reading. The prime influence for them had been the language arts workshop, shown in Figure 7.1, attended by Ron, Cathy, and Irene.

Two main changes occurred in the school that year. These changes are shown in ovals in Figure 7.1. One change was the continued experimentation with alternatives to the basal readers. This change was influenced by a series of workshops that occurred—starting with Wassermann in the early Spring of 1986, followed by McCracken, Johnson, and the reading conference attended by several members of the staff.[1] The workshops encouraged teachers to continue experimenting with alternatives to the basal reading programme. They also served to legitimize such experimentation.

The second change that occurred in the first year involved an activity called theme days. This began in the early Fall when several primary teachers planned the use of small and large group activity to combine Music, Drama and Art. Later in the Spring the intermediate teachers, seeing the success of the programme, suggested that the whole school might well get involved. Two groupings of children were organized—K-3 and 4–7—around the Fine Arts, much as before. And, as before, children broke down into small groups with different individuals providing various experiences for them. This time, however, school board members, parents, and district helping teachers took a part. Soon the whole school became involved and for five weeks the theme of multicultural education became part of the students' lives every Friday.

The concept of theme days caught the imagination of several teachers in the school, and numerous staff meetings were held to work out the details of teacher cooperation across the grades to implement this concept. One of the teachers who was instrumental in starting the project described its influence this way:

> One of the things that made a big change in our staff was theme day. It gave teachers a chance to do whole language for half a day. It was a time to sort of feel your way through, and no one told you what you had to do for that half a day, or full day of theme. It wasn't based on a reading series or on a reading level; there were kids of all grade levels. So you had to come up with something interesting that kids could do at their own rate, and the product wasn't the most important thing, it

was the process. It led to the integrated. So I think that theme day was a really good way to get staff started on many things.

Two results sprang from the theme day experience in the school. First, it further broke down the concept of the basal reader notion. Teachers now saw how they could integrate language arts and other subjects and, therefore were encouraged to experiment further with alternatives to the basal reader. The second outcome was realization of the need for time to plan and to share activities. This led to the implementation of the second Wednesday programme which gave teachers a half-day free from teaching to plan. They developed the notion and took it to the board for approval.

The first year, then, involved developing a new language arts programme. The staff felt that the existing one, having been put together by the previous principal, did not meet the needs of the students at Oceanside. With this new emphasis, the principal and staff took it upon themselves to expand their understanding of the subject through attending the workshops such as those shown in Figure 7.1, undertaking professional reading, and engaging in staff discussions. At this first stage people also talked a great deal about whole language; they talked about a writing school, and they talked about the writing process. These discussions led to the changing of their programme from the use of basal readers to having children write their own stories for reading.

The introduction of 'the writing process' provided the first step for changing the language arts approach that existed in the school prior to this change. The way in which that change came about varied from teacher to teacher. One described the change in this way:

> The first year (in Oceanside) I had grade three, and I used the Ginn readers, but at the same time I was trying to do other things to supplement them—that would make reading more interesting. The pressure was on writing; that was our big goal at the school, to get more writing done. So, I started incorporating a lot more writing than I ever did before. I think that was the major change. But I still used the Ginn as my back up which was sort of my security blanket. And that's the same for all teachers that I've ever talked to. So that year I used the Ginn readers with the criterion tests and mastery tests. But I didn't have any faith in them any more. I just did them because it was something substantial, something that was down on paper that I could show parents when they came in. Then, I started using McCracken's work that year, shortly after they gave their workshop. They came into my classroom and we taped a session in which she took my class and did an exercise with them. And then the next year I had grade three as well. And that was the year that I got rid of the Ginn altogether.

This quotation illustrates in part the struggle that this teacher had in making a change from a structured programme to the alternative approach to language arts that began in Oceanside in the Fall of 1985. It also shows the influence of other teachers in the school and that of the outside consultant when that person made a presentation at a key time in the professional life of the teacher. Parenthetically, it also highlights the not so subtle influence that parents have on classroom practice.

The next school year saw a changed focus. While the emphasis the previous year had been on improving the teaching of reading, the focus in the second year changed to improving writing. Again in-service workshops influenced this change. But the change to writing also affected new developments in the continuation of the theme day and led to further examination of the evaluation process. The second year saw a more reflective cerebral approach with less emphasis on activity and more emphasis on critical examination and the philosophy behind the changes that had occurred; staff talked about how important their own reading had been during this year. Such reading had encouraged a switch from the teacher-centered approach to what the teachers described as a student-centered classroom. And that change came about, according to the teachers, because of the discussion about those readings. This was more of a philosophical shift in view than any particular activity-driven change.

The type of classroom that resulted from this process placed great emphasis on writing. In the classrooms I observed students working with students and with the teacher in making two or three revisions to a written piece of work which would then be redrafted, and on occasions published.[2] It was common to see students in grade six reading their stories to children in the lower grades and their stories could be found displayed around the school. Children in grades one and two wrote their own storybooks. So, by the end of the second year, what a visitor could observe was a very, very different language arts programme than that in which the basal reading programme had provided the focus.

Teachers describe the third year of the project as a consolidation year, having experienced almost frenetic activity in the first year and a period of reading and reflection in the second year. Those ideas now became consolidated in a way that tended to build confidence in the staff. Several of the changes that had begun earlier continued and evolved. The theme day notion continued but was changed to highlight three major themes. The development of evaluation techniques continued with refinement. Two new changes became evident this year. One involved the emphasis on learning styles and the second, the beginning of team teaching. Those who talk about their experiences that year claim that the workshop by Carolyn Mamchur influenced the staff to emphasize teaching and learning styles. The notion of team teaching developed concurrently and the extended experimentation continued. Science and social studies, which had begun to be implemented into the language arts programme, received a boost from another event, a visit by an expert on the writing process, Wendy Strachan.

Part way through my study of the school, and in consultation with the principal and teachers, I invited an expert in the writing process to visit Oceanside and make a comment about the writing programme developed by the staff. She spent two days in the school before Christmas in 1987. She described the writing process that she saw in the school as still being at the initial stage of story writing. She saw little evidence of work in other subjects and little evidence at that time of students using different writing styles. She felt that she could only say that in language arts at Oceanside, significant strides had been made by the teachers to change from a basal reading programme to the use of a quite innovative and exciting language arts programme, but that in her opinion the process was not very advanced.

The teachers and principal did not agree with her assessment, and felt that their innovation was much farther along than her report indicated. They believed that coming as she did in the Fall gave her an incomplete picture of the project. At that time of year many of the teachers were still teaching their classes various ways to organize and present their work. It was felt that had she come in early Spring, story writing would have been behind the students and she would have gained a different impression of the teachers' and students' work. Further, the staff noted that she did not ask for examples of technical or other styles of writing that were available. Nor did she explore with the teachers and students facets of the project that might not have been obvious on her short visit. Thus, the staff first reacted negatively to the notion put forth by this expert that the writing process to this point had dealt mainly with stories.

Perhaps the most important outcome of this visit involved how the staff dealt with what they perceived as a criticism. Much reflection and discussion followed; they began to examine what needed doing in the light of the report on an informal rather than a formal basis. It perhaps was a coincidence that further integration of language arts with science and social studies followed. But, of significance in this incident was the capacity within the staff to deal with the report in the way they did. It became one more opportunity to grow professionally as a staff and to improve their teaching as a result of external input. The key to this growth appeared to be the capacity that had developed within the staff to deal with the dissonance created by the outside expert.

In addition to being a year of consolidation, the third year of the project was also a year of confidence-building for the staff. They now felt that they had something to share with the world that was different and valuable, and as events showed, they were only too happy to share it. The trend toward having the staff involved in workshop activity in and outside the district continued. The staff continued to be involved in district committees, in evaluation, reading and writing and now the success of the school was becoming known in and outside the district. This success resulted in a proposal submitted by the principal to the National Council for Teachers of Reading conference at Coeur d'Lene. This proposal was accepted and the staff spent a good part of that year preparing for the presentation. Against the better judgement of the Superintendent and the conference organizers, six of the teachers on staff attended that conference. But the teachers insisted, pointing out that they had all been involved in the development of the innovation and they all wanted to be a part of making the presentation. They refer to the experience at Coeur d'Lene as having focused their attention and highlighted the more important parts of the innovation. The same presentation was given in their own district and at another.

At the same time, the goal of improving language arts led the staff to explore different avenues of teaching. They attended and hosted workshops on thematic teaching, teaching for thinking, and learning styles. At one point they invited a district counsellor to come in and work with small groups of students using a programme aimed at improving thinking. The project passed into a stage of subject integration where other areas of the curriculum such as science and social studies began to be integrated with each other and with language arts. 'Theme days' soon became 'theme weeks', and through this vehicle the teachers expanded the writing approach to include other subjects. This concept continued to grow so that by 1988, science and social studies were also woven into the language arts programme, and the themes went on for much longer than a single week.

Teachers describe the fourth school year as a year of implementing at the classroom level those ideas that had emerged over the last three years. Some changes took place; old practices began to die out. For example, the concept of theme days, which had been so critical in the first year, now became an innovation that had run its course. Teachers began to discuss whether theme days were actually needed. In many respects they began now to get in the way because much of what they represented were being adopted individually by teachers in their classrooms. The continuing emphasis on refining evaluation procedures to fit the new teaching continued. The team-teaching focus expanded to include the librarian and learning-assistance teachers. Students, too, began to receive a different kind of attention. One concept that began to emerge this year was the notion of student as teacher, where appropriate students took over the role of tutor or teacher of other students. The student-as-teacher concept produced several interesting findings for the teachers. One such finding was that some of the students who had experienced difficulty under certain approaches to teaching developed strategies of learning to cope with these approaches. These strategies of learning became of use to several of the teachers.

This brief description of the school improvement project provides a context for a discussion of a conceptual view of the innovation and the factors contributing to it.

A Conceptual View

By the Fall of 1987 during a visit to the site, I confirmed that the school improvement project itself was a moving target; it had changed considerably over the first two years of observation in the school. And during each visit after that, additional changes seemed to appear. These changes did not occur in a linear straightforward way, nor did each teacher experience them in the same way. To explain the developmental nature of the project, I have devised Figure 7.2. The four layers in the Figure illustrate in part the changes I observed in the school and their relationship to the community over the period of the study. Each level provides a more complex view of the change in the school. The outermost layer, 'improved language arts', provided the starting point for many of the teachers. They talked about whole language, and discussed having changed their teaching from the use of basal readers to having children now write their own stories for reading. For some of the teachers the innovation went no further than that. In the words of one teacher:

> I just am not a person to jump in full force and do something. I have to sit back over a period of time. I will pick up bits and pieces of what I think will work for me. And I have over the past three years taken little bits and pieces, and used them. I don't really see myself as a follower of the whole language approach. I know how to use whole language in my class, but not to the extent of other teachers. I'm not into the really deep structure of it...I use what is offered in the school, but I still have my own biases...I'm not one of your so-called innovators in the school. I just plug along—do the things I want to.

But for others, much more was at stake than simply improving the teaching of language arts. Stage 2 in Figure 7.2 shows some teachers integrating subjects and becoming involved in the writing process. At this stage the larger issues of teaching and learning occupied much of their thoughts and staffroom conversation. They actively contemplated changes that have worked for them, and changes that they were planning to initiate. At this level, they actually

Figure 7.2: *Stages of Instructional Change*

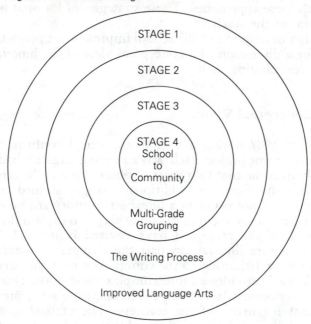

Figure 7.3: *Stages of Reflection*

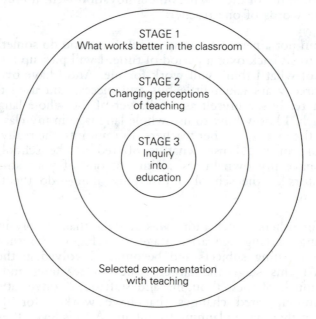

generated changes in their own teaching rather than seeking to adopt someone else's method. The comments of two teachers are pertinent here:

And that was the year I thought that I had finally broken totally free of Ginn and I felt very strong about whole language. And I knew what I believed in and what I didn't for the first time. And I was growing professionally as well, it was really a good year. My second and third years were excellent that way. And then doing our workshop, that just topped everything off and made me feel like a professional. So once you start to feel that you're doing something for the kids and for yourself at the same time a different view of teaching generally... A lot of teachers do things only for the kids; that was me for many years; just working in the classroom. And I thought that was it, that I would always be a classroom teacher, and then the next stage was principal or some other job I guess, in the district, or working for the Ministry. But I didn't think of growing as a professional myself. I didn't realize there was more to work. I went to university and teachers' college, and thought that was all I need to know... But it's not. It's a continuous process.

It was so different from the basal reading approach and some of the things they read out to us, the activities that they used just seemed to be a lot more open-ended and interesting for kids to do. So I started some of that in my own classroom. And then you find that even that... even that's not enough, so you started looking at other things, like the writing process, just trying to use different types of books in your reading programme, that kind of thing, and I guess I'm still evolving in that particular point. It's only two and a half years; I am still working on that process, it's still going on.

These two teachers have begun to see teaching as a changing ongoing activity. In the first situation, for example, the teacher now sees her own professional development occurring as a result of changes she makes to her teaching.

Stages 3 and 4 in Figure 7.2 reflect deeper levels of inquiry into teaching. At level three classes and teacher's work became integrated on a regular basis. The situation had evolved to the point where classes were now grouped together with two teachers working side by side with multiple grades. This stage involved still closer and more frequent interaction among the teachers. Here the staff struggled, experimented and taught themselves to team teach with their colleagues at Oceanside, and to try various types of multi-graded groupings. This metaphorical removal of the walls between their classrooms seems to have been as a result of a momentum that was a real force in the school. One of the teachers describes it like this:

> People share quite freely their ideas and people are really quite excited sometimes, and they will come into the staffroom and talk about something. And you see the excitement in people and you want to be part of that excitement, so you try and learn what the process is so that you can try it in your own room.

The fourth and innermost circle, which I have termed 'from school to community' began occupying more and more of the teachers' time as the change progressed. Here the efforts of the teachers found expression in communicating their work to a larger educational community. Staff became members of committees which took on various district projects. A workshop was presented by the staff to a neighbouring town and to a conference. This level seemed to lead teachers to contemplate the broader issues of education as a whole. Indeed, at this level, the teachers question the role of education in society and their part in it. This stage represents much more personal inquiry into teaching and into their own feelings as teachers. As one moved from the outermost to the inner circles it appeared that the change became more complex and required a deeper understanding.

These four stages of the change that I observed illustrate its complex nature. It reveals not one innovation, but several. I found teachers working at each of the levels illustrated here; the norms of the school were such that those differences were respected. On the other hand, the complex nature of the change required at the innermost levels seemed to provide a challenge for those teachers who wished it. In short, the change provided something for everyone.

But accompanying these observed patterns of change at Oceanside were stages of thinking reflected in the interviews of the teachers and principal, which are shown in Figure 7.3. At the outermost level, teachers appeared concerned about experimenting with new teaching strategies. Their thoughts centred on how this or that practice might be put into place. Others had moved beyond the specific practices themselves to think about how their teaching was changing, or in some cases how it should change. Beyond that the concern focused on a deeper level of inquiry that involved the school, and in some cases education in the more general sense. I inferred from the comments that at times the teachers were dealing with a more fundamental concern which was society itself. So in short, two things were occurring: on the one hand, teachers were changing their practices; on the other certain thoughts appeared to accompany those changes.

With regard to the stages displayed in Figures 7.2 and 7.3, a tempting argument holds that these layers represent stages of teacher practice and development. Indeed, in certain cases evidence would support the argument that some members of the Oceanside staff progressed from the outermost to the innermost circles. Certainly the change itself did appear to move from level 1 to level 4 in Figure 7.2. However, with regard to individual teachers, given the scope of the study, I only claim that I saw people at different levels over the three-year period and that some did in fact seem to move toward the centre of both figures. It also appeared that many of the teachers had worked through earlier stages before coming to Oceanside. But it remains for further thought and inquiry to determine if in fact these are stages of growth, or areas where people find themselves most comfortable. What becomes important in these stages are the implications they hold for change within a school and for teacher development.

As a result of this innovation, a school once considered nearly dysfunctional in terms of teacher growth became a centre in the community, where teachers felt confident enough to display their programme to the public at large. The innovation itself changed over time, as did many of the teachers. This personal growth was not uniformly felt, and while some experienced considerable and profound change within their own development, even those where the change was less acutely felt reported improved practice and a sense of greater proficiency. In terms of student learning, both test scores and student writing support the notion of a much improved school. In British Columbia, the Ministry assess students across the province in one or more subject areas. During the time of this study, scores from this programme were available for science and language arts. In both subjects the school showed significant gains. Further, the school kept records of year-end student writing. These writing samples provided strong evidence of substantial and continued improvement of the students' ability to write.

The Contributing Factors

This study examined school-based teacher development within the context of a project aimed at improving the instructional activity in a school. The two went hand in hand, supported by certain critical factors. The role of the principal and the notion of group process stood out. Other factors also contributed.

The principal, through providing the general conceptual direction for the project and an atmosphere that allowed for trial and experimentation, set an expectation in the school. Within this setting a loosely-coupled group atmosphere developed within the school where both teachers and principal came together to plan, discuss innovation, assess their impact, and simply talk. The change itself, because of its complexity and perceived importance, became a factor. District support provided an ethos within which the staff felt they had support and general direction, but at the same time freedom to explore and make mistakes. Finally, as we saw in Figure 7.1, the availability and use of knowledge and information about teaching and schooling provided an ongoing grist for the activity mill within the school. These factors, which worked in support of the change and teacher development, are discussed below.

The Role of the Principal

During interviews with teachers, the role of the principal was cited repeatedly as a key factor in bringing about and maintaining the change and as a factor in the teachers' own development. An analysis of the transcribed interviews indicated that the principal at Oceanside took certain actions which directly supported the development and implementation of the change, but more importantly, that his attitude toward professionalism and his particular vision of a better education for the children in the school appeared to be the foundation which supported the change.

Support leadership appeared to be instrumental in developing the change strategy and the principal took several actions to support the teachers in the school. These actions included providing release time for teachers, finding money to support their efforts, and taking risks with them by trying out new teaching ideas. Teachers perceived a fairness about him and a willingness to share decision-making with them. He established early the norms of collegiality and interaction and became part of the learning group in the school. The two comments that follow illustrate certain of these points:

> You can't say that you need a really strong administrator or that you need a really strong staff...You need to look at them all. It wouldn't have happened without the principal. But to me, the more powerful way is the teachers. He was an integral part of that, but whatever vision he had would never happen without the teachers pulling together, having ownership, and setting up what they felt would be a group collaborative model.

> I think the vision of what he (the principal) wanted to do has changed the way he behaved as principal, and probably much more than he would have ever expected. Because, although in the beginning he believed in the collegial model, he still thought that, in order for that to happen, somebody had to lead the way. And so lots of the things that he did reflected that sort of conflict. But people on Oceanside staff know him

so well, and they're so used to working with him, that weren't afraid to say, 'Hey, wait a minute! That's not how people cooperate! That's not how you make group decisions!' And pulled him back! So that all the way along I think that there's been as much opportunity for him to grow and change as there has been for the staff.

The last two quotations illustrate the interesting interplay that occurred between the principal and the group of teachers in the school. Reflecting back on their interaction with the principal, the teachers posited the notion that his leadership style had changed during the first year partly as a result of that interplay.

The staff also expressed the view that the principal would 'go to bat for them' if necessary. In short, his commitment lay with them, not the school board office or someone else on the outside. The following comments were made by teachers when asked to describe what they meant when they talked about the supportive role of the principal:

I mean support in terms of the teachers' interests and needs, not the principal's interests and needs. They have to wait...If I needed a day to just sit down and prepare myself, I can have that day to sit down and prepare myself. And I'm not dealt with as if I'm somebody who can't handle my teaching. If I want to go down and buy three books that are just excellent books, that's what I do. Go buy them. Don't come beg, just go get 'em. If I'm interested in developing a workshop in the district, I don't have to go and beg permission. I'm seen as a person who has the rights to do that. I'm a professional, and I'm dealt with as a professional, and not one of his students.

I think the staff knows that (the principal) would just go to the ends of the earth and back for them. Whatever happens, they know he's on their side. And that he does take risks on their behalf. And those things build a sort of rapport as a community that you can't get....

The principal did everything in his power to assist teachers not only in learning different strategies in language arts and integrating them with other subjects, but also in giving the teachers preparation time for implementation. At the same time, other teachers report that they never felt pressure to make changes at a faster pace than they were comfortable with. The changes happened slowly, more slowly than some would have liked, but it seemed to be a necessary pace to ensure the eventual participation of most of the teachers.

Conceptual support proved to be equally as important in bringing about change. The conceptual leadership of the principal (and selected members of the staff) became a significant factor in the developments at Oceanside. The principal showed a type of intellectual persistence regarding the issues surrounding the innovation, and the view of professionalism which guided his actions carried with it certain values about education both for himself and the staff. He spoke about the need to ask if we are satisfied with what we are doing in the schools: to ask how we can empower people to make changes that will bring about better schools for children. He often talked of equality in decision-making among teachers and a valuing of each other's opinion. To him, such an approach should be consistent across the way one runs a school, a classroom, or a district, as can be seen in these comments from two teachers:

> That's his personality; he loves to ask those questions. That's the kind of thinker that he is. And it's not so much that his doubts express a lack of belief in what he's doing, but that it's his nature to explore all the parameters of a problem, to really look at every side of it, to make sure he hasn't missed anything.

> Ron's the type of person who will take your ideas and take them one step further, will work with you on it...So if you have a principal that says, 'Yeah. That sounds great,' and goes next door and you never hear about it again, then I think you're going to have to look in another direction for help.

For Ron, professionalism brought with it a commitment to reform. Such thoughts had been with him for some time. In one interview he recalls his thinking with regard to his work at the Master's level:

> I remember asking questions several times when I was in my Master's course. I would look at a bunch of would-be-administrators going through the hoops in those courses to get the best possible grades. And I knew that when we walked out that door with the diplomas most of us would go right back to doing precisely what we had already done.

What can one learn from examining the principal's role at Oceanside? Simply put, a good principal stands for something that goes beyond mere support. He must be in support of something; he must have a drive to find principles of a substantive nature that speak to the question of what is the substance of a good school. The other observation that one can make from this analysis involves context. Often the literature paints the principal as some sort of guiding light who can lift a school from the ashes of mediocrity by cleverly walking on the water of enlightenment. Papers such as 'The principal as white knight' perhaps create this glowing image. Rarely does the literature point to the importance of the school and district context. As the quotations I have cited point out, the staff provided a conducive atmosphere for the principal; so did the district. Ron as a principal made mistakes over the three years of this study both at the school and district level, but at both levels people recognized his strengths and forgave him. In short, the supportive atmosphere worked both ways, they too provided him with support.

The Power of Group Process

If the isolation typical of most classrooms does not provide a good setting for change and professional development, what then provides a better alternative? The notion that emerges from the Oceanside experience points to the group setting as a powerful vehicle for bringing about change, but with the qualification that certain characteristics must pertain for a group setting to be effective. Certain norms, beliefs, expectations, and support are needed within that group setting for any change to occur. But, in addition, such beliefs and expectations must revolve around instructional matters that those both inside and outside the group see as important. The arguments behind the value of the group in this case go beyond the observations made at Oceanside. Perhaps at this point it would be useful to digress and review some of those reasons.

The first and perhaps most basic reason stems from the fact that men and women are, for the most part, gregarious beings. Why do we go to conventions? Why do we have associations? How many times have you witnessed a house party ending up in one room in your house, usually the kitchen? I suspect the answer is quite simple: we learn, become inspired, and find our identity within the group. Teacher development and school improvement carries with it the same set of needs.

The need for shelter conditions under which the risks necessary for growth to occur provide another factor that underscores the importance of group process. Anyone who has tried something new, whether it is a golf swing, a new pair of skates or a new laboratory procedure, knows that for the first short while (and sometimes for the first long while), one's performance gets worse. For teachers, attempting a new approach to teaching, this can be very unsettling. But, in a group setting the support structure provides time to hone newly forming skills and provides encouragement to help counter initial anxiety.

For teachers, the most logical 'group' involves the school as a unit. Indeed many have argued for the school as the centre for educational reform. Goodlad (1983) has probably argued the most forcefully in this regard. He contends that 'the individual school is the key unit on which to focus for effecting improvement within the formal educational system' (p. 36). That argument, however, rests on the notion that the school can function as an appropriate unit for educational reform. That notion arises more as a well argued item of faith rather than one based on research. Goodlad himself makes this qualification:

> The research necessary to a strong affirmation of the school-based postulate simply does not exist. Both scholars and practitioners cite references adding up to a rather substantial list in arguing for the school as the locus for change. But, on checking these sources, one finds the best of them to be rationales for dealing with the school from the perspective of the hypothesis, not evidence regarding its validity. (p. 37)

Moreover, the literature appears quite slim when it comes to dealing with what the school should look like were it to provide an appropriate setting for teacher development and/or educational change. Perhaps no better illustration of this exists than the eighty-sixth NSSE yearbook bearing the title, *The Ecology of School Renewal*. Here Goodlad (1987) and an impressive group of authors make a convincing case for an alternative paradigm for school improvement. They talk of replacing one-way directives with multiple interactions, rules and regulations with room for decision-making, mandated behaviour with inquiring behaviour, and so on. The alternative set out in the first chapter by Goodlad fails to lift off in subsequent chapters. The reader leaves with the sense that while it may have been a great concept, the knowledge base to effect it remains very weak indeed. The experience at Oceanside suggests that while the school may provide the necessary ethos to support and encourage a change, the group itself within that school offers a more viable and productive notion to account for school change.

One of Oceanside's strengths was surely its collegial approach to change. That the process was characterized by constant and intense interaction among the teachers, and that the principal did not direct the project from above, but instead was part of it, was significant to its success. The ethos that emerged from this carried the staff commitment on from year to year; essentially it was a group process. The tone was set in the school, but the group process drove the innovation.

What occurred in Oceanside went beyond talk and collaboration to include support for risk-taking and in some cases freedom to not collaborate. The group atmosphere produced an ethos which allowed for risk-taking and also for people to go slower at the particular change. This notion can be inferred from the two comments which follow.

And the fact that people on this staff are very cooperative people helped. . . They seem to think nothing of helping each other to develop unit plans and sharing materials back and forth, and that sort of thing, so that has helped a lot too. No one has had to work in isolation. If they run into a problem there is always somebody else that they could go to.

But when someone has dealt with a programme for a long time and has ownership, it's really hard. . . to leave the security of their programmes that were running very well. And I was a real risk person for people on staff. Not everyone was at the same level in terms of how much they wanted to change in that direction. And so people were really nervous about family grouping and looking at how the grades 3, 4 and 5 and people were concerned about report cards, and how would they tell parents. So it was quite a heated debate. . . And we actually had to come back as a staff again to talk about that issue.

The significant point here is that while some confirmation did occur, they did come back to that issue in a way that allowed the staff to move ahead. It was the group support that allowed that to occur. Other things also began to work on the staff, such as classroom visits. As one teacher noted:

I am sure if I went to Bev, or anyone else on staff who has really worked with the writing process a lot more than I have, if I said, 'Bev, would you come in and do a lesson for me?', she would definitely come in and do it. People are that willing to help each other.

The group promoted a feeling of empowerment on the part of the teachers. They saw their parts in the innovation as being central and had a strong sense of ownership over it.

Central to formation of the group at Oceanside was the constant interaction and talk that developed, related both to the change that occurred and to the professional development. Collegiality has become the term to describe such interaction in the school inprovement literature. Little's work in particular pointed to the importance of teachers talking to teachers about instructional matters. The situation at Oceanside supported that notion in part but not in the way that it has sometimes been assumed in the literature. Certainly, in my observations I saw a great deal of teacher–teacher and teacher–principal talk about instructional matters. The interviews confirmed this. For example, when asked about factors that contributed to the change, comments such as the following were made by teachers:

Probably talking, just very informal talking, going out for a drink. Showing the things my kids are doing in the classroom.

And that's the peer interaction part that is so important...being able to hear from other people, 'Well, have you tried this, or that. And this is a good book to read', and keep up to date.

Peer interaction to me is a key that really has to be part and parcel of whatever movement you want to make. Definitely. And with that peer interaction, I would include the workshops...

These three teachers all saw the value of the peer interaction, which the third coupled with the workshops that had taken place. However, others went on to explain just how peer interaction led to changes in their work. In the comment made near the third year of the project, a teacher described how the peer interaction had led to an awareness of the type of change that was needed in science:

I think part of it has been the discussion that's been going on for the last year or so in the area of science. Knowing that science has been an area that has been very weak in the elementary system we decided to take that and figure out what we can do with that, and how we could incorporate that into our language development project. Having individual teachers saying, 'Yes, that is an area that I don't feel comfortable teaching. And it's an area that I want to improve on'. It was an area that we all said, 'Hey, that's exactly what we want to do. That's what we believe in, that's where our philosophy ties in. We want hands-on, we want children to be able to manipulate their environment, and all these kinds of things. That's exactly what science is all about.'

Peer interaction or collegiality became the process by which the group developed within the school.

The Innovation

The literature on school improvement often remains silent on the substance of changes that become the subject of study. It appears almost as though the processes in which teachers engage overshadow the nature of changes they attempt to make. My observations at Oceanside indicate that the very change being attempted there became influential in determining its success. While the teachers did appear to have a shared set of meanings and a common language with which to talk about the change in the school, its complexity seemed to provide something for everyone both in terms of improved teaching and for their own professional development. What existed was a general concept of a change, but one that carried specific meaning for different people. This expressed itself in part by the different perceptions of the change held by different people. Some saw it as a changed language arts programme, one from which they could borrow better teaching techniques. A significant number of people on the staff, who exercised leadership at different stages, and who represented a critical mass, viewed the innovation as something that went far beyond the language arts and indeed as something that went beyond the subjects being taught in the school. They saw it as an opportunity for growth both for themselves and for the students they were teaching. For them it was being engaged in a process of change and improvement and inquiry into their own teaching. While this deep structure remained something of an ephemeral notion throughout my study of the school, it nevertheless held meaning for many of the teachers. And as such the complexity of the innovation became one of its strengths. The complexity was such that it provided a never-ending source of inspiration and engagement for those people. It had now gone far beyond techniques and procedures to a kind of inner notion about what teaching was, how one improved at it, and how one could engage in the excitement of that activity.

Another side of the change became related to its success. Moving from the basal reading programme and providing children and indeed teachers with choice carried with it certain political and social overtones that other types of changes may not have. The principal, for example, made the point that his concern had to do with the relationship between socialization and academic learning and how the individual attitudes of students develop. He continually argued for equality across children and teachers and for their choice in what they were learning. The change that occurred in the school made it possible for the principal and some members of his staff to live out this vision. In short, the principal, and those who felt as he did, brought to the situation certain knowledge and points of view that in themselves acted on the innovation.

The Availability and Use of Knowledge

The importance of applying what we know to the resolution of social problems has long been a concern to social scientists. In fact Glasser (in Louis, 1981) once remarked that civilization was a race between catastrophe and knowledge utilization. One of the instrumental factors directing the shape of the change at Oceanside was the use of information in a variety of forms; it could be said that the change at Oceanside occurred in an information-rich environment. Such an observation might not be particularly startling given today's society. But it should be noted, as I pointed out earlier, that Oceanside was located in an isolated community of 16,000 people. Such information came from two sources, some through direct access to information, and the others through linkages and contacts. On the one hand, the principal and staff read a great deal. In fact, this practice was promoted throughout the district through the periodic distribution of the indexes of journals; staff could then order articles they wished to read. Teachers talked about several benefits of reading in helping them move the project forward. Among the reasons they cited for reading having a benefit were the following: legitimization of change (whether that change was already initiated or being thought about); stimulation to discussion and collaboration with peers; and, obviously as a vehicle for producing new ideas. One of the books that was frequently mentioned was Illich's *Deschooling Society* (1970). The question as to what a book of this nature would do for teachers engaged in this kind of a change was a topic of some discussion at a meeting with teachers. It appeared that Illich's book legitimized challenging the system. In short, teachers who had concerns about the system now saw their concerns echoed in print. Therefore, it became appropriate to continue steps to change the system in which they were working. Schon's *The Reflective Practitioner* (1983) produced a similar advantage but it encouraged teachers to reflect on their practice. The quotation that follows and the teacher's reaction to it illustrate the value of reading in this case. The quotation comes from Illich, *Deschooling Society* (1970:76):

> Schools are designed on the assumption that there is a secret to everything in life; that the quality of life depends on knowing the secret; that secrets can be known only in orderly successions; and that only teachers can properly reveal those secrets.

In response to this quotation Bev writes:

> Writing allows teachers as facilitators to guide students toward finding and sharing their own secrets to allow them to become confident, autonomous learners and teachers. Teachers too need to be learners. We need to listen and observe carefully as students discover and respond to and celebrate their learning. They have lots to teach us. The teachers talk about the staff room as being a forum where they discuss things they've read.

A significant number of the staff maintained contact with people outside the district through various linkages. Many of the staff attended university courses as part of their degree completion. The principal sought to maintain contact with the universities whenever he could. They made visits to other schools which were working with

'The Young Writers Project'. The staff were virtually drenched in workshop activity, some closely related to what they were doing, others more distant.

How did this access to information, and outside linkage direct the change that occurred? One teacher described how reading affected her work in the school in this way:

> (in response to how the particular change came about)...I think mostly through my own professional reading and from observing different things that are happening. I have to use B—as my counterpart here, because I learned a lot from her. But I would say mostly, I have always been interested in actively pursuing new ideas and new strategies and continually doing a lot of professional reading. And so I would always be changing or modifying whatever I was doing, trying to find a better way. I don't think that I am ever perfect and there is certainly a lot more room for improvement.

The interaction between the reading that she did and her contact with other teachers becomes evident in this comment. The interviews also indicated that not all teachers read. But that seemed unimportant because of the intense interaction that continually occurred among staff. What one teacher read would affect others through the process of interaction.

The processing of information was not necessarily smooth; teachers struggled to understand and deal with new ideas and techniques. One teacher describes her initial confusion like this:

> [A workshop leader] spoke to us, in terms of some of the concepts...I didn't really have a background or a real idea of where she was coming from at the time. So when she left I was sort of still in a state of confusion. And at that point she spoke of a one-year unit, a one-year theme, and take off from that into other (ones). And she was talking about the whole unit going from a January to June or something. I can't recall exactly when. In any event it was at that point that I was thinking, you know, this is just ridiculous. I mean, how can you do that with that group of kids with one general topic area.

What did appear to occur as a result of such workshops was further discussion, reflection and interaction. In such a setting any incoming information, whether useful or not, provided a basis for discussion. What appeared to occur in this process was a type of critical adaptation of ideas into the framework of the change that was occurring at the school. That adaptation developed partly through talk and partly through trial and error.

District Support

Although the role that the district played received less attention than the other factors just discussed, it did constitute an important factor both in the overall success of the change and the professional development of the teachers. The district supported the school directly in its participation in an international conference and the carrying out of a research project in the school. One gained the sense that the administrators would make any reasonable attempt to support the school or any particular sub-set of teachers if that request could be justified in terms of benefiting student learning or teacher development. Earlier I noted the retreat for school board and district administrators sponsored by the board every second year. Both the school board member and the superintendent talked about the importance of the retreat in terms of developing district goals. That practice, along with a number of initiatives undertaken by the district staff, had the effect of setting a general direction for the district. At the time of this study, language arts was seen as a district priority, yet within that general goal the district allowed a great deal of latitude for each school. The situation provided flexibility within a tightly coupled system.

The district was tightly coupled. The small size of the district meant that the teachers knew the superintendent and office staff. The board members had direct contact with selected schools. For example, during one of my visits to Oceanside I interviewed a board member who explained to me that his visit to Oceanside reflected a board policy in which each school board member had a certain number of schools he or she visited on a regular basis which enabled them to speak out in support of the school at board meetings. This had been particularly important, he pointed out, when Oceanside had brought forth the request to use alternate Wednesday afternoons for planning. Although the board had expressed concern over this issue, he was able to defend it because he understood why the staff had made the request and he understood the change occurring in Oceanside school. It seemed clear that those at the district level had a vision and were striving for better schools; that a type of professionalism and striving for competence permeated the district. The fact that each school had to produce a set of goals each year, and that principals were regularly evaluated, certainly reflected this professionalism. Those in charge had expectations and they would support schools seeking to achieve goals that furthered those expectations. For example, the Superintendent made this comment in an interview:

> You have to be willing to put your money where your mouth is. In other words, if you want things, you must put money into that. We really do believe that the unit of change is the school, but the district does have to provide a great deal of support for that.

He also discussed developing a general focus through the retreat and other measures from which schools could then create their own goals. But the way in which the district worked to provide support appeared to be quite indirect. Their support often came through the principal. As one teacher remarked:

> The principal will give you support if the district is going to give him or her support. So those two are fairly close together. I think the district support is more related to the principal at the beginning, than it is to the teachers. But it changes over time. I didn't realize the district support the first few years I was here. It wasn't until last year that I really noticed the district was involved in this. But I don't think that Ron would be as supportive initially if he did not have the backing of the district...

The principal, too, acknowledged the importance of support at the school board office for the project occurring at Oceanside. But over and above any kind of overt action, the entire ethos of the district appeared to be nurturing and supportive. Not one person interviewed made any negative comments about the district, and although the teachers saw it occurring at different stages, they generally acknowledged that support from the school board office had been crucial to staff development and change. No one thing or action emerged that would identify 'district support'. Rather, a whole series of small events and happenings added up to the greater whole. Some teachers linked workshops to district support; others sensed that the district commitment to language arts was an important support for them. The overall ethos had produced a sense of confidence that a supervisor best expressed.

> But I feel much better about that now that I've talked to more districts because...we've done so much work in the area of curriculum on our own, that our teachers know so much more about how to teach language arts that they're really ready for the new curriculum. They're going to be able to take those new resources and treat them as resources, instead of treating them as a curriculum. Whereas, in talking to other people who have done pilot studies, they say their teachers are so desperate for new resources. So I feel really wonderful about the district in that respect, because we really have teachers who are going to be ready to teach a new curriculum, and not be swayed by the glossy photos of any publisher's programme.

This supervisor was referring to the new language arts programme that the Ministry of Education had just introduced. These factors worked in support of the change and the professional development of teachers. Taken together they appeared to produce a climate for the developments that occurred at Oceanside. However, some factors appeared to place constraints upon the staff. I end this section by touching on those briefly.

Constraints on Change

Not everything that occurred at Oceanside worked toward productive change. Certain factors, in fact, made the development of the project at Oceanside less than easy. The prevailing norms of schooling within the district and the province worried Oceanside teachers and principal alike who had doubts about whether their project was educationally sound. Seeing that other schools were achieving good results through different means contributed to the intensity and frequency of their collective self-criticism and analysis of their project. While this intense and ongoing reflection on the part of the critical mass of teachers at Oceanside has been cited as one of its strengths, it also drained vital energy. One teacher describes how she was not sorry to be leaving:

> When I think back on being in this school. . .I was very happy to be leaving Oceanside, just because I felt really worn out. I think the teachers here, they put so much out, and where do you get it back? Because it's really hard to get all that energy back. And I wonder where it's going to lead to. Where does it all end? Are people going to have nervous breakdowns, or are they going to find a point where they're just got to stop and take a break from all the workshops, and all the committees, and all this, and all that. I think it's great—it keeps you going in some ways. It can also wear you down pretty fast.

Another factor involved staff turnover. During the three years of the study the teacher turnover at Oceanside reached 33 per cent. This required time for the socialization of new teachers to the ethos of their new school and to their acquaintance with and participation in the project which involved so much discussion at staff meetings. This turnover is an unfortunate characteristic of the profession in general; it may also be ultimately detrimental to any consistent forward movement in education.

Related to these factors is the perpetual and insidious erosion of energy and focus by outside agents that pervades education. The continual change of curriculum by the Ministry, the frequent introduction of new initiatives and priorities by a district, the continual flow of one-hit change agents through the district, the exposure through reading, courses and workshops to new and interesting teaching strategies, while playing a part in the attempts to improve education, also contribute to its fragmentation. The district, for example, by introducing a system of evaluation for principals, could easily detract from a 'risky' school innovation project such as the one at Oceanside. What the staff seemed able to do during the duration of this study was to accommodate this external input within a group setting in the school, which not only provided a forum for reflection and discussion but also shelter-conditions within which to take risks. Such risks seemed necessary if the development that was occurring among teachers was to find expression in practice. However, without this critical mass it would have been difficult for the change at Oceanside to develop or indeed to stay on track.

Implications for Teacher Development

The case study just presented carries several implications for teacher development. This section offers five points.

1.   The school improvement project at Oceanside demonstrates the close relationship between school improvement and teacher development. The teachers talked continually about their own professional growth and the changes they had made to their practice. Both occurred within the context of a school change which they also saw improving their instruction. While it may be argued that teacher development is an end in itself, the Oceanside experience suggested that it can be enhanced if it goes on within the context of a school improvement project that links professional growth to practice. Further, the change at Oceanside would hardly have occurred without ongoing teacher development. The implications here become obvious: plans for change within schools must be accompanied by plans for professional development.

2.   Assuming the link between school improvement and teacher development for the moment, a further implication arises with regard to the types of innovations and change efforts schools take on. Earlier, I pointed out that the school improvement plan itself—its complexity and diversity—became a major factor supporting the change. The literature on school improvement frequently leaves the impression that an innovation is an innovation is an innovation. This case study and previous work suggest strong links between the change itself and teacher development. The implication here suggests that the change being attempted must be taken into account when thinking about teacher development. Some changes produce more opportunities for teacher development than others.

3.   Teachers had highly varied and independent perspectives on the particular change. As such the teachers at Oceanside, who brought their own meaning to the change that occurred, differed little from

most teachers and other professionals. This observation has been made before in other jurisdictions. Clandinin (1986) argues that we must first understand teachers' practical knowledge and build on that. She contends that teachers have been asked to implement other people's intentions, an approach that has failed. Similarly, Gran (1990) cites research in Sweden to show that while the wishes of central authorities could be rather easily transferred to district officials and school leaders (principals), they did not transfer well to teachers.

The implications here suggest that people outside the classrooms such as school administrators, Ministry officials, university professors and all the others who see school improvement as something occurring as a result of their stating their own intentions and values, will find themselves frustrated and disappointed. Plans based on such intentions and values are almost sure to fail. Districts can perhaps set general guidelines for reform, but the nature of that reform and the specifics of its implementation must be left to teachers. Improvements in our schools rest largely on the shoulders of teachers and principals and their development as professionals.

To illustrate, I comment on one piece of the current literature which, though it appears to have the correct sentiments, goes about things in the wrong way. Caldwell and Wood (1988) begin by pointing out that:

> school-based improvement holds the promise of producing substantial positive change in our schools, yet it is a complex process involving new expectations and roles and a reorientation in the way we think and operate schools at the district level. It means moving many decisions about improvement out of the central office and into the schools. (p. 50)

So far so good. But then the authors go on to present a flow chart showing all the arrows coming down from the district with teachers not even mentioned. The board selects goals, identifies procedures for planning, etc. Teachers, when they do get mentioned, are to work collaboratively with principal and central office staff and 'to assist in the implementation of these programmes' (p. 53). In short, the authors describe a very top-down model of school-based improvement which misses the point that they appeared to express earlier, i.e. the need for teachers to be involved centrally in initiating the process and the product. That model will do little for teacher development in the sense in which we seem to be thinking of it today. The type of school-based development that I have considered in this Chapter places most of the onus on the principal and teachers to initiate and sustain school improvement and teacher development on an ongoing basis. This takes a very different view of teacher development from the positions taken by authors such as Caldwell and Wood.

4.   The perspective of the principal often varied from those of others on his staff when the project began in 1985. It appeared that these perspectives did play a part in how teachers viewed the change occurring in the school. The constructivist view of learning, an area receiving attention in the literature of late, argues that learners come to any situation with their own conceptual understanding whether that be a science concept held by a third grader, or a notion of how teaching should occur held by student or teachers. In this view, learning how to integrate subjects or use a multi-graded approach becomes a process of conceptual change in which the construction first held becomes changed and developed. This view implies that any change within a school must begin with an understanding of what constructions teachers first have about teaching and learning and proceed from there. Teacher development then becomes a process of conceptual change whereby the construction first held becomes changed and developed.

5.   Peer interaction was seen as a major factor in promoting the change at Oceanside. Much collaborative work grew out of this interaction. The talk among teachers also provided a forum to test ideas and to receive feedback. Others such as Little (1986) have also identified the importance of collegiality in implementing innovations. Providing ways that school staffs can become more collaborative about their work may well be a beginning step in engaging a staff in a school improvement process. It creates a collaborative culture from which curriculum and pedagogical reform can occur. Except in very special circumstances, it is difficult to see much change occuring outside collaborative efforts or outside the reference to some group.

But a caveat must be placed on this statement. Hargreaves and Dawe (1989) have warned against the concept of contrived collegiality, in which bureaucratically driven systems attempt to 'create' collegiality through imposed practices such as peer coaching. While such programmes may be a starting point, in and of themselves they are not sufficient. Collegiality takes time to develop and must come from within the school as it did in Oceanside. The sharing of views among teachers must occur in a natural and genuine way. It cannot be legislated.

6.   Leadership in these situations remains essential. The project at Oceanside saw leadership at different levels. The school superintendents and the consultants provided support and assistance at different times. The principal's role proved to be critical, as I have already discussed. Often forgotten within a school situation like this is the role played by teacher leaders within the group. Many implications could follow from this, but two in particular seem to stand out. If we are serious about school reform and teacher development, then the people who occupy the position of principal become critical. Since so much

has been written about the principal's role, little more need be said. However, what did appear key to the success of the innovation in the Oceanside situation was the instructional and substantive leadership provided by the principal. Second, the role played by the central office in this situation appeared critical to its success in very subtle but important ways. That role is probably among the most undervalued and understudied.

7. The title of this Chapter implies that the school provides the context for teacher development. Indeed nothing that has been said takes away from that assertion. But as we saw in this case, the group processes that occurred within the school were critical to the teachers' development. The group may well provide a better focus for understanding why some schools provide much better settings for teacher development and change than others.

In closing, I wish to insert a word of caution about generalizing these findings to other settings without looking carefully at the context. This Chapter rests primarily on the experience of one school and my interpretation of what those experiences mean *vis-à-vis* the literature on school improvement. However, generalization will occur; it always does. But that responsibility rests with the reader. Stake and Easley (1978) once argued that the case study is a valuable research approach because it presents results in a way that relate to the epistemological understanding of the reader. This study from which I drew in this Chapter is no exception.

Notes

1 International Reading Conference held in Vancouver.
2 The notion of publication in this case involved preparing a table of contents for the book and a dedication; the book would then be bound in a hard cover.

References

CALDWELL, S.D. and WOOD, F.H. (1988) 'School-based improvement: Are we ready?', *Educational Leadership*, 46, (2), pp. 50–3.

CLANDININ, D. (1986) *Classroom Practice: Teachers Images in Action*, Philadelphia: Falmer Press.

DAVIS, G.A. and THOMAS, M.A. (1989) *Effective Schools and Effective Teachers*, Boston, Allyn and Bacon.

FULLAN, M. (1985) 'Change process and strategies at the local level', *The Elementary School Journal*, 85, 3, pp. 391–420.

GOLDBERG, M.F. (1984) 'An update on the National Writing Project', *Kappan*, 65, 5, pp. 356–7.

GOODLAD, J. (1983) 'The school as a workplace', in GRIFFIN, G., *Staff Development*, NSSE Yearbook, Chicago, University of Chicago Press.

GOODLAD, J. (1987) *The Ecology of School Renewal*, NSSE Yearbook, Chicago, The University of Chicago Press.

GRAN, B. (1990) 'Research on Swedish teacher training', in TISCHER, R. and WIDEEN, M. (Eds.) *Research in teacher education: International Perspectives*. London: Falmer Press.

HARGREAVES, A. and DAWE, R. (1989) 'Coaching as unreflected practice: Contrived collegiality or collaborative culture?', Paper presented to the American Educational Association, San Francisco.

HECHINGER (1983) *The New York Times*, 6 June.

HUBERMAN, A.M. and MILES, M.B. (1986) 'Rethinking the quest for school improvement: Some findings from the DESSI study', in LIEBERMAN, A. (Ed.) *Rethinking School Improvement*, New York, Teachers College Press.

ILLICH, I. (1970) *Deschooling Society*, New York, Harper and Row.

LITTLE, J. (1986) 'Seductive images and organizational realities in professional development', in LIEBERMAN, A. (Ed.) *Rethinking School Improvement*, New York, Teacher College Press.

LOUIS, D. (1981) 'External agents and knowledge utilization: Dimensions for analysis and action', in LEHMAN, R. and KANE, M. (Eds.) *Improving Schools*, Beverly Hills, Sage.

MILES, M. (1984) 'The role of the change agent in the school improvement process', Paper presented at the annual meeting of the American Educational Research Association, New Orleans.

SCHON, D. (1983) *The Reflective Practitioner*, New York, Basic Books.

STAKE, R. and EASLEY, J. (1978) 'Case studies in science education', a Project for the National Science Foundation, University of Illinois.

STEIN, M.K. and WANG, M.C. (1988) 'Teacher development and school improvement: The process of teacher change', *Teaching and Teacher Education*, 4, pp. 171–87.

STRACHAN, W. (1988) *Report to the Principal and Staff of Kantana School: Reactions to Writing Program*, Burnaby, Simon Fraser University.

WIDEEN, M., CARLMAN, N. and STRACHAN, W. (1986) *Problem-Focused Coursework As A Model For In-service Education: Case Studies of Teacher-Initiated Change*, Project Report, Burnaby, Simon Fraser University.

Chapter 8

Teacher Performance Appraisal and Staff Development

Edward S. Hickcox and Donald F. Musella

The Context

Issues surrounding the evaluation of educational personnel have been central in both the study and practice of supervision for a long time (Darling-Hammond, Wise and Pease, 1983). In the United Kingdom, there is considerable discussion and activity on matters relating to appraisal (Department of Education and Science, 1986). At the same time a vast amount of literature has accumulated about staff development. Staff development, with its accompanying sets of concepts and language such as mentoring, coaching, peer assistance and the like, seems to be riding a crest of popularity among educators interested in school improvement and the improvement of teaching.

It is only natural to think that teacher supervision and evaluation can be superimposed into staff development models. A common assumption about evaluation or appraisal for teachers is that its fundamental purpose is improvement in teaching. Staff development, in its most central aspects, also deals with the improvement of teaching, and the melding of the two strands would seem easily accomplished. Wood and Lease (1987) have undertaken an attempt to link staff development, supervision and teacher evaluation. They argue that core elements of staff development such as readiness, planning, training, implementation and maintenance are coterminous with pre-planning, objective setting, classroom activities and follow-up, often listed as components of effective evaluation processes. Fessler and Burke (1988) support this position: 'The assessment of teacher professional growth needs and the planning of staff development strategies are components of the same process or links in the same chain' (p. 14).

A major intent of this Chapter is to suggest that while there are certainly areas of overlap, both conceptually and practically, between performance appraisal and staff development in schools, the links are not so easily established as might first be imagined, given the similarities in language and the sharing of common goals. Part of the difficulty lies in the traditional ways in which teacher evaluation has been practised and part in characteristics of emerging models of evaluation.

An early conceptualization by Dale Bolton (1973) is useful in establishing the links between performance appraisal and teacher development. Bolton conceives of personnel supervision as consisting of a series of related processes. The first step is recruitment and selection of individuals to the system. The next step consists of assigning the teacher to a role, providing in-service training (or development), and evaluating. This step is cyclical in that development and evaluation are continuous activities. The third supervisory phase is the 'exit' system whereby it is determined that an individual's development is not appropriate to the situation, and steps are taken to re-assign or terminate the individual's relationship with the organization.

The connection between teacher development and appraisal, using this conceptualization, occurs principally in the interaction between assignment, training, and evaluation. Bolton, however, does not focus extensively on the teacher involvement aspects of training, so much a part of our thinking these days; nor is he particularly concerned about issues surrounding personal growth in teachers as well as professional growth. Rather, he takes a much more top-down functional approach, focusing on the importance of achieving organizational objectives, with the objectives having been set in essence by the organization, or at the organization level.

A quick glance at the Bolton model suggests that the connection makes sense. The tenets of teacher development fit nicely into performance appraisal models. This is the reaction of writers such as Wood and Lease (1987). Developments in teacher appraisal, however, indicate a much more complex relationship between emerging teacher evaluation models and teacher development.

Staff Development

What is Staff Development?

The initial problem with staff development, as with performance appraisal, lies with the lack of clarity of differing purposes and definitions. Staff development, long known as in-service education, can take place in a variety of settings, can include an almost limitless number of activities, and can be conducted to achieve many differing objectives.

The National Education Association (1966) listed nineteen different types of in-service staff development activities, from professional reading to the standard after-school workshop. In an attempt to overcome what he described as the uselessness of this approach to in-service education, Ryan (1987) developed the following definition: 'Those activities planned for and/or by teachers designed to assist them in more efficiently and effectively planning and attaining designated education purposes' (p. 3).

However, Yarger, Howey and Joyce (1980), in recognizing that one general definition does not assist in defining the teacher's role in staff development, identified five general types or modes for inservice:

1 Job-embedded, which emphasizes 'hands on' experience to improve teaching skills while working with children
2 Job-related, which is closely related to the job, but does not take place during teaching
3 General professional, which consists of experiences to improve general competence, but is not tailored as closely to specific needs as the above experiences
4 Career/credentialed, which helps one obtain a new credential or prepare for a new role.
5 Personal, which facilitates personal development that may or may not relate to teaching (pp. 14–15).

What are the Purposes of Staff Development?

This summary of types, considered along with the differing purposes of staff development, point to the problems of melding staff development with performance appraisal. Consider the following purposes as they relate to the different types of in-service.

Although staff development programmes vary widely in context and format, they generally share a common purpose. Specifically, they are designed to 'alter the professional practices, beliefs, and understanding of school persons toward an articulated end' (Griffin, 1983:2). In most cases, that end is the improvement of student learning. In other words, staff development programmes are a systematic attempt to bring about change—change in classroom practices of teachers, change in their beliefs and attitudes, and change in the learning outcomes of students' (Guskey, 1986:5)

One purpose of in-service staff development is to bring about changes mandated from above. For example, the Board of Education, upon recommendation from the Ministry of Education, introduces a new programme that requires some or all of the teachers to make some changes, either in methods or content. The obvious follow-up procedure is to introduce in-service staff development programmes to assist the teachers in making the necessary changes. In some cases, assistance external to the school is employed. In others, within-district consultants are given this responsibility.

A second purpose of staff development is to make changes to solve a specific school problem. For example, the school staff has decided that changes are needed in the math programme; there is common agreement that the students are not doing as well in this school as in other schools in the district. In this case, the needs assessment by staff led to the selection of a new math programme. As a consequence, it was decided at the school level that staff development was needed to assist teachers in implementing the new math programme. In this situation the district math consultant is often turned to for assistance.

A third purpose is to change a specific teacher's behaviour because of perceived ineffectiveness. This decision is most often the result of the performance appraisal of the teacher by school principal, vice-principal, and/or a supervisory officer. The staff development process in this case is an individual programme, often with assistance by the school administrator and/or support staff employed by the district.

A fourth purpose is to solve an individual problem. For example, the teacher has identified a teaching problem that he/she wants to solve. The teacher usually initiates a programme of assistance; the type of activity undertaken can take one of many forms, from an informal discussion with another teacher to a formal course of study.

Yet another purpose is to gain promotion to another position. There are many sources of programmes directed to assist teachers who wish to move to other positions. Some school districts conduct their own programmes for those who aspire to positions of greater responsibility. For example, the district may offer a programme for people identified as future school principals which consists of weekly or bi-weekly sessions where current administrators and outside personnel speak on issues of importance in administration. More sophisticated efforts in this direction involve regular courses, utilizing in-basket techniques, assessment centre techniques as well as readings and assignments.

What are the Purposes of Performance Appraisal?

Consider now the purposes of performance appraisal. Most school boards list two sets of purposes in their performance appraisal policy and procedures: (1) to improve teaching, and (2) to ensure accountability. Various words are used to convey these two basic purposes. However, the purposes of performance appraisal of teachers in most school boards can be reduced to these two intentions—improving performance and ensuring that employees are serving the system well (i.e. being able to show others that the system is holding others accountable for effectiveness on the job).

Given the many purposes of staff development, and the quite divergent purposes of performance appraisal, it is understandable that the link between performance appraisal and staff development is difficult, if not impossible to establish. How can accountability and staff development procedures co-exist given these differences in purpose?

Who are the Key Players in Staff Development and Performance Appraisals?

Another area of conflict among staff development activities and between staff development activities and performance appraisal procedures arises in the designation of key actors in the process. There is much evidence and support for extensive teacher involvement in staff development. Rubin (1969) found that 'a practising teacher is the best possible trainer of teachers' (p. 9). Current interest in coaching and mentoring is reflective of this notion (Hargreaves and Dawe, 1989). In a meta-analysis on a number of studies, Lawrence (1974) reported that:

1 School-based programmes in which teachers participate as helpers to each other and planners of in-service activities tend to have greater success in accomplishing their objectives than do programmes which are conducted by colleges or other outside personnel without the assistance of teachers (p. 11).
2 School-based in-service programmes that emphasize self-instruction by teachers have a strong record of effectiveness (p. 12).

The research and literature support the use of teachers as staff developers given that certain conditions exist (Wu, 1987).

In the performance appraisal process, the supervisor is the key actor. The supervisor (principal, vice-principal) initiates the process, collects the data, judges the data, provides feedback to the teacher, makes recommendation for improvement (change), and is responsible for reporting this to his/her superordinates and for follow-up activities to ensure the intended change (although not many do this). In fact, all performance appraisal systems include a major role for a person in a superordinate role, even though many indicate the main purpose is to improve teacher performance.

What is needed are some changes both in performance appraisal and in staff development procedures which can accommodate these differing, often conflicting, purposes.

Approaches to Teacher Appraisal

Traditional Appraisal

Current practices in teacher appraisal have been well documented in Canada, the United States, and the United Kingdom. (Darling-Hammond, Wise, and Pease, 1983; Lawton, Hickcox, Leithwood, and Musella, 1986). In broad outline, traditional appraisal of teachers in public schools involves the following activities:

1   The teacher will be notified, sometimes in writing and sometimes verbally, that an evaluation is coming up. The school principal is generally responsible for such notification.

2   The principal will arrange a pre-evaluation conference with the teacher, sometimes at the teacher's convenience but not always. At this meeting, which probably will be held in the principal's office, the principal will indicate what it is he (most principals are men) will be looking for when he comes to observe class. He may ask the teacher to indicate objectives for the lesson to be observed. The meeting may last from five minutes to an hour, although the average tends to be less than one half-hour.

3   The principal will come to the class at the designated time. He will sit in the back of the classroom during the lesson and take notes while the teacher is teaching. If it is an elementary classroom, he will likely move around the room quite a bit, interacting with the students, looking at notebooks and sometimes even taking over the class.

4   Following the observation, the principal will arrange a post-observation meeting with the teacher, most often quite shortly after the observation. He probably will have prepared some sort of draft document for examination, or at least he will have the notes of his observation. Generally at this meeting, the principal reports on his visit, indicating most often the good things he observed (good from his perspective), and sometimes indicating areas where he observed practices not quite appropriate. The teacher will react to the suggestions, and may seek advice about particular matters of concern. If the report the principal has prepared is the final report, he will ask the teacher to read and sign the report, indicating not so much agreement as acknowledgement that the report has been read.

5   If the report is not in final form, the principal will prepare it after the post-observation conference and will send it to the teacher for examination. The teacher will have the chance to respond in writing to the report if she wishes. Most reports contain positive, supporting comments. Suggestions for improvement are minimal, in most cases. A copy of the report is retained by the teacher, and a copy goes into the teacher's personal file at the school and probably at the central office. One Ontario school board used to let the teacher determine whether the written report was to be kept for the files. If he or she felt it was not appropriate, then it would be torn up, an act which might have given pause to a principal who had spent some hours in preparation. No record exists of whether any reports were ever torn up, and the policy has been changed since.

A question to be asked about the traditional approach to appraisal is whether it reflects the basic assumptions of staff development models, i.e. an emphasis on cooperation, collegiality, and decisions from the bottom up rather than from the top down (Dawe, 1989). An exhaustive inquiry into the state of the art in Ontario (Lawton *et al.*, 1986) indicates a lack of emphasis on cooperation and collegiality in both the policies on performance appraisal and the practice of performance appraisal in school systems. For example, it was reported that most teacher-evaluation cycles are carried out by the school principal and, in the case of probationary teachers and those in difficulty, by the superintendent. Pre-conferences occur in a little more than half of the evaluations carried out, and these are often short meetings. Very few respondents reported systematic follow-up. The stated purpose in most policies for appraisal was the improvement of instruction (or some variation), but there was little evidence that improvement actually occurred. In fact, a large majority of teachers reported that the appraisal experience had not resulted in any improvement, or in very little improvement, in their instructional behaviour (Lawton *et al.*, 1986).

Traditional performance-appraisal approaches also tend to be narrowly focused, concentrating for the most part on classroom performance rather than on a broad reflective examination of teaching life. Further, traditional approaches almost always mix appraisal for professional-growth procedures with appraisal for making a judgement. In fact, it is common for the same set of procedures to be used for both kinds of appraisal in spite of evidence to show that the hierarchical aspects of the judgemental appraisal blunt any strong sense of collegiality and professional cooperation growing from the effort to bring about growth. The traditional approach is a technical-rational approach with an emphasis on standardization across widely disparate situations, attention to record-keeping, and written reports.

This is not to argue that the traditional approach to supervision, as described here, is necessarily dysfunctional or negative. The point is that the traditional approach does not seem to fit too well with the ideas of staff development with its emphasis on collegiality, cooperation, and professionalism.

Emergent Approaches to Appraisal

The strong evidence that traditional approaches to evaluation have not been effective in improving instruction (among other problems) has motivated the development of alternative appraisal patterns, some elements of which seem more congruent with the central notions of staff development models (Hickcox, 1988).

These emergent approaches have some of the following characteristics:

1 Supervision for growth or improvement is separated for the most part from supervision for making a judgement. In a sense or ideally, there are two separate sets of procedures, often called tracks. There are crossover points. For example, an individual may be on a development track and because of a shift to a new school, or a move to a different grade level, he or she may be moved to a judgement track. The anticipated effect of the separation of the procedures is to remove the threat of dismissal or a negative rating from the great majority of teachers whose jobs are not really on the line. The development track, in theory at least, is supposed to be collegial and non-threatening.

2 Notions of coaching and mentoring are often built into the developmental procedures (Joyce and Showers, 1982; Hargreaves and Dawe, 1989). Some school boards in Ontario and elsewhere are making a serious effort to promote peer coaching. Extensive in-service efforts are made to train participants in coaching skills, and resources are used to free teachers and supervisors from classroom responsibilities in order to receive this training.

3 There is a shift in emphasis from observation of classroom performance to broader concerns with the nature of teaching itself, with career development, with programme concerns. An interesting discussion of peer coaching by Dawe (1989) describes a kind of hierarchy ranging from coaching in classroom techniques advocated by Joyce and Showers to ideas of reflective practice developed by Schon (1987).

4 There is a move away from the highly structured, rational, linear characteristics of the traditional approaches to a less hierarchical and in a sense less organized set of procedures. In emergent policies, for example, written reports are not required after every evaluation cycle.

5 Ideally, emergent appraisal patterns are a move toward professionalism for teachers, professionalism in the sense of promoting autonomy, independent thinking, reflective practice, and the assumption of responsibility by the individual for both personal and professional growth.

It is not the purpose of this paper to evaluate whether emergent patterns of teacher appraisal are working, whether growth is actually occurring. Several experiments are under way in Ontario, and a number of problems are already evident. There is the matter of trust among teachers about whether the central administration really is prepared to rely on classroom teachers for their own evaluation. There are time problems, and skill-development problems, among many others. Hargreaves (1989) has dealt extensively with notions of time in schools, pointing out that differing patterns of behaviour relative to time, carried by teachers and principals in schools, is a source of tension and potential conflict. The purpose here, however, is to establish any connections between performance appraisal and staff development, as currently conceptualized, and to discuss these connections in terms of the impact on teaching and learning (Wallace, 1989).

What Changes Need to be Made?

Changes in Staff Development

The major change to staff development is one that leads to greater accountability. The concept of 'bottom–up' staff development, that is, starting and ending with the teacher, is well supported in the research and entrenched in the vast literature based on experience (Bond and Dykstra, 1967; Edmunds and Frederickson, 1979; Fisher *et al.*, 1980; Purkey and Smith, 1983). The problem for the practising supervisor-educator is to ensure some accountability in all aspects of in-service staff development. The connection between experiences and activities and improved teaching should be made more obvious. Further, the procedures should be directly related to the purposes of the staff development. For example, is it not possible to involve teachers in a 'bottom–up' process even though the change has been mandated from above? Further, is it not possible to hold the key players responsible for improved outcomes, given the purpose is to improve performance? Accountability could and should be one of the major criteria for assessing all forms of staff development, whether individual teacher-initiated or board-initiated (Elliott *et al.*, 1981).

Accountability can be introduced along with the many suggested changes in staff development. These many attempts at improving teaching do not have to operate without reference to documented gains in student learning and/or positive changes in the teacher's classroom practices, attitudes and beliefs. In fact, the model Guskey (1983) offers is based on the position that 'evidence of improvement (positive change) in the learning outcomes of students generally precedes and may be a prerequisite to significant change in the beliefs and attitudes of most teachers' (p. 7).

The other changes in staff development are well documented and quite in vogue at the present time. The concepts are familiar to those currently responsible for assisting teachers. One need only review the table of contents in *The Journal of Staff Development* to get a feel for contemporary thinking in staff development. Here are a few titles: 'Teachers as Staff Developers'; 'Mentoring: A Means by which Teachers become Staff Developers'; 'Instructional Growth through

Peer Coaching'; 'Teachers as Leaders'; 'Staff Development through Professional Reading and Discussion'; 'Changing School Culture through Staff Development'; 'Using Networks to Promote Staff Development'; 'Strengthening Teachers' Reflective Decision Making'; 'Collegial Support Networking'.

Changes in Performance Appraisal

The changes that must be made in performance appraisal to strengthen the link with staff development are: (1) to reduce the emphasis on accountability; and (2) to adopt the procedures considered to be most critical to effective staff development.

Reducing emphasis on accountability is done in several ways. First, one could move to a multi-track set of procedures. The objective here is not to treat all teachers the same, in other words, not to use the same criteria and procedures for performance appraisal for all teachers. For example, one track is for probationary teachers for whom a decision must be made with respect to permanent contract. Another track includes teachers of whom change is demanded in order to retain the position as teacher in the district. Another track, one which includes the largest number of teachers, includes experienced teachers judged to be competent.

Another approach to reduced accountability is to reduce the number, or remove entirely, records of performance. If the purpose is to improve teaching, is it necessary to have a completed evaluation form, signed by the teacher and principal, retained in central office files? If all information is directed to improvement, then the content and forms of information must be adjusted to meet this purpose. Yet another approach to reduced accountability is to place more emphasis on the key staff development principles (such as those indicated above) and less emphasis on superordinate review.

Fessler and Burke (1988) summarize these themes well in providing three key recommendations: (1) teachers should be encouraged to engage in self-assessment; (2) the teacher and supervisor should engage in frequent sharing and conferring sessions; and (3) staff development activities should be based on growth needs agreed on by teachers and supervisors.

Thinking about Teaching and Development

Connections between performance appraisal and staff development activities, then, are not seen in the traditional patterns of performance appraisal. In the emergent patterns and beyond, however, there are some linkages:

Collegiality

The focus on collegiality in terms of coaching, mentoring, and peer coaching is common to appraisal and development. Referring again to the Bolton conceptualization, this occurs in the in-service or training component of his supervisory system.

For collegiality to have any meaning it has to occur naturally, or it has to be a natural part of the dominant culture of the organization. There is some sense, even in the most enlightened of appraisal systems, that collegiality and cooperation are forced. The notion of contrived collegiality is relevant here (Hargreaves and Dawe, 1989). Forced cooperation is a contradiction in terms. The staff development language, at least, seems to describe a much more informal and natural occurrence, such as might occur among professionals. Also, it does not seem to be mandated. Even in emergent appraisal systems being piloted in school boards, there is a sense that meetings have to occur among parties paired as 'coaches' or 'mentors' because meetings are mandated by the policy (Wallace, 1989).

Another approach to teacher control of development is offered by Smyth (1989). While strongly disagreeing with the Madeline Hunter approach to clinical supervision, he provides us with an 'educative or emancipatory' view of clinical supervision. He sees the process highlighting the relationship between reflection and practice and how teachers can actively intervene in their own teaching so as to challenge, if appropriate, the conventional wisdom of established practices. He relies heavily on Goldhammer's original intention of clinical practice (Goldhammer, 1969:54), grounded in a view of the 'importance of "inquiry", "analysis", "examination", and "evaluation" that are "self-initiated" and "self regulated"' (p. 55).

By moving staff development and performance appraisal closer together, we have included ways of improving teaching by placing responsibility and judgement with the teacher through self development while assuring some means of outcome-related judgements.

Professionalization

Collegiality is embedded in professionalization, considered in a broad sense. Professionalization implies, among other things, a considerable amount of freedom for the individual in terms of both personal and professional development, in terms of the individual assuming responsibility for what he or she does on the job to carry out the job. While professionals in organizations (such as universities) are constrained by general directions mandated from outside, by codes of ethics, and by certain standards of competence, they make their own decisions about the content of courses, the method of course delivery, the frequency and nature of colleague interaction, and activities designed to improve performance. They are accountable in terms of achieving tenure and promotion over the course of a career, but these steps most often focus on productivity over a fairly long period of time.

At the public school level, it is difficult to imagine such a situation coming to pass in a highly developed state, and it is not at all certain that it should, given the responsibility for teachers in schools to transmit knowledge, attitudes, and beliefs rather than to create knowledge. Certainly in Ontario, the central government authorities and the school boards are going to continue to mandate both the content of curriculum and its delivery for the foreseeable future. To this extent, the freedom, and ultimate professionalization of teachers, will be constrained.

At the same time, those involved with staff development and with performance appraisal should attempt to build in as many factors as possible that would increase the degree of professional autonomy possessed by teachers.

Trust

In order for approaches to either staff development or performance appraisal to have any hope of bringing about genuine improvement in teacher performance, or in attitudes teachers have about themselves and their work, some measures will have to be considered to increase the level of trust. Especially in large districts, teachers tend to be cynical about the continual onslaught of new initiatives designed to 'make them better'. For one thing, a teacher's day is so taken up with the intensity of dealing with the small events involved in interaction with young people that there is little time or, more importantly, energy left to work on either staff development activities or performance appraisal follow-up (Wallace, 1989).

Teachers will look for things which might have an impact on their actual classroom activities in a narrow sense. They are no longer much impressed by highly organized efforts on the part of central office personnel to change their way of doing things in any marked way. And they feel quite strongly that such efforts are designed not to meet whatever personal or professional objectives they might have, but rather to serve some ambition of trustees or senior administrators.

A radical approach which might serve as an interesting discussion point is to argue that we should cease formal performance appraisal practices which are laid on from above, and we should avoid those aspects of staff development which emphasize instilling system objectives and system development programmes into the schools. Instead, we could inform teachers that we would like to know from them what they need from the organization, and we could try to provide as much of that environment as possible, allowing more or less free rein to teachers to develop according to individual needs and individual decisions.

References

BOLTON, D. (1973) *Selection and Evaluation of Teachers*, Berkeley, McCutchan Publishing Co.

BOND, G.L. and DYKSTRA, R. (1967) 'The cooperative research program in first grade reading instruction', *Reading Research Quarterly*, 2, 4, pp. 5–142.

DARLING-HAMMOND, L., WISE, A.E. and PEASE, S.R. (1983) 'Teacher evaluation in the organized content: A review of the literature', *Review of Educational Research*, 53, 3, pp. 285–328.

DAWE, R. (1989) 'The organizational images of teachers and school implicit in experiences of peer coaching: An exploratory study', Informal paper, available from the author, Dept. of Educational Administration, the Ontario Institute for Studies in Education.

DEPARTMENT OF EDUCATION AND SCIENCE (1986) *Better Schools: Evaluation and Appraisal*, London, Her Majesty's Stationery Office.

EDMUNDS, R. and FREDERICKSON, J.R. (1979) *Causes of Effective Schools*, New York, Board of Education.

ELLIOTT, J., BRIDGES, D., EBBUTT, D., GIVSON, R. and NIAS, J. (1981) *School Accountability*, London, Grant McIntyre Limited.

FESSLER, R. and BURKE, P.J. (1988) 'Teacher assessment and staff development: Links in the same chain', *The Journal of Staff Development*, 9, 1, pp. 14–18.

FISCHER, C.W., BERLINER, D.C., FILBY, N., MARLIAVE, R.S., CAHEN, L.S. and DISHAW, M.M. (1980) 'Teaching behaviors, academic learning time and student achievement: An overview', in DENHAM, C. and LIEBERMAN, A. (Eds.) *Changing School Reading Programs*, Newark, DE, International Reading Association.

GOLDHAMMER, R. (1969) *Clinical Supervision: Special Methods for the Supervision of Teachers*, New York, Holt, Rinehart and Winston.

GRIFFIN, G.A. (1983) 'Introduction: The work of staff development', in GRIFFIN, G.A. (Ed.), *Staff Development*, Eighty-second yearbook of the National Society for the Study of Education, Chicago, University of Chicago Press.

GUSKEY, T.R. (1986) 'Staff development and the process of teacher change', *Educational Researcher*, May, pp. 5–12.

HARGREAVES, A. (1989) 'Teachers' work and the politics of time and space', Paper presented at the annual meeting of the American Educational Research Association, San Francicso.

HARGREAVES, A. and DAWE, R. (1989) 'Coaching as unreflective practice: Contrived collegiality or collaborative culture?', Paper presented at the annual meeting of the American Educational Research Association, San Francisco.

HICKCOX, E.S. (1988) 'Performance appraisal in context', in HICKCOX, E.S., LAWTON, S.B., LEITHWOOD, K.A. and MUSELLA, D.F. (Eds.) *Making a Difference through Performance Appraisal*, Toronto, The OISE Press.

JOYCE, B. and SHOWERS, B. (1982) 'The coaching of teaching', *Educational Leadership*, 40, October, pp. 4–10.

LAWRENCE, G. (1974) *Patterns of Effective Inservice Education*, Tallahassee, FL, Florida Department of Education.

LAWTON, S., HICKCOX, E., LEITHWOOD, K. and MUSELLA, D. (1986) *Development and Use of Performance Appraisal of Certified Education Staff in Ontario School Boards*, 1, Toronto, Ministry of Education.

MCLAUGHLIN, M. and PFEIFER, S. (1988) *Teacher Evaluation: Improvement, Accountability, and Effective Learning*, New York, Teachers College Press.

NATIONAL EDUCATION ASSOCIATION (1966) *Inservice Education of Teachers: Research Summary 1966–S1*, Washington, DC, NEA, Research Division.

PURKEY, S.C. and SMITH, M.S. (1983) 'Effective schools: A review', *Elementary School Journal*, 83, 4, pp. 427–52.

RUBIN, L.J. (1969) *A Study of the Continuing Education of Teachers*, Santa Barbara, CA, University of California.

RYAN, R.L. (1987) *The Complete Inservice Staff Development Program*, Englewood Cliffs, NJ, Prentice-Hall, Inc.

SCHON, D. (1987) *Educating the Reflective Practitioner*, London, Jossey-Bass Limited.

SMYTH, J. (1989) 'Problematising teaching through a critical perspective on clinical supervision', Paper presented to a symposium on *Counter Begemonic Views and Practices in Teacher Evaluation: International Perspectives*, at the annual meeting of the American Educational Research Association, San Francisco.

WALLACE, J. (1989) *Personal-Professional Growth: Self, Situation, and Teacher Image*, Unpublished Ph.D. dissertation, Department of Education, University of Toronto.

WOOD, F.H. and LEASE, S.A. (1987) 'An integrated approach to staff development, supervision, and teacher evaluation', *The Journal of Staff Development*, 8, 1, pp. 52–5.

WU, P.C. (1987) 'Teachers as staff developers: Research, opinions, and cautions', *The Journal of Staff Development*, 8, 1 pp. 4–6.

YARGER, S.J., HOWEY, K.R. and JOYCE, B.R. (1980) *Inservice Teacher Education*, Palo Alto, CA, Booksend Laboratory.

Chapter 9

Teacher Development and Educational Policy

Judith Warren Little

Inquiry into teachers' professional development reflects two quite different points of departure. A first path, and the one most frequently trod, follows teachers' progress in mastering the complexities of classroom practice. Though dominated by a concern for the implementation of specific pedagogical or curricular innovations, these inquiries have also pursued broader curiosities about how teachers learn to teach, how they mature intellectually and professionally, and how they sustain engagement in their work over time.[1] A second path, less well developed, draws attention to the organizational and occupational conditions that affect teachers' incentives and opportunities to learn. This emerging body of research places professional development in the context of teachers' work, seeking the connections between the social organization of teaching and the professional development of teachers. These inquiries highlight the organizational contexts of teaching and the structure of teachers' careers. They attend less to discrete programmatic innovations than to the larger pattern of policies, practices, and circumstances that affect teachers' professional obligations and opportunities.[2] In this essay I pursue the second path, relying on data from a one-year study of staff development in thirty California school districts to illuminate the local policy choices that enable or constrain teachers' learning.

The policy orientations and strategies that govern teachers' professional development are largely implicit, revealed by the 'dollar choices'. Assumptions about teachers and teaching are made apparent in the organization of staff development resources, in the obligations to which teachers are held, and in the opportunities they are afforded. By examining the entire configuration of professional development activities and opportunities (rather than specific programmes), this paper renders these implicit policy choices accessible to discussion and debate. By employing a comprehensive model of public and personal investments as a framework for policy analysis, it also demonstrates the shortcomings of a policy confined to the orchestration of staff development 'programmes' and enlarges the range of domains in which professional development policy might productively operate. Using specific forms of investment as a point of departure, the paper (1) confronts the limitations and possibilities that reside in formal programmes of locally-sponsored staff development; (2) re-examines the assumptions linking salary advances to formal educational attainment; (3) underscores the workplace conditions that enlarge or diminish teachers' 'opportunity to learn' during the salaried work-day; and (4) speculates on the forces that sustain a delicate balance between institutional and personal contributions to teachers' professional development. In combination, these arguments suggest a framework for policy and practice that is responsive both to teachers' career interests and to a broader public interest in the quality of the teacher workforce.

The Staff Development Policy Study

The Staff Development Policy Study[3] provides a descriptive inventory of the policy and programme choices reflected in local staff development, based on detailed, comprehensive programme and cost data on actual staff development activities. For purposes of this study, we modified Moore and Hyde's (1981) definition of staff development slightly to include 'any activity that is intended partly or primarily to prepare paid staff members for improved performance in present or future roles in the school district...The term staff member is limited in scope [to include] all certificated personnel and teachers' aides' (Little *et al.*, 1987:1). From interviews with district administrators, staff developers, and principals, we constructed a profile of actual staff development activity—the array of opportunity ordinarily available to teachers over a one-year period. Data were collected on more than 800 discrete staff development activities. For each designated 'activity' (for example, a seminar series on the state's math curriculum framework or a one-day workshop on science instruction in the elementary grades), we collected information on: content; number and type of participants; duration; format; time spent in planning; roles of teachers, administrators, or external consultants; type of evaluation; funding sources; and costs associated with substitutes, stipends, materials, consultants, travel, or facilities. To gather these detailed activity records, we conducted extensive interviews with 280 district staff developers and 97 principals in the 30 case study districts. In addition, we collected the locally bargained contract, salary schedule, official long-term plans, and other documents related directly or indirectly to staff development policy and practice.

To ensure that teachers' own voices were heard, we completed telephone interviews with over 460 randomly selected teachers in 30 districts. The twenty-minute interviews concentrated on teachers' accounts of both productive and disappointing professional development experiences during the preceding year and on teachers' perceptions of their districts' investment in professional growth. In addition, a mail survey was sent to 1000 elementary and secondary school teachers selected randomly from the statewide teacher population. Approximately 75 per cent of the teachers returned completed surveys (N=749); many appended long notes. Teachers responded from 48 of California's 58 counties and over 300 school districts, large and small. This included teachers at all grade levels and at all levels of experience (though nearly three-quarters of them had eleven or more years' experience). As a group, the teachers closely mirrored the ethnic profile of the state's teacher workforce. Through the telephone interviews and the statewide mail survey, individual teachers contributed their views of the content, format, and value of staff development opportunities in which they had participated during the preceding calendar year. They described the range of their activities, the quality of those activities and their perceived impact on teaching. Teachers described opportunities for professional development during the salaried work-day, and characterized the level of support for professional development they received from school administrators and colleagues.

Together, the case studies and mail surveys provide data on the prevailing pattern of professional development opportunities and on teachers' judgements about them. This comprehensive study of professional development policy and practice offers a model for assessing current policy and practice and for inventing alternatives for the allocation of resources.

Public Investment in Teacher Development: The Prevailing Patterns of Policy and Practice

By their deployment of funds, policy makers and administrators communicate the general status that teachers' professional development occupies within the broader array of district priorities. Taken as a whole, the amounts recorded here are hardly exorbitant. When one eliminates the part played by salary advances linked to the accumulation of coursework credits or the award of advanced degrees (see below), formal professional development accounts for less than 1.5 per cent of classroom support costs, or about $1200 per teacher[4]—a modest investment by most corporate standards. But these patterns of resource allocation convey not only the general value attached to teacher development; they also communicate particular images of teachers and teaching, and specific conceptions of what it means to develop professionally. They suggest the relative importance given to teachers in their various roles as individual educators, as members of a school faculty, as participants in a wider professional community, or as employees of an institution with its own needs and requirements.

Figure 9.1: Elements of Investment in Teachers' Professional Development

Component 1: Current monetary expenditures associated with producing formal professional development activities: leader time, consultants, substitutes, stipends, facilities, materials.

Component 2: Opportunity cost associated with reduced instructional time; investment in opportunity to learn during the salaried work-day.

Component 3: Present value of teachers' future salary increases accrued as a result of staff development.

Component 4: Participants' own investment of uncompensated time and out-of-pocket expenses.

The flow of dollars opens up some opportunities, while others are foregone.

Our analysis of professional development opportunities is organized by a conception of investment made up of four components (Figure 9.1).[5] Individually, each component points up certain characteristic aspects of professional development policy and practice. Taken together, the four components yield a more penetrating analysis of the possibilities and limitations of professional development than one is able to obtain by focusing on isolated activities or narrowly conceived programme budgets. The first component encompasses all current monetary outlays associated with the production or other support of formal activities. These are the expenditures that policy makers and administrators typically include under the rubric of 'staff development costs'. They include the salaries of administrators or specialists who are responsible for staff development planning or delivery; substitute teachers; participant stipends; fees for external presenters or consultants; materials and facilities; and other routine costs of producing staff development activities.

A second element is the estimated monetary value of reduced instructional time resulting from staff development activities that occur during regularly scheduled instructional time (for example, a pupil-free day).[6] In the concern for lost instructional time is embedded the entire issue of teachers' professional time and the organization of opportunity to learn in the salaried work-day and work-year.

A third element of public investment is the present value of future salary increases that result from credits that teachers acquire when they participate in university coursework or other credit-bearing staff development activity. In the link between the salary schedule and formal educational attainment reside the dilemmas surrounding professional development incentives. To what degree, for example, do individual incentives and rewards yield wider institutional benefit (most prominently, improved classroom performance)?

Finally, we constructed an estimate based on teachers' average salary to represent the value associated with the uncompensated time that teachers devote to district-sponsored or school-sponsored staff development activity. Teachers' voluntary contributions of time and money also form part of the total investment in professional development. The nature and extent of those contributions may serve as a barometer of teachers' organizational and occupational commitments. Collectively, these four components enlarge the boundaries of 'professional development" as it is conventionally defined in educational administration and policy analysis and more fruitfully balance the interests of individuals with the requirements of institutions.

Programme Expenditures and the Staff Development Market-Place

Current monetary expenditures (that is, the costs associated with formal programmes) present the most accessible point of departure for debating and potentially altering the premises and aspirations associated with teachers' professional development. At the time of the study, these expenditures represented about three-quarters of all investments exclusive of teachers' salary increments, or about $900 per teacher. How are these resources organized, and what conception of professional development do they suggest?

Staff development across the thirty districts is a largely centralized enterprise in which institutional priorities and prerogatives dominate (on this point, see also Moore and Hyde, 1981; Schlechty and Whitford, 1983). Despite speculation about the future of site-based management or other forms of decentralized decision-making, most decisions about the what, when, how, and who of staff development still reside in central offices. The greatest share of districts' current monetary expenditures, fully one-half, is devoted to the salaries of administrators or specialists who spend some or all of their time on deciding staff development priorities and in designing or conducting formal staff development activities for an audience of teachers. Of every ten hours spent by teachers in locally-sponsored staff development, nine hours are devoted to activities conceived and led by such specialists. Classroom teachers, by contrast, account for leadership in no more than 10 per cent of formal staff development activity. In actual dollars, and in the control exercised over the content and form of professional development, investments (costs) are concentrated on leaders rather than learners. The thirty case-study districts spent an average of nearly $900 per teacher on locally-sponsored staff development activity during a one-year period, or slightly less than 1 per cent of the costs of supporting the average classroom.

Consistent with these patterns of expenditure, mechanisms of influence and authority serve to centralize decisions that govern the content and form of staff development. In effect, staff development policy and programme choices reside at considerable distance from the classroom. To some extent, teachers exert influence when they elect to participate in some activities and not others (most are voluntary) and when they complete post-hoc evaluations of specific activities. Ironically, even those mechanisms designed to enlarge teachers' influence tend to reinforce the status quo. Periodic 'needs assessments', by which individuals presumably influence the course of staff development planning, frequently begin with an inventory of topics or offerings on which the district is already prepared to expend resources. By voting with their feet, patronizing some activities more than others, teachers progressively refine an inventory of offerings in ways that make it appear ever more attractive and responsive, even while it perpetuates a training paradigm grounded largely in a skill-dominated conception of teaching. Post-hoc evaluations aid specialists and trainers in becoming more polished, but provide no means for examining the larger rationales that underlie the activities in the first place.

One cannot help but be struck by the extent to which public investment in teacher development has taken the form of 'service delivery' fed by a nearly inexhaustible market-place of packaged programmes and sophisticated presenters. This service delivery mode has certain corollary features. Conceived as discrete programmes, staff development places a premium on the simplification and standardization of content. That this press toward standardization is essentially in conflict with widely-acknowledged conceptions of adult learning has not escaped the attention of some staff development specialists. These specialists report a gradual decline in their reliance on 'generic pedagogy' and an increase in efforts to tailor offerings to the needs of specific subject areas or grade levels. Nonetheless, most administrators responsible for approving staff development expenditures stated a predilection for 'well-packaged programmes'.

A service delivery model requires a certain economy of scale. To attract a sufficiently large pool of participants, programme developers concentrate on form over content. The largest share of programme resources is devoted to workshop-style offerings in which appealing materials and a fast-paced round of individual or group exercises secure favourable satisfaction ratings from participants. A demand for high participation rates also makes individual 'sign-up' more likely than the deliberate recruitment of school-based teams who expect to work together both during and after structured events. Although teachers report attending at least one event in a team with other teachers from their own school, team-oriented staff development remained more the exception than the rule.

In their attempt to forge a closer, more meaningful link between newly introduced skills and classroom circumstances, staff developers have emphasized 'coaching'. In principle, coaching supplies the classroom-based consultation that increases rates of measurable change.[7] Under such conditions, teachers may more readily detect the benefits that follow from changed practice; Guskey (1987) argues that shifts in belief and commitment follow rather than precede practice and are contingent on the benefits that teachers observe directly in their work with students. In practice, however, the coaching strategy is rendered problematic in two ways. Among the activities charted in our thirty districts, coaching was proposed far more often than it was actually practised. As described by staff developers, nearly two-thirds of professional development activity was accompanied by offers of classroom-based follow-up. It was actually required as a condition of participation, however, in only about one-quarter of district activities and in less than one-fifth of school-level activities. Judging by other related research,[8] the prospects that coaching will actually occur and will achieve the intended results are much greater when teachers make an explicit commitment to participate. Optional follow-up tends to mean no follow-up. Most teachers (about 60 per cent) report having spent no more than ten hours on all combined follow-up to professional development over a one-year period. Those who spent the most time in follow-up (fifty hours or more) also claimed the greatest impact on their teaching, but their numbers were small (8 per cent of the teachers). Coaching is also made problematic by an emphasis on observation and feedback that may not be consonant with teachers' own apparent preferences for useful follow-up. In one of the first tests of coaching,[9] teachers reported that joint planning and problem-solving, in addition to classroom observation and feedback, enabled them to ascertain the 'fit' between new ideas and established practice. This is precisely the kind of time-intensive involvement that proves difficult for external specialists to sustain.

Despite official support for classroom follow-up and 'coaching,' the service delivery model displays low capacity to involve teachers closely in the investigation of their own classrooms, or to assist them in achieving a fit between new ideas and established practice. Classroom-oriented consultation is arguably more manageable and productive when organized as mutual support among faculties accustomed to collaborative work. Approximately one-third of staff development hours are spent in activities that might be called 'school-based,' but few reveal any conception of the participants as a faculty.[10] Present service-delivery strategies reinforce the idiosyncratic, individualistic character of teachers' work. In the most favourable construction, teachers confront new ideas and materials as 'independent artisans'[11] who enjoy substantial freedom to decide whether and how to apply new ideas. But under current configurations of professional opportunity, the artisans' supply of new ideas is represented largely by the menu of workshops and presenters. Rarely are teachers granted the resources to develop a context-specific course of action that follows from close scrutiny of their own or others' classrooms, or from the array of new developments in a subject-matter field. Nor are teachers often invited to take the perspective of a department, grade-level team, or entire staff charged with making collective choices about the fit between proposed content and existing beliefs and practices.

Teachers are thus cast in a fundamentally passive role with regard to the content and format of professional development, typically serving as audience for a performance staged by others. Recall that teachers accounted for less than 10 per cent of all 'planning, development, and leading' hours associated with local staff development in the thirty case-study districts and that on the whole, district-sponsored activity is the province of specialists. While the design of actual staff development activity may engage teachers in hands-on activities, role playing, and application exercises, their fundamental role remains passive. To participate in activities and exercises designed by someone else is a different matter altogether from assuming intellectual command of the entire enterprise. Few were the instances in which teachers emerged as true students of teaching and learning, engaged in inquiry of their own making. A lengthy and varied menu of staff development offerings gives the appearance of honouring the diverse interests and circumstances among the teacher population. At root, however, individual initiative is constrained by the more general centralization of resources and decision-making above the level of the school. Asked about their preferences, nearly four-fifths, of teachers who completed the mail survey agreed that teachers *should* provide staff development. Less than one-fifth said they now work in schools where teachers frequently lead staff development activities. Only one in four teachers said they had had an opportunity to lead at least one activity during the one-year period, with opportunities markedly less visible to teachers in large districts.[12]

To be sure, we found no difficulty in unearthing idiosyncratic examples of innovative strategies that reflected more ambitious views of teaching, and that were more fully integrated into the lives of teachers and schools.[13] Such approaches were highly regarded by teachers, administrators, and policy makers. In virtually all districts, in various regional service centres, and in special university projects, we found teachers engaged with their colleagues and with subject-matter experts on matters of genuine intellectual and practical import. Such ventures seemed substantively rich, respectful of teachers' knowledge and circumstances, and alert to institutional obligations toward children. But they also consumed a relatively small proportion of public resources devoted to teacher development. While a few innovative programmes engage teachers in the rigorous investigation of teaching and learning, calling upon them to exercise informed professional judgement about curriculum and instruction, the modal pattern reflects a relatively narrow, technical view of teaching and a passive view of teachers as learners. Celebrated exceptions notwithstanding then, present practices of local professional development operate powerfully in the direction of centralization of resources and decision-making, specialization of staff development roles, standardization of staff development content, and context-independent conceptions of teachers and teaching.

A service delivery model dominates the use of programme resources, to the general exclusion of other strategies. Few districts have explicit, policy-driven decision rules that reserve a proportion of resources for other modes of professional development, and that balance sophisticated skill training with, for example, support for teacher-initiated joint work during the salaried work-day. By comparison with the apparent clarity of training objectives, the aims of teacher work-groups may appear diffuse and their outcomes uncertain. By comparison to the crisp pace of a training sequence, the progress of collaborative teacher groups may seem slow. And by comparison with the polished skill of experienced presenters, teachers who lead workshops or study groups may appear clumsy. In this manner, skill training designed by others comes to dominate over teacher-initiated study and experimentation.

On the whole, the present pattern of investment communicates an impoverished view of teachers, teaching, and schools. Celebrated innovations compel attention, but account for a relatively small proportion of allocated resources. The larger pattern of expenditures tells a different tale. Compared to the complexity and immediacy of classroom demands (and rewards), professional development is often a remarkably low-intensity enterprise. It occupies little of teachers' time, squeezed along the margins of teachers' ordinary work. It requires little of teachers by way of intellectual struggle or emotional commitment. It takes only the most superficial account of teachers' histories or present circumstances. Teachers' motivation to learn is further dampened and their opportunity to learn further constrained by the present organization of roles (the separation of teachers from specialists) and by the organization of time scheduled to align with programmatic exigencies rather than with the ebb and flow of teachers' lives in schools.

'Opportunity Costs' and the Allocation of Teachers' Professional Time

The emphasis on locally-sponsored training activities or university coursework tends to obscure the extent to which the impact of formal professional development activities is dependent on the motivation and opportunity to learn that teachers find in the salaried work-day. Formal staff development occurs around the margins of teachers' time. It competes for teachers' attention and energy with the classroom obligations that dominate the work-day and the school year. Public concern for protecting instructional time is reflected in local school board policies regarding release time, minimum days, and pupil-free days. It is mirrored in teachers' general reluctance to use extensive release time even when it is offered.[14]

The Staff Development Policy Study assigned an opportunity cost, based on teachers' average salary, whenever professional development activities reduced the amount of regularly scheduled instructional time. Under provisions of state legislation, eligible schools were permitted up to eight pupil-free days. Most school boards, it appears, endorse the use of pupil-free days (about three-quarters of the districts surveyed), and nearly all districts permit teachers to take professionally-related release time. Nonetheless, teachers and administrators alike have been sparing in their use of out-of-classroom time. Pupil-free days were used to conduct 27 per cent of the participant hours recorded among the thirty case-study districts. On average, teachers used only about twelve hours, or two days, of pupil-free time during a one-year period. They employed a substitute teacher for another eight hours. Altogether, pupils lost less than 2 per cent of regularly-scheduled and regularly-staffed instructional time to teachers' structured professional development activity. This is arguably less than is routinely lost through various distractions in the ordinary school day.

At heart, however, this construction of opportunity cost signals the importance of more fundamental questions surrounding public expectations regarding teachers' time, teachers' responsibilities, and the scale of public investment in the teacher workforce. The investment model, by concentrating on formal activities designated as professional development, inevitably obscures some of the most important decisions that affect professional development motivation and opportunity. In particular, it excludes from consideration the way in which school staffing formulas and teacher workload affect the time and energy teachers can devote to getting better at their work. As calculated here, 'opportunity cost' directs attention to 'lost instructional time'. An alternative is to direct attention to the opportunities for student learning and for teacher development that are created or diminished by the ratio of in-class to out-of-class time, and to examine how the balance of the two fosters or inhibits teachers' intellectual, emotional, and professional maturation.

Time is in short supply in schools; out-of-classroom time for teachers is especially scarce. Staff development competes for teachers' time and attention with other obligations, most with greater immediacy. Yet teachers argue that their most productive involvements in staff development occur during official work time, when they are freed both from the pressing obligations of instruction and from other out-of-school commitments. The major options for districts are pupil-free days, when pupils remain home while teachers work; release time, when pupils are instructed by substitute teachers; and extended duty days or contract years. An additional option, managed at the school site, is to design teaching assignments and schedules to permit regular, daily interaction among pairs or groups of teachers working together; data collected from teachers and administrators suggest that this is a relatively uncommon arrangement. Teachers enthusiastically endorse the idea of special time to confer with colleagues, but 80 per cent of those surveyed for this study say they rarely or never are granted time specially designated for this activity. In secondary schools, where preparation periods are commonly a part of the master schedule, teachers who are out of class during the same period may choose to spend that time together. However, there is no guarantee that teachers who have reason to develop ideas or materials together will be free at the same time. In elementary schools, even individual preparation time is uncommon.

The dilemma is not easily resolved. If the entire pool of 'programme dollars' devoted to local professional development—about $900 per teacher—were re-allocated toward a reduction in ordinary workload, it would not stretch far. At the average hourly salary rate, a reduction of one period a day in a high school teacher's workload would cost nearly five times that amount.[15] Nonetheless, some schools more than others configure teachers' work in ways that support a 'learning-enriched' environment.[16] Teachers' appraisals of formal professional development and its effects suggest why it is important to do so.

The main differences between supporters and critics lay not in the length of their teaching career, their formal education, or the communities in which they worked, but in the daily teaching environments they described and in the role teachers typically assumed in formal staff development activities. Overwhelmingly, the teachers who proved most consistently enthusiastic about professional development were also those who worked in schools that made both formal and informal learning an integral part of teachers' work. Enthusiasts were more likely to describe a school in which administrators provided both symbolic and material support, where professional development was embedded in the ongoing activity of teaching and learning in the school, and in which teachers themselves played an active role in determining content and form. Further, these were schools in which the time for teacher-to-teacher consultation and classroom observation was systematically carved out of otherwise crowded days. Such accounts suggest that there are serious limits to our ability to improve professional development by investing more resources on widening and deepening the market-place offerings.

A strategy that combines the resources of external activity and the resources of a supportive workplace arguably stretches the capacity of each. A well-organized faculty can exploit the advantages of a wide range of activity, and can more readily overcome the limitations of inadequate programme design and limited external resources. Positioned better to pursue the institutional development that Fullan (1990) advocates, the faculty also overcomes some of the main limitations of market-driven staff development—the passive roles of teachers and the absence of attention to individual and organizational histories, present circumstances, or possible futures.

Salary Increments and the Problem of Professional Development Incentives

An individual's professional development presumably yields benefits that encompass personal success and satisfaction, professional prestige, and objective career advantages including higher compensation. The last of these is at the heart of the teacher–compensation element of the investment model: the present value of the future salary advances that teachers obtain as a result of their continuing formal education. Linking formal education to salary advances by the use of a uniform salary schedule is a widespread feature of American school governance. The arrangement has survived periodic assaults[17] to become firmly embodied in personnel policy, reinforced by collective bargaining. It is such a taken-for-granted practice that it appears unavailable for policy consideration, with the consequence that policy debates surrounding professional development focus almost exclusively on the much smaller pool of discretionary resources represented by 'programme' dollars.

By including this aspect of professional development investment in the model, we prompted considerable controversy. The sources of controversy were two. First, the resources dedicated to salary advances cannot be reallocated in the same sense that programme resources might be. During the Staff Development Policy Study, superintendents and union representatives joined forces on the study's advisory board to argue that it would be counter-productive to entertain any policy initiative that had the prospect of lowering basic levels of teacher compensation. To do so would be to weaken further the power of schools to attract and retain a capable workforce. Second, proposals for altering the specific conditions of salary advancement have tended in recent years to focus on a shift from formal preparation (university degrees and course credits) to classroom performance as the measure of merit. The anticipated difficulties surrounding merit pay or other forms of performance-based compensation have led educators to resist any efforts to open up discussion and debate surrounding the present criteria and procedures for salary advancement. In this instance, we intended to support neither a reallocation or reduction of basic compensation, nor a shift from preparation to performance as the basis for salary increases. Rather, we proposed that the practice of basing salary increases on formal educational attainment nonetheless deserves scrutiny on two grounds: the sheer scale of investment, and the import of the underlying purposes and claims surrounding teachers' professional development.

   Salary advances that teachers accrue as a result of advanced university courses, or more recently through salary credits awarded by
districts, constitute taxpayers' largest investment in teachers' staff
development, accounting for nearly two-thirds of the total resources.
When future salary increments are added to current programme expenditures, the total taxpayer investment exceeds 4 per cent of total
education funding. Although 'access to new ideas' ranks highest
among the incentives for teachers' participation in professional development, salary advantage remains a powerful motivator. Among
teachers surveyed in the Staff Development Study, close to half of
those enrolled in course work reported that a main reason for doing so
was to gain credits on the salary schedule. Teachers statewide
accumulated an average of two semester units during a one-year
period, with an (average) combined value in 1987 of approximately
$2800.
   A critical examination of present assumptions, practices, and
consequences does not inevitably yield proposals to substitute
performance-based increases for those based on formal education. The
recommendations outlined by Conant, for example, would strengthen
assurances that the university experience was of sufficient depth and
rigour and was plausibly linked to a teacher's present or future work
in teaching. Conant proposed awarding salary credit only for coursework aligned with a coherent programme of study leading to an
advanced degree and pursued during blocks of time reserved for study
(summer or sabbatical leave). He proposed further that no salary
credit be awarded to teachers for coursework taken toward an administrative credential; presumably, the financial reward for such coursework is obtained when a person actually secures an administrative
post. Such a policy might slow the rate at which salary units are
acquired, but make the claims about the worth of those units more
uniformly credible. Assuming it is desirable to maintain the present
pace of career (salary) advancement, districts could combine provisions for university-derived credit with provisions for other forms of
participation in professional development to which equally sound
quality controls were applied. For example, one might argue that
sustained participation in an organized subject-matter collaboration or
network, or in the activities of a subject-oriented professional association, requires an investment of time and thought equivalent to a
credit-bearing course, and perhaps comes closer to meeting the standard of 'relevance' to the work of teaching.[18]
   In principle, there is no reason that teachers might not satisfy
their own interest in greater compensation while adding to their
intellectual depth and breadth and to their professional capacities in
classroom, school, and occupation. In practice, however, this principle is compromised in several ways. Many of them were described by
Conant a quarter-century ago, but are confirmed by these and other
recent data. First, the incentive structure is weighted toward the first

stages of the teaching career. University-course enrolments have declined steadily over the past fifteen years; among teachers surveyed in the Staff Development Policy Study, only about one in three was enrolled in coursework.[19] Although one might construct multiple and varied explanations for the decline, it corresponds with a steady increase in the average age of the teaching force. In most states, teachers may acquire sufficient credits to reach the ceiling on the salary schedule in approximately twelve to fifteen years. Without claiming that universities are the sole source of new knowledge and creative thought, they are inescapably a major force to which the public looks in judging the adequacy of teacher preparation. Teachers most likely to be 'out-of-date' through long tenure in the classroom are, under present arrangements, those with the fewest material incentives for university coursework. The subsidy for university study resides almost exclusively in the salary schedule; rarely do teachers receive tuition subsidies or other assistance with out-of-pocket expenses.

The incentive structure places a premium on easily acquired units, those least likely to stretch a teacher's intellectual capacities or contribute substantially to a teacher's curricular and instructional repertoire. Expedience displaces genuine intellectual interest; quantity of course-taking takes precedence over coherence of programme. Although many districts limit the rate at which credits can be accrued, it remains the case that course content may be less salient than ease of completion, accessibility, and scheduling in accounting for teachers' enrolment decisions. The incentive toward easily acquired units, combined with difficulties of scheduling, pushes teachers away from subject-area classes outside of departments of education that may contribute most to 'current knowledge' and that may be most credibly linked to teaching assignments. In a review of issues surrounding teacher compensation, Stern (1986) argues that 'the potential advantage of basing teachers' pay on education may be lost if that education is not relevant to what teachers actually do, or try to do' (p. 303).

The incentive for long-term university study, already weakened by the 'front-loaded' earnings profile embedded in the salary schedule, is diluted further as districts begin to award semester unit equivalents for participation in a wide range of district-sponsored activity. The salary-education link is less firmly tied to institutions of higher education than in the past. Districts confront two difficulties: uncertainty regarding the quality of coursework that qualifies for salary credit; and the felt need to concentrate scarce resources on district priorities. Increasingly, they have responded to both by awarding salary credits for locally-sponsored activities. (District-awarded units contribute to salary advances within a district, but are not transferable from district to district.) Acknowledging that teachers are motivated to earn credits from some source in order to advance on the salary schedule, these districts have viewed district-sponsored credits as a way to ensure quality control and to forge a connection between credit-earning

Judith Warren Little

activity and district priorities. Of thirty district contracts reviewed, one placed specific limits on the ratio of district units to university units; four permitted both university and district units, but did not specify a ratio; and three accepted only semester units earned at an institution of higher education. Other contracts made reference only to semester units or quarter units required to advance on the salary schedule, with no stated restrictions on institutional source.

In effect, districts expand the resources devoted to equipping teachers with the 'local knowledge' they require to succeed with local students; they correspondingly reduce the share of resources most clearly linked to teachers' careers and to the pursuit of subject-specific knowledge. In so doing, they gain control over the content of activity for which they subsequently compensate teachers but lose some of their capacity to encourage individual initiative and to subsidize teachers' external exploration of knowledge advances. Teachers' incentive to remain current in the field is thereby diminished. The schools' ability to sustain a well-prepared workforce is further skewed in the direction of short-term priorities and accommodation of local circumstances.

More vigorous policy debate might productively clarify the way in which individual and institutional goals are supported or compromised by the present link between teacher compensation and professional development. In principle, salary rewards for formal education serve as the district's major vehicle for ensuring a workforce that possesses a reasonable standard of current knowledge, remaining up-to-date with advances in the subject disciplines and in knowledge related to teaching and learning. The present arrangement is also the system's most obvious accommodation to individual career interests and initiative; its justification derives partly from the prospect that forays in postgraduate education help to sustain a teacher's energy and enthusiasm over the long term. It is thus potentially an important piece of a comprehensive configuration of professional development obligations and opportunities, one in which individual and institutional interests clearly intersect. The thrust of this argument is not to displace the salary advantage attached to formal professional development, but to examine the ways in which the link between salary and education now serve, or might serve, a range of individual interests and institutional purposes, and in which the salary subsidy for formal education fits as part of a larger configuration of public support for teachers' professional development.

Teachers' Contributed Time and the Balance of Individual and Institutional Commitments

Personal responsibility for continuing education is an established tradition in the professions and in higher education. In exchange for time

184

and money devoted to up-grading knowledge, skills, and professional reputation, individuals secure continued certification under state law and qualify for career advancement and greater compensation. Individuals invest in their own professional development when they volunteer time outside the salaried work-day to enrol in university or college coursework, attend professional conferences, participate in workshops, join informal study groups, or keep abreast of professional reading. In addition, they incur out-of-pocket expenses for tuition, travel, conference fees, books, and other materials.

Teachers' contributions to their own staff development are substantial. In the thirty case-study sites, approximately one of every five hours that a teacher spends in district or school staff development is volunteer time—time spent outside the salaried work-day, with no compensation in the form of stipends or salary credit. At the district and school levels, then, staff development costs are offset substantially by the value of uncompensated participant time. (Volunteer time amounts to about $500 per teacher.) Further, this estimate is conservative, based only on records of teacher time associated with locally-sponsored activity. It does not take into account the time that teachers spend on activities they undertake fully on their own, with no district subsidy or compensation. Nor does it record the out-of-pocket expenses that teachers incur when they enrol in university coursework, invest in books or journals, or pay their own way to professional conferences.

The available data provide us with few clues to the nature and magnitude of teachers' personal contributions to their own professional growth. It seems likely, however, that some aspects of teachers' personal investments are of considerable policy interest. Personal expenditures of time and money are differentially burdensome to beginning and experienced teachers, to unmarried teachers and those raising young children (or sending children to college), to teachers in resource-rich urban areas and teachers in remote rural schools. The burdens may be compounded or eased by local workplace conditions; teachers in resource-poor schools may choose to spend discretionary dollars on classroom supplies rather than conference attendance.

Although we have no direct evidence to this effect, it seems probable that a delicate balance obtains between institutional and individual commitments. Teachers who see their institution committing resources to their development may be more amenable to contributing some of their own; teachers who perceive the institution to be withholding resources for teachers' development may find little incentive to compensate with their own time and money. Leaving apart variations in personal circumstances, one might speculate that teachers' independent contributions may be greater where (1) local staff development budgets balance support for institutional initiatives with direct subsidies for individually-initiated professional development; (2) the rewards and incentives for professional development are clear and varied; and (3) school workplace norms favour continuous improvement. To the extent that these speculations are supported, they hold implications for the distribution of programme resources, the structure of extrinsic and intrinsic career rewards, and the exercise of school-level leadership.

Conclusion

This essay examines the prevailing configuration of professional development policies and practices, assessing the conceptions of teachers and teaching they communicate and the prospects they have for enhancing teachers' motivations and opportunities to learn. A four-component investment model shows the distribution of actual investment and illuminates the policy issues embedded in professional development funding. Each of the four elements of the model reveals specific aspects of the policy problem surrounding professional development. That problem, at its broadest, is how to pursue the professional development of teachers in ways that best yield benefit for children. It encompasses the obligations to which teachers are held, the opportunities they are afforded, and the rewards they reap. Three of the four domains represented in the investment model (excluding only teachers' personal contributions of time and money) lend themselves directly to policy intervention: the form and content of activities associated with designated staff development programme monies; in modest ways, the distribution of 'opportunities to learn' in the salaried work-day; and the nature of the linkage between professional development and teacher compensation.

Policy reformulation might begin by embracing a broadened conception of professional development that accounts both for individuals' inclinations or experiences and for institutions' interests and requirements. Professional development policies and practices might then be evaluated, both prospectively and retrospectively, by the degree to which they appear congruent with multiple dimensions and purposes of professional development—both individual and institutional. First, professional development can be judged by the growth in knowledge, skill, and judgement that teachers bring to their work in the classroom. By this standard, the test of effective development is whether teachers come to know more about their subjects and their students, and to attempt more in teaching them. University coursework, professional conferences, district-sponsored skill workshops, classroom consultation, observation by peers or administrators, independent sabbaticals, teacher networks, and acquired habits of professional reading all have been described as routes to expanded intellectual breadth and depth. Less frequently considered are the ways in which teaching assignments themselves stretch (or shrink) teachers' understanding, or the way in which the patterns of work among colleagues cause teachers to broaden or narrow their curricular and instructional alternatives.[20]

Second, professional development might be judged by the contributions teachers make to a professional community. In this conception, professional development is linked to one's collective responsibilities, and to one's capacity and propensity to fulfil them. By this standard, the test of effective professional development is whether experienced teachers engage collectively in examining the direction and quality of the educational enterprise beyond the classroom, and whether less experienced teachers are systematically prepared to do so. Some of this preparation is accomplished in conventional ways. Through coursework and workshops, teachers can acquire the knowledge required to evaluate texts and tests, interpret test scores, or compose the school or department policies that govern course design, curriculum scope and sequence, student grading, or the use of classroom time. In the same manner, they can develop facility in group participation and group leadership, enabling them to make productive use of scarce time together. Other requirements of preparation cannot be satisfied by formal instruction or simulated experience, but only by access to real-time opportunities for collective planning and decision-making.

Finally, individual professional development can be witnessed in the evolution of a teacher's career. Recent developments in the organizational theory literature offer an alternative orientation toward career, one that takes its point of departure from the work itself and that accounts for the meaning of work in persons' lives. By this conception, teachers would be treated as members of an 'occupational community'[21] whose participation in professional development ventures would vary in substance, form, and intensity over the span of a career in teaching. In this broad conception, then, professional development opportunities might be expected to affect—and to reflect—at least three dimensions of an individual teacher's life: in the classroom, in the staffroom, and in the unfolding of a career. The constructs of teacher as classroom instructor, colleague, and member of an occupational community provide three standards for judging the nature and consequences of professional development.

Despite its profoundly personal character, schoolteaching is nonetheless institutional work. Whatever images persist of the privacy of individual classrooms and the autonomy accorded to individual teachers, teachers remain employees of districts and schools. These districts and schools have an independent stake in the professional development of the teacher workforce. We also make certain assumptions about the institutional stake that schools and society have in a well-prepared, well-supported, and professionally committed teacher workforce. The institutional purposes of teachers' professional development are directly bound to the collective competence of a faculty and to a school's capacity for steady improvement. These purposes may be rendered more or less urgent by conditions external or internal to the school; they may be served well or badly by the prevailing configuration of professional development opportunities; and they may be congruent or in conflict with the professional interests, needs, and commitments of individual teachers.

First, schools have a stake in ensuring that teachers have adequate local knowledge to succeed with a particular student population, in a particular school, pressed by quite distinct community expectations. Variations among schools are many and consequential for the teachers who work in them. Local staff development may be judged in part by its capacity to equip teachers for local circumstances. Second, schools have a stake in hiring and maintaining a workforce that boasts current knowledge, up to date in curriculum, pedagogy, and other matters affecting student learning and development. Neither policy makers nor researchers have devoted much attention to learning how teachers add to their own knowledge of a field, or to charting the paths by which advances in the disciplines come to the attention of teachers.

Professional development also serves programmatic institutional agendas, serving to move intended change forward or to introduce a measure of stability in times of turmoil.[22] In the past two decades, schools in the United States have experienced the effects of desegregation (with and without busing), mainstreaming of the handicapped, a flood of non-English speaking immigration, back to basics and forward to critical thinking, more rigour in graduation requirements with less tolerance for high drop-out rates. The importance of both short-term skill training and long-term problem-solving opportunities to the fate of such efforts has been well-established, but the resources devoted to such activities remain relatively meagre.[23]

Finally, schools have a stake in equipping teachers to make judgements that are well-informed and productive for students. By teachers' own accounts, they make independent decisions about what and how to teach, and they learn most of what they learn on the job in the course of day-to-day work. Thus, the district gains the best return on its salary investment when it finds the means to give teachers timely and useful feedback on the work they do, thus making 'learning by experience' a more certain venture. At issue here are the link between professional development and teacher evaluation or 'accountability,' and the prevailing norms among teachers regarding commentary on one another's work.[24]

Together, teachers' professional interests and schools' institutional requirements form the basis for criteria on which professional development resources might be allocated and their effectiveness assessed. In pursuit of strategies consistent with this broadened conception, governing boards, administrators, and teachers' associations might adopt resource allocation principles and mechanisms that more explicitly account for the diversity in teachers' professional interests, circumstances, and maturation, and that more consistently favour teacher initiative and leadership. A more productive balance might thereby be achieved between teachers' individual and collective interests and the interests and requirements of the institution. The same groups might engage in a more deliberate discussion and debate about the nature of professional development activities that contribute toward salary advances; in consequence, the range of credit-bearing activity is likely to be broadened but linked more closely and persuasively to teachers' own work.

Policy makers and administrators might profitably abandon the evaluation of isolated staff development activities in favour of selected studies—conducted with and by teachers—that trace the development of persons, schools, and ideas. Evaluation in our case–study districts typically produced a small set of 'satisfaction' measures associated with selected activities, but offered little insight into comprehensive patterns of involvement and impact. A revised stance toward programme and policy evaluation could take meaningful account of the classroom, school, community, and career contexts that shape teachers' curricular and instructional choices. Both the obligations and the opportunities of professional development would come to rest more closely with teachers, without compromising legitimate institutional interests.

In sum, this is an argument for a principled strategy of professional development that expresses a coherent but comprehensive view of teacher development and that relies on resource allocation criteria to accommodate both the teacher's individual interests and the institution's stake in a well-prepared workforce. It is fruitfully guided by a framework that encompasses teachers' professional maturation and commitments, the collective competence and maturity of a staff, and the school's institutional capacity to serve students and communities.

Notes

1 Contributors to the skill training and training implementation literature include Joyce and Showers, 1981; Mohlman, Coladarci and Gage, 1982; Sparks, 1983, 1986; Smylie, 1988; and Guskey, 1986. Illustrative of the range of literature on learning to teach and the evolution of teachers' knowledge and identities are Feiman-Nemser and Buchmann, 1986; Huberman, 1989; Measor, 1985; Nemser, 1983; and Nias, 1989.

2 Characteristic of this perspective are Moore and Hyde, 1981; Schlechty et al., 1982; Schlechty and Whitford, 1983.

3 The Staff Development Policy Study was conducted over a fifteen-month period as a joint project of the Far West Laboratory for Educational Research and Development and Policy Analysis for California Education (PACE), with funding from the California Postsecondary Education Commission. My thinking on the policy and cost aspects of teachers' professional development has benefited from discussion with my colleagues on the larger study, especially David S. Stern, James W. Guthrie, and Michael W. Kirst.

4   Details on the amount and distribution of resources are provided in Little *et al.* (1987) and in Little (1989).

5   For further discussion of the rationale underlying the four-component investment model, see also Stern, Gerritz and Little (1989). For purposes of this essay, the order of elements has been altered but the definitions remain the same.

6   We imputed a figure for lost instructional time only when pupil-free days or minimum days were devoted to staff development. For purposes of these estimates, we did not consider the use of a substitute teacher a reallocation of instructional time.

7   For the earliest statement of this argument, see Joyce and Showers, 1981. The popular appeal of the coaching rationale is suggested by the frequency with which professional journals have devoted articles and special issues to the topic (for example, 'Staff Development Through Coaching', special issue of *Educational Leadership*, *44*, 5, February, 1987).

8   For example, Little (1984), McLaughlin and Marsh (1979).

9   Showers, 1982; see also Showers, 1984.

10 On this issue, see also Little, 1984, 1987.

11 Huberman, 1988:3.

12 The present surge of interest in 'site-based management' may shift the locus of decision-making about staff development closer to the school and classroom. In these data, however, school-based choices regarding the content and form of staff development look very much like those now made more centrally, placing a premium on the purchase of services from external experts and the delivery of packaged training.

13 For example, Gray and Caldwell, 1980; Kreinberg, 1980.

14 The same phenomenon is reported by Berman and Gjelten (1984) in their evaluation of the implementation of California's School Improvement Program.

15 This estimate assumes that reductions in load are achieved by altering the actual permanent FTE allocation, or the teacher-student ratio at the school level (not necessarily a change in class size). It would be misleading to estimate the costs of a reduced workload on the basis of lower rates associated with substitutes for three reasons. First, most districts are already at the limit of the available, capable pool of substitutes. A solution based on a 'reserve pool' of substitute teachers is simply not feasible. Second, there is well-documented community resistance to a high volume of substitute use associated with teachers' professional development; in parents' eyes, release time is a sacrifice of instructional quality. Third, release time is not a genuinely reduced workload in the eyes of teachers; indeed, it generates an additional planning and preparation burden. Teachers themselves do not want to take large amounts of release time and thereby compromise the sense of responsibility they have to a class to which they are officially assigned.

16 Rosenholtz (1988:80) employs multiple social organizational dimensions to distinguish between learning-enriched and learning-impoverished environments.

17 Most prominently Conant, 1963.

18 For example, see Nelson's (1986) discussion of the Urban Math Collaboratives.

19 For the most recent available national figures see National Education Association (1987).

20 For example, see Sprinthall and Thies-Sprinthall (1983).

21 Van Maanen and Barley (1987) contrast this orientation with conventional definitions of career that centre on a linear trajectory in which career development is measured mainly by objective advances in status and income (promotions).

22 On the role of staff development in school change see McLaughlin and Marsh, 1979; Fullan, 1982, 1989. On the organizational maintenance functions of staff development, see Schlechty and Whitford, 1983.

23 On the allocation of district resources in support of implementation, see Farrar, 1988.

24 McLaughlin and Pfeifer (1988) address the relationship between teacher, evaluation, accountability, and effective teacher learning; Little (1987) summarizes the conditions that support or inhibit teachers in providing feedback on (or evaluations of) one another's teaching.

References

BERMAN, P. and GJELTEN, T. (1984) *Improving School Improvement: A Policy Evaluation of the California School Improvement Program, Vol. 2: Findings*, Berkeley, Berman Weiler Associates.

CONANT, J.B. (1963) *The Education of American Teachers*, New York, McGraw-Hill.

FARRAR, E. (1988) *Environmental Contexts and the Implementation of Teacher and School-based Reforms: Competing Interests*, Paper presented at the annual meeting of the American Educational Research Association, New Orleans.

FEIMAN-NEMSER, S. and BUCHMANN, M. (1986) *Knowing, Thinking, and Doing in Learning To Teach: A Research Framework and Some Initial Results*, Leuven, University of Leuven.

FULLAN, M. (1982) *The Meaning of Educational Change*, New York, Teachers College Press.

FULLAN, M. (1990) 'Staff development, innovation and institutional development', in JOYCE, B. (Ed.), *Staff Development*, Alexandria, ASCD.

GRAY, J. and CALDWELL, K. (1980) 'The Bay Area Writing Project', *Journal of Staff Development*, 1, 1, pp. 31–9.

GUSKEY, T. (1986) 'Staff development and the process of teacher change', *Educational Researcher*, May, pp. 5–12.

HUBERMAN, M. (1988) *Teacher Professionalism and Workplace Conditions: Conceptions of Teachers' Work and the Organization of Schools*, A memorandum prepared for the Holmes Group Seminar, September.

HUBERMAN, M. (1989) 'The professional life cycle of teachers', *Teachers College Record*, 91, 1, pp. 31–57.

JOYCE, B. and SHOWERS, B. (1981) *Teacher Training Research: Working Hypotheses for Program Design and Directions for Further Study*, Paper presented at the annual meeting of the American Educational Research Association, Los Angeles.

KREINBERG, N. (1980) 'The EQUALS Program: Helping teachers to become researchers and problem solvers', *Journal of Staff Development*, 1, 1, pp. 19–30.

LITTLE, J.W. (1984) 'Seductive images and organizational realities in professional development', *Teachers College Record*, 86, 1, pp. 84–102.

LITTLE, J.W. (1987) 'Teachers as colleagues', in RICHARDSON-KOEHLER, V. (Ed.),

Educators' Handbook: A Research Perspective, New York, Longman, pp. 491–518.

LITTLE, J.W. (1989) 'District policy choices and teachers' professional development opportunities', *Educational Evaluation and Policy Analysis*, 11, 2, pp. 165–79.

LITTLE, J.W., GERRITZ, W.H., STERN, D.S., GUTHRIE, J.W., KIRST, M.W. and MARSH, D.D. (1987) *Staff Development in California: Public and Personal Investment, Program Patterns, and Policy Choices*, San Francisco, Far West Laboratory for Educational Research and Development.

MCLAUGHLIN, M.W. and MARSH, D.D. (1979) 'Staff development and school change', in LIEBERMAN, A. and MILLER, L. (Eds.), *Staff Development: New Demands, New Realities, New Perspectives*, New York, Teachers College Press.

MCLAUGHLIN, M.W. and PFEIFER, R.S. (1988) *Teacher Evaluation: Improvement, Accountability, and Effective Learning*, New York, Teachers College Press.

MEASOR, L. (1985) 'Critical incidents in the classroom: Identities, choices, and careers', in BALL, S. and GOODSON, I. (Eds.), *Teachers' Lives and Careers*, London, Falmer Press, pp. 61–77.

MOHLMAN, G.G., COLADARCI, T. and GAGE, N.L. (1982) 'Comprehension and attitude as predictors of implementation of teacher training', *Journal of Teacher Education*, 33, 1, pp. 31–6.

MOORE, D. and HYDE, A. (1981) *Making Sense of Staff Development: An Analysis of Staff Development Programs and their Costs in Three Urban School Districts*, Chicago, Designs for Change.

NATIONAL EDUCATION ASSOCIATION (1987) *The Status of the American Teacher, 1985–1986*, Washington, DC.

NELSON, B. (1986) 'Collaboration for colleagueship: A program in support of teachers', *Educational Leadership*, 43, 5, pp. 50–2.

NEMSER, S. (1983) 'Learning to teach', in SHULMAN, L.S. and SYKES, G. (Eds.), *Handbook of Teaching and Policy*, White Plains, NY, Longman.

NIAS, J. (1989) *Primary Teachers Talking: A Study of Teaching As Work*, London, Routledge.

ROSENHOLTZ, S. (1989) *Teachers' Workplace*, New York, Longman.

SCHLECHTY, P.C., CROWELL, D., WHITFORD, B.L., JOSLIN, A.W., VANCE, V.S., NOBLIT, G.W. and BURKE, W.I. (1982) *The Organization and Management of Staff Development in a Large City School System: A Case Study*, Chapel Hill, NC, University of North Carolina.

SCHLECHTY, P.C. and WHITFORD, B.L. (1983) 'The organizational context of school systems and the functions of staff development', in GRIFFIN, G. (Ed.), *Staff Development: Eighty-Second Yearbook of the National Society for the Study of Education*, Chicago, University of Chicago Press, pp. 62–91.

SHOWERS, B. (1982) *The transfer of training: The contribution of coaching*, Eugene, OR, Centre for Educational Policy and Management, University of Oregon.

SHOWERS, B. (1984) *Peer coaching: A strategy for facilitating transfer of training*, Eugene, OR, Centre for Educational Policy and Management, University of Oregon.

SMYLIE, M. (1988) 'The enhancement function of staff development: Organizational and psychological antecedents to individual teacher change', *American Educational Research Journal*, 25, 1, pp. 1–30.

SPARKS, G.M. (1983) 'Synthesis of research on staff development for effective teaching', *Educational Leadership*, November, pp. 65–72.

SPARKS, G.M. (1986) 'The effectiveness of alternative training activities in changing teaching practices', *American Educational Research Journal, 23,* 2, pp. 217–25.

SPRINTHALL, N.A. and THIES-SPRINTHALL, L. (1983) 'The teacher as adult learner: A cognitive-developmental view', in GRIFFIN, G. (Ed.), *Staff Development: Eighty-Second Yearbook of the National Society for the Study of Education,* Chicago, University of Chicago Press, pp. 13–35.

'STAFF DEVELOPMENT THROUGH COACHING', special issue of *Educational Leadership, 44,* 5, February, 1987.

STERN, D. (1986) 'Compensation for teachers', *Review of Research in Education, 13,* pp. 285–316.

STERN, D.S., GERRITZ, W.H. and LITTLE, J.W. (1989) 'Making the most of the district's two (or five) cents: Accounting for investments in teachers' professional development', *Journal of Education Finance, 14,* Winter, pp. 19–26.

VAN MAANEN, J. and BARLEY, S.R. (1984) 'Occupational communities: Culture and control in organizations', *Research in Organizational Behavior, 6,* pp. 287–365.

Chapter 10

Universities in Partnership with Schools and School Systems: Les Liaisons Dangereuses?

Jean Rudduck

The Image of the University

Opportunities for in-service education can be as much a means of controlling the direction of teaching as of liberating the thinking and practice of teachers. The development of centralized authority in education makes it increasingly possible to use in-service as a form of deliberate intervention to achieve particular ends: we are experiencing this in England at the moment as money and time are made available by the Government specifically to support teachers in the rapid implementation of new policies for the national curriculum and for assessment of nationally-set attainment targets.

The role of the university[1] in the further professional education of teachers is complex. The university seems to have freer rein at times when the state authority approves the attempt to raise the professional status of teachers through the advancement of knowledge, but at other times, when the state has a more conservative agenda, the university's role is constrained. The ambiguity of its relationship with schools has been sustained by crude assumptions about theory and privilege, and those who, at any time, want to minimize its influence on education can readily reconstruct the old mythology of the ivory tower.

Ironically, in relation to in-service events, the notion of privilege has, in the past, been consciously promoted as a means of emphasizing the professional importance of the teaching community. For instance, the first University of London Vocation Course for teachers, directed by the widely-respected educationalist, Professor John Adams, made the following offer: 'A whiff of the old university atmosphere amid all the comforts of the twentieth century is here put within the reach of every enterprising teacher' (Rudduck, 1979). Well-known speakers gave lectures, and social occasions had a touch of grandeur. There is a strange blend of patronage and sense of service in the wording of the lengthy brochure:

Teachers are so much given to planning out things for others that they stand in particular need of a period in which they can, for once, leave the planning to others...To do work in a carpeted room is a most welcome change...Teachers stand in special need of mixing as much as possible with mature minds...in order to counteract the schoolroom atmosphere. (Rudduck, 1979)

The occasion, it is confidently claimed, 'will coruscate with enthusiasms; it will give its members new energy and new life; it will make all who attend it conscious of the power that lies within them' (Rudduck, 1979).

The conference represented a celebration of professionalism at a time when teaching was far from being a graduate profession. Interestingly, the organizers were at pains to point out that the programme would be delivered by people who were 'not only experts in their subject, but working experts...as far removed from "mere theorists" as could be' (Rudduck, 1979). There was already, in the educational press, a familiar debate (which has continued over the years) about the relative merits of 'theory' and 'practice' in the education of new and experienced teachers. The *Education Expositor* (September 1854) carried a series of letters from a reader who condemned initial teacher training programmes for aiming to produce 'proficient scholars' rather than 'accomplished teachers', and the *Times Educational Supplement* (September 1920) reflected current criticism of in-service courses: 'Many teachers think that [they] should be more vocational in character and that they should have more direct bearing upon the particular problems which a teacher has to face in school' (Rudduck, 1979).

In the late 1960s and early 1970s the concern was, once again, with the need to update teachers' curriculum knowledge, and subject specialists in universities led teams whose task it was to produce new curriculum courses and teaching materials. In time, the preoccupation with curriculum development gave way to a concern for teacher development, and to the extent that this shift of emphasis was expressed through such slogans as 'research-based teacher education' and 'the teacher-as-researcher-movement', university staff played a key role. That role has been less obvious in relation to the trend towards school-based curriculum development which, in the UK, preceded the move towards stronger centralization of curriculum control. In the free-market training culture that is dominant here at the moment, and outside the formal structures, which continue, for validating learning and conferring higher degrees on teachers, university staff are now one of several groups of 'expert' consultants who are setting up their own stalls to attract business as schools come to have greater control over their own in-service budgets. In such a market situation the simplistic profile that survives from an early mythology and which presents universities as elitist and remote from practice is disturbingly dysfunctional.

Frameworks for Teacher Development

This section outlines four frameworks for teachers' professional development that have been important, at one time or another, during the last twenty years.

1 High Degree Programmes

Before university staff became involved in the curriculum development movement of the late sixties and early seventies, their main encounters with practising teachers were as students who chose to enrol on university-based higher degree programmes (whether one year full-time or part-time over several years) and who, in doing so, were, by and large, buying support for their own personal and intellectual development. They were also, of course, buying into a traditional university culture. Only relatively recently has criticism of the academic paraphernalia of that culture been vociferously expressed by its own members. Stenhouse (1980) was one of the spokespersons for reform:

> What is required of the universities is that they...recognize forms of research alternative to the still dominant tradition of scientific positivism with its emphasis on experimental and survey procedures conducted on samples in field settings and giving rise to 'results'. Among these alternative forms are experimental or descriptive case studies which may be based upon the teachers' access either to the classroom as a laboratory or to the school or classroom for participant observation. In Britain, standards for these research paradigms are now in process of being worked out at masters' and doctoral level...this alliance with universities is important for teachers because it provides access to a pattern of...study, right up to the level of doctorate, which turns one towards one's professional work rather than away from it, and offers a systematic training in the appropriate research skills as well as a grasp of the theoretical issues applicable to...practitioner research.

There is, now, ample evidence that this re-orientation has been achieved in most university departments of education. Interestingly, as assessed work for higher degrees became more practice-oriented, schools and school systems (which, in England, often make a contribution to the costs of a teacher's course of study) tried to influence the issues that might be addressed by 'their' teachers in assignments and dissertations. They did this in order to ensure that there was local relevance and some practical benefit. Universities, while maintaining some ambivalence towards the idea that students' and tutors' traditional freedom to determine the content of their studies was being questioned, nevertheless accepted the challenge of supporting personal professional development in the context of school and system priorities. An embryonic notion of partnership was thus established, although somewhat uneasily at first.

2 Curriculum Development Projects

Two decades back, university staff started to play a leading role in the up-dating of curriculum content by designing and directing curriculum projects. Ideally their contribution extended beyond design to support in implementation, and project directors might see their role as ensuring that the curriculum development projects which they had been invited to lead were realistically founded and were being introduced in ways which respected the epistemological and procedural principles which gave them structure. There were clearly problems in defining and managing the working relationship between university-led curriculum development teams and teacher-led school-based implementation teams. In England, the movement suffered, I think, from some of the technocratic/bureaucratic assumptions that marred its progress in the States. In its extreme form the model was arrogantly simplistic and neglectful of a school's sense of its own identity. The concern was with the mass-produced package and its secure conveyance through the system. The ownership of meaning tended to remain with the project's originators. Schwab (1984) summarizes the situation in his caricature of a curriculum project as something 'decided in Moscow and telegraphed to the provinces'. The problems are to do with the authority and, consequently, the perceived integrity of the product as something to be adopted rather than adapted.

Had the curriculum development movement been preceded rather than followed by the teacher-as-researcher movement, reactions might have been more fearlessly robust. Teachers might have seen or been helped to see that the generalizations that the descriptive pedagogy of a curriculum project embody are in fact working hypotheses that have to be tested in local conditions. They might also have seen or been helped to see that curricula should not be regarded as 'good' or 'right' but instead as interesting and therefore 'worth examining'. But in order to examine them and see what they had to offer that might be of value in the varying circumstances of different classrooms, teachers needed to comprehend the logic of the thinking that gave form to the pedagogy and its teaching materials. It was important to find ways of inviting teachers into the world of deliberation that the curriculum developers inhabited so that they would, to some extent, be able to reconstruct the process of development: in this way they would be in a better position to respond critically to the product. A tradition of curriculum critique is not, however, firmly established within the teaching profession and an understanding of the dilemmas that shape the process of curriculum construction has not always been seen as an important pre-condition of intelligent experimentation. Instead of bringing practitioners in on the inside story of curriculum development as a way of establishing an equal literacy, curriculum developers have often chosen, instead, to act like 'columnists and commentators' (Schwab, 1956) who are protectively selective in their disclosures of the logic of the ideas they report:

> They give neither all the reasons they have considered nor all the interrelations among those they present. They over-simplify the sugar-coat. They select only the kinds of reason which experience has taught them are presently accessible to readers. (Schwab, 1956)

Thus, important opportunities for extending the curriculum literacy of practitioners were lost.

Another problem for implementation was that in-service courses designed to prepare teachers to work on the new curricula frequently recruited only one teacher from a school rather than a working group of teachers, and shared meanings were not built up. In the privacy of the teacher's own classroom it was all too easy for the regularities of past practice to creep back and stifle the innovation. We have also to remember that in the days of the curriculum development movement projects were, in the main, concerned with separate bits of the curriculum. There was no coherent framework of principles across projects: at most they were linked by a loose commitment to discovery and inquiry learning methods. The effects were inevitably piecemeal. The curriculum development movement could not, by virtue of its project structure, address itself to the task of holistic curriculum development. This task was left to the school-based curriculum development movement.

3 The School-Based Curriculum Development Movement

For all their weaknesses, the departure of the big projects was an intellectual loss. What was distinctive about them was that their central teams had the time to tackle fundamental curriculum issues in ways that are often beyond the scope of school-based teams whose members have, usually, a full teaching load. Teaching requires such energy that significant and coherent curriculum development is unlikely to be achieved without time and space to distance oneself from everyday routine, and without opportunities for focused and crucial dialogue with people who can offer different perspectives on the task of curriculum change. School-based curriculum development sounds good, said an observer recently: 'All our liberal reflexes resonate when we hear about schools developing their own curricula' (Gordon, 1987:29). But, he added, it is difficult to do well. School-based curriculum development promises local relevance—what Schwab (1984:310) describes as a sense of 'a particular locus in time and space, with smells, shadows, and conditions outside the (school) walls which may have much to do with what is achieved inside'. This is the obvious and seductive strength of school-based curriculum development. But one pays a price for such intimacy. The limits of possibility may be determined by expectations rooted in a familiar past. Ways of thinking may be constrained by routine patterns of perception that support routine patterns of behaviour, and ambitious alternatives may not easily be considered. The price of local relevance may be, given the conditions under which teachers generally attempt school-based curriculum development, either lack of pedagogic coherence and rigour, or an unwitting conservatism. Overall, I remain somewhat sceptical, even at the best of times, about the intellectual coherence of courses of study constructed by busy teachers in their own school setting—unless initial and in-service teacher education programmes are deliberately preparing teachers for the task of curriculum development by fostering critical judgement as well as technical competence (see Lewy, 1987; Sabar and Silberstein, 1987). In England, these are not the best of times, and the climate is no longer supportive of school-based curriculum development: the agenda has been taken out of teachers' hands by the imposition of a new national framework for the curriculum; at the same time, the universities' influence on teacher education is being artfully contained. A new mood of anti-intellectualism functions to protect Government policy which is, contradictorily, radical in the extent of its reforms and consistently conservative in its values and direction. Indeed, the pace of legislated change is so rapid that teachers scarcely have time to get the new structures into perspective, let alone develop a balanced view of their strengths and weaknesses. As Hargreaves and Reynolds (1989) have said: 'There is greater pressure toward productivity, but less opportunity to reflect on the worth and rationality of what is being produced' (p. 23). In such a climate it is crucial that universities try to find some ways of rebuilding their partnership with teachers, schools and local school systems.

4 Practitioner Research

Illich, writing about the democratization of knowledge, distinguishes between science, or research, *for* the people, and science, or research, *by* the people. Practitioner research, although clearly exemplifying the move towards 'the people' has still, in most of its forms, been developed with the support of university staff.

One form of teacher research grew out of the curriculum development movement. Some curriculum projects were conceived as offering a set of hypotheses, with supporting classroom materials, for teachers to work on experimentally in their own settings (see Rudduck, 1988). These projects provided structures which would help teachers focus intelligently on different sets of educational issues, taking into account personal and local contexts of practice.

Another form of practitioner research cast the teacher in the role of major audience of so-called 'academic' research; this was not a passive role, however, for, as Stenhouse (1979), a strong advocate, argued: 'using research means doing research'. As Cronbach (1975) said: 'When we give proper weight to local conditions, any generalization is a working hypothesis, not a conclusion'. Researchers were, in Stenhouse's view, obliged to communicate whatever they had to say to teachers in ways that would enable them to sharpen their understanding of the conditions of learning.

A popular, if loosely-defined, means of effecting teachers' professional development has been through participation in action research. In the action research mode, the university researcher is not normally leading the action, but, instead, playing an advisory role, helping teachers to define the nature of the problem or aspiration that is to provide a framework for their action, and guiding them through appropriate strategies for gathering and analyzing data and using new insights to modify practice. Support and training could be offered either through university staff acting as coordinators of research initiatives which involved different groups of teachers (see Hull *et al.*, 1984), or through teachers enrolling on higher degree courses which were specifically designed to help them gain confidence and competence in conducting school- or classroom-focused research. Without strong but sympathetic university guidance (research is, after all, our distinctive stock-in-trade) practitioner research can lack impact:

> By developing primarily as a form of teacher-controlled classroom research, [it] has managed to create for itself the image of a popular 'grass roots' movement which neither threatens, nor is itself threatened...Such practitioner research runs the risk of addressing trivial questions, lacks cumulative power, and offers no collective, radical challenge. (Adelman and Carr, 1988)

Lawn (1989:147–161) aspires to a kind of research that moves out from 'small-scale problems in particular classrooms' to look at schools and schooling; he urges that individual inquiry be strengthened by the group commitment of authentic action research. The dimension which transmutes individual enquiry into research—for research has an important communal aspect—is the linking of teachers' own insights and concerns with frameworks for thinking that the wider community of educational researchers is always engaged in constructing.

But whatever form practitioner research takes, it supports professional development by helping teachers to see things afresh that habit has made ordinary. Teaching is, in some respects, subject to routinization, and teachers all too often come to see only what they expect to see, transcribing the surface realities of classroom interactions, and constantly reconstructing the familiar past in its own image.

As Ruth Jonathan (1987:586) observes, school improvement is not merely a matter of 'rapid response to changing market forces through a trivialized curriculum' but a question of dealing with the deep structures of school organization and the habits and values they embody.

Summary

Before moving on to new ground let us pull together some ways, outlined in this section, in which university staff have learned to work productively with teachers during the last ten years or so and which have allowed the barriers of the theory/practice divide to begin to be dismantled.

University staff have worked with teachers on curriculum development projects, at both national and local levels. They have also worked closely with teachers on research initiatives, ensuring that those who participate benefit from the insights that the research yields. Teachers are also more likely now to be regarded as a significant audience for research reports, and the style of reportage is often more vivid and accessible.

Universities have supported the development of teacher research and the role of teacher as researcher partly as a way of demystifying and democratizing research and partly as a way of exploring new ways of learning from practice. University courses have largely moved away from the old transmission model and are now more ready to take teachers' concerns as starting points for inquiry, and to endorse assignments that are practice-based and even collaboratively produced.

But the main achievement in our learning is that we are beginning to see change not simply as a technical problem, but as a cultural problem that requires attention to context and to the creation of shared meaning within working groups in schools.

We have supported change by working with key individuals in the hope that they would stimulate development in their own settings, but we have also worked with groups of teachers from individual schools on problems or possibilities that are part of that institution's own agenda. But rarely, until recently, has a university attempted the more complex task of contributing systematically to district-wide change. Such a way of working depends on the building of effective partnerships between schools, the school district or local authority, and university staff. It is an ambitious and challenging strategy for change, and in the next section I shall outline the bold attempt of one local education authority in England to develop, in partnership with its schools and its university and polytechnic, a district-wide programme of curriculum change.

An Example of University—School System Partnership

The partners in this account[2] are Sheffield Local Education Authority, Sheffield schools and Sheffield University/Polytechnic.[3] The scheme was initiated by the Local Authority, and its manifesto for change, which it circulated to all schools, was intended to be inspiring:

> The time is right for a radical reappraisal. . .(previous developments) have been. . .little more than attempts to enliven the curriculum by tinkering at the margins. . .more time must be spent in collaborative learning, with pupils negotiating their own learning experiences. . .assessment and monitoring can no longer be subcontracted to an examination system immersed in the 'cult of the fact'. We must develop a far more relevant portrayal of pupil experience (and achievement). (Rudduck and Wilcox, 1988:160)

The Sheffield Initiative was designed to allow schools ample room for their own local colour but it was premised on a common core of concerns: equality of opportunity, the integration of subject experience, active learning, and greater student control over and understanding of their learning programme, progress and achievement. The Initiative was committed to changing the whole curriculum in ways that would meet the needs of all students.

The proposal for change was not opposed by schools. Some school principals justified their ready acceptance on the grounds that the Initiative represented a set of social and moral imperatives for change that all schools could not but welcome; others projected their ownership of the core values: 'The programme is based on what *we* have said we wanted for *our* schools'. It became increasingly clear, in time, that the local Initiative was working towards goals that were different in many respects from those that the Government had in mind for schools. What is reassuring is that the schools and the Local Authority are, so far, pretty confident of holding on to their purposes while being seen to be working within the broad framework of the new Education Reform Act. Teachers' autonomy has not been totally undermined, it seems!

The key strategy for change was a programme for all schools which would release teachers from classroom teaching to work on 'commissions' drawn up by their school and intended to represent its priorities for change within the common, broad framework of concerns identified by the Local Authority. In the first year, five teachers from each of the 36 high schools (a smaller number from the elementary schools) each had a full year's release to work together as a school team. Thereafter, the number of teachers released was, for financial reasons, cut back to two from each school. Other key features of the strategy for change were, first, the establishing of clusters of schools so that collaborative planning and better use of resources could be undertaken across schools; and second, some teachers who had had a year's release were taken into a specialist group set up to give support in particular curriculum areas and to develop the new system of assessment.

The 'release' arrangements took an unusual form. Whereas in the old days a teacher would disappear to the university for a year to study there for a Master's degree, here, teachers would spend two or three days a week pursuing their curriculum commissions with support from university tutors, and two or three days in their own schools working with their colleagues. In this way, the teachers did not lose touch with their colleagues and the anxieties and suspicions that normally surround re-entry were minimized: 'All right clever clogs, you were out last year and now you're back. You can show us how it's done.' Although such comments did not entirely disappear (for there was still some suspicion about why certain teachers had been selected for 'a year off'), the antagonism was reduced.

The scheme has undoubtedly generated excitement and raised the general level of awareness of the key principles of the local reform programme. Importantly, it has generated new structures for dialogue within and across schools and it has celebrated teachers as the agents of change: resources are being used not to bring in outside experts as the instruments of change but, to use Kanter's (1983) term to 'groom' insiders to handle the responsibilities of change themselves. University staff made a dual contribution, as 'trainers-cum-tutors' and as 'researchers'. As *trainers-cum-tutors*, they were responsible for working with teams of seconded teachers from particular schools and they offered support with the content of the school commissions, helped to raise awareness of cross-curricular issues such as equal opportunity, and helped teachers understand the process of change within their own institutions. The teachers involved were encouraged to use their experience of change as the basis for credits in a higher degree programme, and the opportunity to submit assessed work was another important factor in helping teachers to reflect on their activities in a more systematic and organized way and to recognize their insights and achievements. As *researchers*, university staff worked with teachers and schools to try to understand the broader issues of school-centred innovation and to feed back insights emerging from formative evaluations.

What did we learn about the process of supporting district-wide change, and about the possibilities of partnership? First, we learned that district-wide attempts at curriculum reform need slogans which can quickly establish an emotional commitment (intellectual commitment has to be built up later). Sheffield's slogan was 'ownership'. As Popkewitz *et al.* (1982) have said: 'A slogan works in education in a manner similar to the functioning of a slogan in the political world. A word...provides a way of symbolizing...[the] values and aspirations of a group' (p. 2). The term 'ownership' made people feel that they were participating in worthwhile communal action and it gave the action a sense of majority mandate. It worked because it had a good democratic ring to it—and because it remained largely undefined. Slogans work best if they are 'a hazy hugger-mugger of ideas and sentiments from which (people) can draw consolation and the ease of a good conscience' (Dunlop, 1979:43). The idea of ownership served as a rallying cry and, later, provided an important critical perspective for analyzing the problems of school-centred innovation.

The aspiration towards corporate commitment to change was ambitious in the sense that the habits and structures that hold traditional procedures and relationships in place are not easily dismantled; ownership as a symbol of the democratization of power provided a useful organizing concept for reflection and research.

Second, we learned that you can't expect all schools to make progress at the same rate: progress, of course, means different things to different schools and district-wide change is therefore an untidy process. The starting points for schools are very different for they are dealing with the different legacies of their past ways of thinking about learning and about achievement. The crux, as Fullan (1982) has said, is how new shared meanings can be constructed when teachers and schools are 'part of a gigantic, loosely organized, complex, messy social system' (p. 79). We can't expect change to be steady, neat, or even always to be facing forward! It is quite an achievement if we can all hang on to the initial commitment to change 'despite poor local fit and general system stress' (Huberman and Miles, 1984:297).

Third, we all had to learn that progress takes time. To use Smith *et al.*'s (1986) phrases, we had to face the fact that the Alternative of Grandeur—the vision we had, and needed to have at the outset of the Initiative—was giving way to the more sober and modest Alternative of Gradualness. Teachers who were on release for a year fulfilled the practical tasks they were set by their schools, but they came to see that delivering a new teaching scheme or a new set of learning resources could not guarantee change that was more than skin-deep. They duly modified their expectations of what they might achieve: 'To do this is going to take a little longer than we first imagined'; 'We are changing the world—shovelful by shovelful'. This realism brought a new understanding of the long-term and corporate nature of institutional change. Teachers came to understand more about the process of change in their own settings and the psychology of change among their own colleagues:

> I don't really believe that people don't want to relate to change. I think that they are a bit scared of how they might face up to it. I think some people are reluctant to move from secure ground.

> I think I'm more sensitive to the management of change, and attentive to the feelings involved.

> You have to create a climate where people matter and are speaking to people like people and not like animals...That's got to be understood; it's got to be felt, and felt by a group of people, a bigger group, to take that change along.

These are all hard-won insights into the process of change. They are sometimes offered with a touch of disappointment that change is so slow and so tough a process, but many teachers have learned something that the fragmented constructions of the curriculum development movement could not give—insight into the demanding task of facing and managing the continuous experience of change, including its everyday strains and internal politics.

Fourth, we learned that you can't develop shared meaning about the curriculum and about students' rights without giving attention to the structure of power relationships and trust within individual institutions. As Andy Hargreaves (1982) has said, 'Is democracy a realistic goal as long as Heads (school principals) retain final and long-standing responsibility for the decisions that are taken within schools?' In the Sheffield Initiative, teachers had been commissioned by their schools to facilitate the task of change. Once they had shifted their perception of the task from the delivery of product to the understanding of process, they began to see the complexities of change and how people and power relationships are at the heart of it: 'It's taken us half a year to realize that the task of curriculum change is about changing colleagues'. Teachers took responsibility for trying to create better opportunities for dialogue but they were at the same time wary of assuming executive power in a system that had not formally given them power. There were some compromises. While teachers took on the role of facilitating more open debate, they remained uncertain about their right to act outside the areas of their traditional responsibility and they were reluctant to open up and confront the issue of power relations: 'I'd wriggle on the word power; it sounds threatening'; 'I always get a bit uncomfortable about power'; 'I'm anxious not to give the impression of being on an ego trip and forming a power base. I don't think it's at that level'; 'We haven't been a power group. We've worked with the structure because if we set ourselves up as important people—I don't think that would be the way of doing it'.

The teachers who had been released to spearhead change had achieved a certain power through understanding, but it was not clear how they could use this power in situations where formal managerial power, operating through a hierarchy of roles, still existed. The task was to change the culture of the school. What this meant for a conventional school staff was that the ideology of separatism had to be replaced by an ideology of collegiality. But as Bates (1987) reminds us, it is not easy for insiders to examine the micro-politics of their own institution. Space has to be made and a structure created which will 'enable the articulation and where possible the resolution of conflicts contained within the cultural politics of the school' (p. 85). Management teams needed more help and support in accepting a role that offered leadership in critical analysis. The local authority, once it understood the problems, responded by giving special support to senior management teams in schools to help them work with their own seconded teachers to build a collective confidence in the possibilities of change and to clarify their own role in the process.

Tangerud and Wallin (1986:56) argue that very little school improvement can take place *unless* the existing power structures have been analyzed and a realistic strategy for action developed. The real world, of course, is not as neat nor real people as patient as these writers think they are. In Sheffield, the analysis followed on the heels of the action, and the continuity of successive cycles of teacher release seems to be a good strategy for enabling retrospective analysis and for supporting reflection-in-action, provided that the commitment to understanding the problem of change at district, institutional, group and individual levels can be sustained. Overall, more people came to understand that 'real change requires intellectual effort' (Kanter, 1983:23).

One could say that the story of the Sheffield Initiative is of teachers who became potentially radical but who stepped back a little from the hard edge of change as they confronted the traditional authority structures of their institutions and the dilemmas of interpersonal power relationships. It is also a story of the difficulty of achieving rapid system-wide developments and an acknowledgment of the importance of setting a steady pace, sustained by concerted effort and commitment, if overall change to the culture of schools and their communities is seriously addressed. And it is a story which underlines the significance of the commitment to reflection and communal understanding that the university, backed by the Local Education Authority, sought to contribute to the partnership.

The Conditions and Benefits of Partnership

The fact is that in the Sheffield Initiative, the lead time for planning was so short that the conditions of partnership were not properly worked through in advance. Moreover, the national mood was volatile and plans could be subject to sudden upheaval: indeed, fairly early on, the Government introduced new rules that dramatically affected the structure of in-service provision and made the university's contribution more problematic. However, it is possible, from the example, to see some of the advantages of such a partnership.

First, the university can offer help with specialist content in curriculum areas where staff have a particular expertise. By and large, however, it seems helpful if we can subdue our content-linked image and highlight our process skills: the skills of analysis and interpretation, of disclosing meaning, of building group commitment and understanding, and, importantly, of helping teachers, schools and local authorities to comprehend the culture of their own learning.

Second, the partners can use the combined skills available to them to offer schools, or groups of schools, support with the crucial task of understanding their own progress and achievements. Rarely have schools, in my experience, been able to develop good strategies and structures for understanding what and how teachers are learning from practice, and what they need to know about in order to improve their practice. University staff can make a useful contribution here by using qualitative and quantitative research techniques to help schools and school boards gather and use relevant information: for example, how community perceptions of a school may be changing; how staff attitudes and practices are developing in relation to a new teaching strategy; what language the school is using to talk about education; or what criteria it is using to understand and make judgements about its own performance.

Third, the university and the school board together can provide a secure environment for justifiable educational experiment in which both new and experienced teachers can feel supported in trying out new ideas; they will need explicitly to signal their readiness to protect a climate in which educationally justifiable risk-making is valued more highly than never trying anything different.

The coherence and usefulness of such partnerships will depend on the following things:

- the readiness of the partners to give up their traditional mythologies about each other, and learn to respect each other's strengths and recognize each other's needs and conditions for professional survival
- building a shared commitment to well-judged change, to exploring alternatives and to pushing back the limits of possibility in learning

- building a shared commitment to clarifying principles and purposes, and to understanding the social and political contexts in which those purposes and principles are set to work
- accepting a shared perception of teaching as one of the 'impossible professions'—impossible because it has 'ideas which admit no easy realization, [and] goals that are often multiple, ambiguous and conflicting' (Sykes and Elmore, 1988:81)
- recognizing that the pace of worthwhile change—change that achieves new cultural coherence and significance—is relatively slow and that ways have to be found of keeping up the momentum.

These are not easy commitments. Gunnar Berg has recently said that 'the basic condition of professionalization is that it must be sanctioned by the environment in which it is carried on' (1989:81). The present scene in England is not one that readily supports such commitments, and schools, local authorities and universities need to plan how best they can work together in a spirit of determination and common purpose.

The Role of a University Department of Education in Troubled Times

> Any approach to teacher education which does not encourage teachers to reflect critically on their own educational views and on the nature of education as it is realized in the institutional setting of schools will be either inherently conservative or dangerously doctrinaire. (Carr, 1986:6)

A major dilemma for university departments of education here in England is how, in the present climate of anti-intellectualism, to find ways of maintaining a relationship with teachers that does not fall short of the standard that Carr, rightly, sets for us.

University staff are now subject, as are teachers in schools, to new systems of surveillance and control, including staff appraisal, and performance analysis is used as a basis for selective central funding. The threat of cut-backs in finance and staffing makes us vulnerable to market forces in the same way that schools now are, and the danger is that this vulnerability may make us cautious where earlier we would have been more courageously defiant about the nature of our distinctive contribution to teacher education.

In relation to research, for example, we may be wary about how far to go in criticizing Government policy—and yet that has been a traditional and important responsibility of the university. It seems to me that we must keep our courage and sustain our commitment to the rigorous analysis of educational policy. In particular, we have to place on our research agenda the determinants of the research process itself (see Lundgren, 1988:18). This is a period in which administrators have considerable power to decide what research is to be financed, and it is crucial that we understand what values are constraining or directing the focus of enquiry. Such research will enable us to see more clearly 'how knowledge *about* education is created and how a language *about* education is established'—in short, how research is currently endorsed 'by being "cogged" into the state apparatus' (Lundgren, 1988).

And then there are the uncertainties about how we might work with teachers on mandated reforms that we do not fully agree with on educational grounds. Should we put all our efforts into supporting teachers in England to implement the new national imperatives, helping them to get on with and make the most of the task that Government has set them? This approach could, if we are not careful, take us close to incorporation and the loss of impetus to question and challenge. Alternatively, we could offer sustained critique and opposition. Inglis (1989:129) puts the case forcefully:

> What they (teachers) now need from their 'intellegentsia' in the schools of education, graduate courses, in-service education and training, and teachers' centres, which have (all) done so much to bring them status and space for reflection, is a theory of explicit resistance to the new authoritarianism, combined with a continuing duty to pupils.

But, as David Hargreaves (1989) has warned: 'Without alternative visions, critique deteriorates to mere criticism' (pp. 214–15). We need, I think, to combine both positions while trying to avoid undue compromise! We need to have '*usable* intellect and imagination' (Silberman, 1970:380) and our responsibility must be to give teachers support while keeping open the prospect of alternative structures and values. It is up to the university, in troubled times, to keep alive what Aronowitz and Giroux (1989) have called 'a language of possibility', and to make sure that all those who work in local partnerships to improve the quality of education, are able to go on speaking that language.

Notes

1 In England, education departments in universities, polytechnics and colleges all make a contribution to teacher education. Not all countries have such a diversity of provision and so, to avoid confusion, I have used the word 'university' throughout this paper. I hope that readers from other institutions of higher education in England will accept this simplification.
2 This section of the paper draws closely on an account of the Sheffield Initiative written by Jean Rudduck and Brian Wilcox; Brian was Chief Adviser of

the City of Sheffield Education Department (see Rudduck and Wilcox, 1988). Data were collected in interviews conducted by Jean Rudduck and Alan Skelton. A more recent account of the progress of the Sheffield Initiative is available in *Learning to Change* (Clough *et al.*, 1989).

3 In the Sheffield Initiative, Sheffield Polytechnic's Department of Education was involved on the same basis as Sheffield University's Department of Education and was an equal partner in the scheme. I have (see note 1) tried to avoid confusing readers from other countries and I use the term 'the university' to refer to both institutions.

References

ADELMAN, C. and CARR, W. (1988) 'Whatever happened to action research?', Paper presented at the British Educational Research Association Annual Conference, University of East Anglia, August, Mimeo.

ARONOWITZ, S. and GIROUX, H. (1986) *Education under Siege*, London, Routledge and Kegan Paul.

BATES, R.J. (1987) 'Corporate culture, schooling and educational administration', *Educational Administration Quarterly*, 23, 4, pp. 79–115.

BERG, G. (1989) 'Educational reform and teacher professionalism', *Journal of Curriculum Studies*, 21, 1, pp. 53–60.

CARR, W. (1986) 'Recent developments in teacher education: A response', Paper presented at the Conference on Teacher Research and INSET, University of Ulster, February, Mimeo.

CARR, W. (1989) 'Action research: Ten years on', *Journal of Curriculum Studies*, 21, 1, pp. 85–90.

CARR, W. (Ed.) (1989) *Quality in Teaching: Arguments for a Reflective Profession*, Lewes, Falmer Press.

CARR, W. and KEMMIS, S. (1983) *Becoming Critical: Knowing Through Action*, Geelong, Deakin University Press (reprinted by Falmer Press, 1987).

CLOUGH, E., ASPINWALL, K. and GIBBS, R. (Eds.) (1989) *Learning to Change: An LEA School-Focused Initiative*, Basingstoke, Falmer Press.

CRONBACH, L.J. (1975) 'Beyond the two disciplines of scientific knowledge', *American Psychologist*, 30, pp. 116–27.

DUNLOP, F. (1979) 'On the democratic organization of schools', *Cambridge Journal of Education*, 9, 1, pp. 43–54.

FULLAN, M. (1982) *The Meaning of Educational Change*, New York, Teachers College Press.

GORDON, D. (1987) 'Autonomy is more than just the absence of external constraints', in SABAR, N., RUDDUCK, J. and REID, W. (Eds.) *Partnership and Autonomy in School-Based Curriculum Development*, Occasional Papers 10, Sheffield, University of Sheffield Division of Education Publications, pp. 29–36.

HARGREAVES, A. (1982) 'The rhetoric of school-centred innovation', *Journal of Curriculum Studies*, 14, 3, pp. 251–66.

HARGREAVES, A. and REYNOLDS, D. (Eds.) (1989) *Education Policies: Controversies and Critiques*, Lewes, Falmer Press.

HARGREAVES, A. and REYNOLDS, D. (1989) 'Introduction: Decomprehensivisation', in HARGREAVES, A. and REYNOLDS, D. (Eds.), *Educational Policies: Controversies and Critiques*, Lewes, Falmer Press, pp. 1–32.

HARGREAVES, D. (1989) 'Educational policy and educational change: A local perspective', in HARGREAVES, A. and REYNOLDS, D. (Eds.), *Educational Policies: Controversies and Critiques*, Lewes, Falmer Press, pp. 213–17.

HUBERMAN, A.M. and MILES, M.B. (1984) *Innovation up Close: How School Improvement Works*, New York, Plenum Press.

HULL, C., RUDDUCK, J. and SIGSWORTH, A. (1984) *A Room Full of Children Thinking*, London, Longmans for the Schools Council.

ILLICH, I. (1981) *Shadow Work*, Marion Boyars Publications.

INGLIS, F. (1989) 'Theory and tyranny: The strange death of democratic England', *Cambridge Journal of Education*, 19, 2, pp. 123–30.

JONATHAN, R. (1987) 'Review Essay on S. ARONOWITZ and H. GIROUX, Education under Siege', *Journal of Curriculum Studies*, 19, 2, pp. 584–7.

KANTER, R.M. (1983) *The Change Masters: Innovation and Entrepreneurship in the American Corporation*, New York, Simon and Schuster.

LAWN, M. (1989) 'Being caught in schoolwork: The possibilities of research in teachers' work', in CARR, W. (Ed.), *Quality in Teaching: Arguments for a Reflective Profession*, Lewes, Falmer Press, pp. 147–61.

LEWY, A. (1987) 'Can teachers produce high quality curriculum material?', in SABAR, N., RUDDUCK, J. and REID, W. (Eds.), *Partnership and Autonomy in School-Based Curriculum Development*, Occasional Papers 10, Sheffield, University of Sheffield Division of Education Publications, pp. 84–6.

LUNDGREN, U. (1988) '"Social engineering": Practical versus disciplinarian knowledge in Swedish post-war educational planning', *Studies of Higher Education and Research, Newsletter of the Research on Higher Education Program, Sweden*, 6, 1–23.

POPKEWITZ, T.S., TABACHNIK, R.B. and WEHLAGE, G. (1982) *The Myth of Educational Reform*, Wisconsin, University of Wisconsin Press.

RUDDUCK, J. (1979) 'A study of traditions in the development of short in-service courses for teachers', unpublished Ph.D. Thesis, University of East Anglia.

RUDDUCK, J. (1988) 'Changing the world of the classroom by understanding it: A review of some aspects of the work of Lawrence Stenhouse', *Journal of Curriculum and Supervision*, 4, 1, pp. 30–42.

RUDDUCK, J. and WILCOX, B. (1988) 'Issues of ownership and partnership in school-centred innovation', *Research Papers in Education*, 3, 3, pp. 157–79.

SABAR, N. and SILBERSTEIN, M. (1987) 'Can we train teachers to improve the quality of curriculum materials?', in SABAR, N., RUDDUCK, J. and REID, W. (Eds.), *Partnership and Autonomy in School-Based Curriculum Development*, Occasional Papers 10, Sheffield, University of Sheffield Division of Education Publications, pp. 87–96.

SABAR, N., RUDDUCK, J. and REID, W. (Eds.) (1987) *Partnership and Autonomy in School-Based Curriculum Development*, Occasional Papers 10, Sheffield, University of Sheffield Division of Education Publications.

SCHWAB, J.J. (1956) 'Science and civil discourse: The users of diversity', *Journal of General Education*, pp. 132–43.

SCHWAB, J.J. (1970) 'The practical: A language for the curriculum', Paper given at the AERA Annual Conference and printed by the National Education Association's Centre for the Study of Instruction.

SCHWAB, J.J. (1984) 'The practical 4: Something for curriculum professors to do', *Curriculum Inquiry*, 13, 3, pp. 239–65.

SILBERMAN, C.E. (1970) *Crisis in the Classroom: The Remaking of American Education*, New York, Vintage Books.

SMITH, L.M. *et al.* (1986) *Educational Innovators: Then and Now*, Lewes, Falmer Press.

Jean Rudduck

STENHOUSE, L.A. (1979) 'Using research means doing research', in DAHL, H., LYSNE, A. and RAND, P. (Eds.), *Pedagogikkens Sokelys: Festskrift til Johannes Sandven*, Oslo, Oslo Universitets Forlaget.

STENHOUSE, L.A. (1980) 'The teacher as focus of research and development', in HOPKINS, D. and WIDEEN, M. (Eds.) (1984), *Alternative Perspectives on School Improvement*, Lewes, Falmer Press.

SYKES, G. and ELMORE, R.F. (1988) 'Making schools manageable', in HANNAWAY, S. and CROWSON, R. (Eds.), *The Politics of Reforming School Administration* (special issue of *The Journal of Educational Policy*, 3, 5, pp. 77–94).

TANGERUD, H. and WALLIN, E. (1986) 'Values and contextual factors in school improvement', *Journal of Curriculum Studies*, 18, 1, pp. 45–61.

WESTBURY, J. and WILKOF, N.J. (Eds.) (1978) *J.J. Schwab: Science, Curriculum and Liberal Education—Selected Essays*, Chicago, University of Chicago Press.

Chapter 11

Beyond School District-University Partnerships

Nancy Watson and Michael G. Fullan

Both schools and universities have attempted to bring about improvements in teaching and learning, without much success (Fullan, 1991; Sarason, 1990). Schools are routinely criticized for their inability to alter the learning experiences of students and to improve the working conditions of teachers, while faculties of education are seen as irrelevant to schools. At the same time, universities are seen as neglectful of faculties and colleges of education and teacher education.

Persistent problems have accompanied attempts at reform in both types of institutions. Introducing innovations, revising curricula, changing structures, bringing in new leadership—all seem to reinforce the notion that the more things change the more they remain the same. In this context, collaboration between school systems and universities has been increasingly advocated as a potentially more powerful strategy for improving education (Gross, 1988; Sirotnik and Goodlad, 1988). While we will argue that people have underestimated how very deep such changes are, we will also claim that basic change in the relationship between schools and universities is a *sine qua non* of educational reform.

Although school improvement and teacher development are often approached separately, we argue that the two are inextricably related. Staff development can be a strategy for implementing specific improvements, but more importantly, it can also be a strategy for basic organizational change in the way schools operate (Fullan, 1990).

Thus two assumptions are central to rethinking the relationship between schools and teacher development:

- Teacher education or teacher development is a career-long continuum from the earliest through the latest stages of being a teacher.
- Teacher development and school development must go hand in hand. In general, you cannot have one without the other.

In order for these two assumptions to be realized there must be major institutional changes in school systems and faculties of education, and in the relationships between them. As we shall see, we are talking about changes not only in the *cultures* of these two traditional types of institutions, but also in their *cultural relationships*. The latter raises acute and complex problems for change and improvement, because the cultures of school systems and the cultures of universities differ from each other in basic and profound ways.

In this chapter we will examine a major district–university partnership called the *Learning Consortium*. The Learning Consortium is based on a comprehensive framework of partnership among four large school districts and two higher education institutions in the greater Toronto area (see Fullan, Bennett and Rolheiser-Bennett, 1990). We will first briefly consider the literature on district–university collaboration in order to identify the key issues and themes involved. Second, we will look at the Learning Consortium as an example of such a school–university partnership. Third, we report and comment on some of the activities in the Learning Consortium (both collectively and in the partner organizations) over its first three years of operation. Fourth, we discuss the main issues and dilemmas we have identified through our experience with one particular partnership venture.

Finally a word about the title of the chapter. District–university partnerships should not be seen as just the latest project. We use the term 'beyond' advisedly to emphasize that district–university partnerships represent a new and ongoing way for schools and faculties of education to relate to each other. Successful partnerships bring benefits through their joint initiatives, but perhaps more crucial in the long run, through the organizational and educational changes that are sparked by such joint ventures. Successful partnerships are difficult to achieve, but have great promise for lifting attempts at reform to a qualitatively higher level of effectiveness.

1 Partnerships: A Look at the Territory

Successful field-based teacher education programmes, at the pre-service, induction or in-service level, blend the best of theory and practice. However, such a task cannot be carried out successfully by universities or school systems alone: both need to be involved. Goals such as better educational inquiry and better professional teacher preparation should involve both university and school educators, since research and professional practice bear directly on what goes on in both kinds of institutions (Brookhart and Loadman, 1989). Because existing organizations are not designed to plan or implement collaborative programmes involving several stakeholders, organizational 'hybrids' such as school–university partnerships are a particularly exciting possibility for filling the gap. As Goodlad observes:

The argument for school–university partnerships proceeds somewhat as follows. For schools to get better, they must have better teachers, among other things. To prepare better teachers (and counsellors, special educators and administrators), universities must have access to schools using the best practices. To have the best practices, schools need access to new ideas and knowledge. This means that universities have a stake in school improvement just as schools have a stake in the education of teachers. (Goodlad, 1985:6)

Collaboration is necessary where parties have a shared interest in solving a problem that none of them can resolve alone. Collaboration makes sense where stakeholders recognize the potential advantages of working together—they need each other to execute a vision they all share, and they need the others to advance their individual interests. Such a partnership represents an ideal, a goal toward which collaborative ventures can aspire, although the literature often reveals that partnerships are more limited in practice.

Much of the literature represents descriptions or case studies of individual partnerships (e.g. Conyers 1988; Kennedy 1987; Piscolish *et al.*, 1988; Sinclair and Harrison 1988; Williams 1988), with few comparisons to enable the development of conceptual frameworks, although there are exceptions (Gross 1988; Havelock 1985; Mickelson *et al.*, 1988; Rudduck 1992; Sirotnik and Goodlad 1988). In the present paper, we will try to develop a framework for understanding school–university partnerships and their outcomes.

In discussing such partnerships, terminology becomes crucial. As Clark (1988) has pointed out:

One of the complications of investigating this subject is that different terms are used to describe similar activities, and on the other hand, different meanings are attached to the same term. Authors speak of partnerships, collaborations, consortiums, networks, clusters, inter-organizational agreements, collectives, and cooperatives, frequently without definition and often without distinguishing their chosen description from other possible terms. (p. 33)

Mickelson *et al.* (1988) report that 'collaboration, cooperation, and partnership are terms that are often used synonymously in the literature when describing joint ventures between schools and universities' (p. 4). They go on to suggest that collaboration is most frequently used because of the 'proactive, coequal, problem-solving image it conveys' (p. 4).

Barriers to collaboration have been noted and described by virtually all those who have explored the field. Gray (1989), for instance, identifies conflicts over plans for how a vision should be carried out, problems in implementing agreements, and difficulties in overcoming the barriers created by different institutional cultures.

In order to resolve such problems, certain conditions seem necessary. Sirotnik and Goodlad (1988) have identified three conditions as essential for setting up collaborative relationships:

- a moderate degree of dissimilarity among partners
- the potential for mutual satisfaction of self interests
- sufficient selflessness on the part of each partner to assure satisfaction of self interests by all (a symbiotic relationship)

These three criteria, particularly the last, are more likely to serve as goals toward which partnerships can strive, rather than descriptions of actual partnerships in action.

In examining the notion of collaboration, Gray (1989) identifies five critical features. She concludes that:

- Collaboration implies interdependence, an ongoing give and take.
- Solutions emerge by dealing constructively with differences. Partners must work beyond stereotypes to rethink their views about each other.
- Collaboration involves joint ownership of decisions.
- Stakeholders assume collective responsibility for future direction of the domain.
- Collaboration is an emergent process: through negotiations and interactions, rules for governing future interactions are actually restructured. (p. 11)

Organizational Structures and Processes

In most cases where school–university partnerships have been organized, some forms of cooperation already existed between the partners. Why then formalize the relationship? Havelock (1985) argues that the structure developed provides a coordinating framework for integrating a variety of efforts and resources to achieve identified common goals, and by weaving together the power of many institutions, we increase the chance that initiatives will actually make a difference. Once such a decision has been made, the partnership needs to develop structures for 'making decisions, allocating resources, proposing and developing projects, keeping track of activities, etc.' (Sirotnik, 1988:8). Within these categories, issues of governance and administration that must be dealt with include: financial arrangements, appointing a coordinator or director, deciding on membership of governing committees, agreeing on channels for communicating information, and so on.

Perhaps more important than the type of structure in school–university partnerships is the process through which the partnership develops—the way its members work together. Gaining commitment, developing trust and ownership, communicating openly and effectively, recognizing and resolving problems: all these are vital. One organizational feature that deserves note is the issue of type and degree of planning. Anderson and Cox (1988) for example, support the idea of emergent planning as opposed to a high degree of detailed pre-planning. Sirotnik (1988) concluded that getting involved in actual activities dealing with fundamental educational tasks is crucial in new partnership initiatives. As writers such as Clark (1980) have pointed out, it is more common for interesting goals to emerge from human activity than for them to direct these activities in the first place. Reflecting on initial actions is what helps objectives to become clearer, and more detailed plans to evolve. In other words, collaboration is an emergent process, and as we have suggested elsewhere, the best advice may be to 'start small, think big' (Fullan, 1991).

Relating to the Broader Organizational Context

Rarely have those writing about school–university partnerships explored organizational variables beyond looking at the structure of the partnership arrangement itself, and in some cases looking at activities in schools. What is missing is an examination of how the new partnership fits within the framework of school system and university operation. School innovations are more likely to succeed when closely linked to a system focus. Similarly, school-university partnerships, to be effective, need to influence the classroom, the school and the wider school system, as well as the system of teacher education. New initiatives need to be coordinated and integrated with existing priorities. Indeed, since most school improvement efforts are fragmented, the most effective new initiatives will be ones that actually synergize and focus the activities of the institution.

Organizational Cultures: Different Worlds of Field and University

Virtually every writer who has written about school–university partnerships has pointed out that schools and universities are different worlds, and that the cultural and operational differences, between them mean that collaboration is fraught with miscommunication, misunderstanding, and other difficulties. Hargreaves (1989) captured the differences when he referred to schools as the 'world of commitment' with universities as the 'world of questioning'. Another writer phrased it as follows:

Public schools are held captive by legislative and board directives and are almost daily asked to expand their roles to meet
such emergencies as substance abuse, racism, fragmented families, and sexually-transmitted diseases—to name only a few.
On the other hand, universities are insulated so well from the
vicissitudes of governmental decision makers that they are
often held captive by a form of lethargic scholasticism. Those
differences become painfully obvious when attempts are made
to create partnerships between universities and public schools.
(Ervay & Lumley, 1989:10)

Brookhart and Loadman (1989) suggest that the cultures of
universities and school systems differ on four key dimensions: (1)
work tempo and the nature of professional time, (2) professional
focus, from theoretical to practical, (3) chosen reward structure, and
(4) sense of personal power and efficacy. For school teachers compared to university professors, work tempo is more immediate and
short-term; the focus of concern is more practical and applied; rewards are tied up more in the reaction of pupils rather than larger
projects and publications; and their sense of personal power and efficacy is less well developed. These differences become magnified when
strong forms of collaboration are undertaken—when decisions and
activities are jointly planned, carried out, and assessed. However, it
should be noted to the extent that university faculty in colleges of
education work directly with student teachers, their professional culture may be more similar to that of schools.

In summary, we can learn from each other, but we also need to
change some aspects of both types of cultures. A real difference in
focus in the two types of organizations justifies to some extent the
differences between them, since universities have as part of their
primary mandate the production of knowledge, while schools by the
very nature of their mission are more concerned with day-to-day
practical issues. Nonetheless, working in isolation from each other,
both schools and universities tend to accept uncritically their own
views of education. In working together, universities may become
more focused on outcomes and accountability, while schools and
school systems may become more reflective and coherent in their
approaches. Working closely together requires not only communication and understanding, but also shifts in behaviour. It is difficult to
avoid stereotypes and build on an acknowledgment of differences,
but commitment to a partnership, with constant interaction around
joint tasks, may lead to reconceptualizations of responsibilities, to the
mutual benefit of both.

What have we said so far about the desirability and nature of
district-university collaboration?

- Schools/school systems and universities (at least faculties of education) need each other to be successful.
- They are dissimilar in key aspects of structure, culture and reward systems.
- Working together potentially can provide the coherence, coordination, and persistence essential to teacher and school development.
- Both parties must work hard at working together—forging new structures, respecting each other's culture, and using shared experiences to problem-solve by incorporating the strengths of each culture.
- Strong partnerships will not happen by accident, good will or establishing *ad hoc* projects. They require new structures, new activities, and a rethinking of the internal workings of each institution as well as their inter-institutional workings.

Partnerships are thus serious endeavours to bring about new institutional development—to work together to make one's own institution more effective at addressing valued mandates hitherto neglected or poorly achieved.

Goodlad (1988) signals the scope of these efforts when he lays down essentials for structuring each partnership. These include:

- a governing board
- a modest secretariat paid from the partnership budget
- an operating budget providing both money and assigned personnel from participating institutions, with sufficient funds for the task
- top-level endorsement and support from each institution
- task forces or working parties to develop strategies for addressing critical problems of improving schools and the education of educators
- an orderly process of endorsing and encouraging all projects and activities undertaken in the partnership
- documentation, analysis, and communication of successes and failures (and reasons)
- arrangements for sharing information, ideas, and resources within and across partnerships (p. 28).

Sirotnik and Goodlad (1988) make a point that is easily overlooked; that 'the nature of these synergistic processes and their outcomes is not at all clear' (p. 218). In other words, we are engaged in a *social experiment*. A basic assumption is that together we will attempt and discover through inquiry and problem-solving better ways of doing things. The agenda then must be 'specific enough to bind participants in a common enterprise but general enough to allow for individuality and creativity' (p. 219).

A Conceptual Framework

Based on a consideration of what has been written about school–university partnerships, the following is proposed as a simple framework for making sense of any such partnership venture:

- *Context*: What is the background, the history of cooperation between the partners? How did the partnership come about? What is the nature of the organizations? What were their reasons for joining?
- *Rationale*: What is the underlying purpose? What objectives does the partnership have? What reasons are there for assuming a partnership will be successful in this case?
- *Structure*: What are the organizational arrangements? How is the partnership governed? What are the mechanisms and procedures for making decisions, communicating with each other, coordinating initiatives and so on?
- *Focus*: What is the agenda? What is the vision, the content, the issue the partnership has decided to address? What does the partnership actually do?
- *Process*: How does the partnership develop over time? What are the relationships among the members? What is the balance of power and influence? How are issues of centralization and decentralization dealt with? How do organizational cultures interact?
- *Beyond the partnership*: As the partnership progresses, what happens? Are there substantial changes taking place in the partner organizations (school systems and universities)? What is the impact of the partnership on both short-term and long-term goals of each institution?

Although the resolution will differ in various partnerships, these issues need to be considered and dealt with. The factors that must be addressed include:

- the meaning and type of partnership and collaboration
- interaction of the different organizational cultures involved
- managing the change process
- integrating the school-university partnership with prior policy and initiatives
- fostering ongoing inquiry and evaluation, and ensuring that they feed into ongoing work

Table 11.1:   *Organizations in the Learning Consortium*

Boards	Students	Teachers	Schools
Dufferin-Peel	61,000	3,300	96
Durham	52,000	3,100	102
Halton	44,000	2,600	82
North York	59,000	3,700	142

University Members	Students	Faculty	
FEUT	1200 (B.Ed.)	100	
OISE	700 full time	150	
	1600 part time		
	(grad.)		

- capitalizing on opportunities for synergistic outcomes
- allowing for both change and permanence in the partnership.

In looking at any given partnership, the relative importance of different factors changes. For instance, in a context favourable to partnership, in which organizations are building on a history of cooperation, there is more leeway in setting the agenda. In other situations, determining a clear focus would be essential as a first step in a partnership venture. However, although there may be different starting points, a common agenda is to establish permanent partnerships between schools and universities.

2   The Learning Consortium: Background, Objectives and Context

The Learning Consortium is a teacher development partnership formed by four school boards in the vicinity of metropolitan Toronto (the Dufferin-Peel Separate School Board, the Durham Board of Education, the Halton Board of Education, and the North York Board of Education), together with the Faculty of Education at the University of Toronto, and the Ontario Institute for Studies in Education. The Consortium commenced in 1988. Table 11.1, indicates the size of the organizations that have joined together in this partnership arrangement.

A variety of factors led to the formation of the Learning Consortium, among them:

- As part of a wide-ranging review of teacher education in Ontario, a position paper on teacher education (Fullan & Connelly, and Watson 1990) was widely circulated throughout the province, suggesting both increased collaboration

among those involved in teacher education, and the importance of the teacher education continuum.

- School boards, already active in developing high quality professional development programmes, were interested in collaborating with each other and with universities to support
  these initiatives, and to go beyond what they were already
  doing.
- The Faculty of Education, University of Toronto, was beginning a process of renewal, following a long period in which
  there had been few resources and little growth.
- There was interest in developing closer links between the
  Ontario Institute for Studies in Education and the Faculty of
  Education.

Context

The context in which the partnership developed was a positive one,
favourable to innovation and growth. Teacher education in Ontario,
including pre-service and in-service phases, was not seen to be in
crisis. On the other hand, the system was not seen as particularly
effective. The latter, combined with a growing need for more
teachers, a better knowledge base, and the appointment of new leaders
at all levels of the system, including the partner organizations, generated an impetus for reform. Such a favourable context represented a
'window of opportunity' for all six member organizations to build on
their individual accomplishments, and to re-focus for the future.

Rationale

The aim of the Consortium is to improve the quality of education in
schools and universities by focusing on teacher development. Recall
the two basic assumptions: teacher development is a career-long continuum; and teacher development and school improvement go hand in
hand. It was explicitly recognized that realizing these two assumptions, taken together, would require greater system development and
coherence. School districts and the universities would have to change
in ways that provided greater system support and coordination within
their organizations as well across institutions.

Structure

The initial commitment was for three years, during which each partner agreed to contribute money, time and personnel to support what
soon became an expanding and increasingly complex set of initiatives.

The Learning Consortium was formed as a partnership based on a pooling of resources and on shared decision-making among the members. During the first year the group established a framework for collaboration, carried out a range of initiatives, and built a foundation for working together in the future. The primary decision-making body is a Planning Group, composed of one representative from each of the six member organizations, with meetings chaired by a Consortium Coordinator, a full-time employee hired by the partnership. A Steering Group composed of the Directors of the school boards and of OISE, and the Dean of the Faculty of Education, meets annually to review the year and suggest priorities for the future.

Focus

On the basis of the assumptions concerning teaching as life-long learning, and the necessity of viewing teacher development as inextricably linked to school improvement, the Consortium set out:

- To plan and initiate new programmes that incorporated the two basic assumptions
- To monitor and document these programme developments
- To engage actively in the growing knowledge-base on teacher development and school improvement by drawing on it as well as contributing to it through dissemination.

Such a focus set out our overall agenda, but we were also committed to launching specific initiatives. Through processes both serendipitous and deliberate, we began with an emphasis on cooperative small-group learning, a theme which provided a concrete agenda to get us under way, and influenced other programme developments over the two years. By the beginning of Year 3, in-service professional development programmes, such as summer institutes on cooperative learning and peer coaching, had been supplemented by the development of a pre-service programme, by conferences on such collaborative approaches as mentoring, induction, and peer coaching, and by other programmes offering perspectives on school improvement and change. At first glance, such a set of teacher development initiatives might seem somewhat unrelated to each other. However, the Consortium attempted to link these programmes by paying attention to consistent themes which weave through the various initiatives, themes such as: teaching as life-long learning; fostering collaboration in the school; and a focus on instruction as the link between teacher development and school improvement.

In addition to formally established activities and programmes, a variety of less formal practices evolved, also aimed at integrating a set of varied Learning Consortium activities. These encompassed:

the networking, reflective and monitoring strategies of the coordinator, the bridging and implementation action taken by the Planning Group members within the unique culture of their respective organizations, and the emerging linking and school improvement efforts by Summer Institute participants in their schools. (Thiessen, 1989:5)

By the third year of operation, Consortium activities had evolved (although not as smoothly as that word might suggest) into an inter-connected web within and across the six organizations. As an integral part of the Learning Consortium work, ongoing documentation and evaluation of activities was undertaken, with the results made available to the Planning Group (e.g. Thiessen, 1989; Scane and Watson, 1990; Watson *et al.*, 1989).

Process

Although some attention was given to structures and procedures at the beginning of the partnership, the priority was more on getting some initial activities under way. Such a *modus operandi* was based partly on the notion that a broad agenda combined with specific initial activities would encompass the kind of developmental or evolutionary planning needed, while at the same time addressing the need for short-term accountability felt particularly by the school board representatives.

The Planning Group meets each month, with the agenda emphasizing implementation of joint programme initiatives. More recently the Planning Group has set aside time to focus on discussion of interesting programmes and ideas in each organization, on considering knowledge arising from research and evaluation, and on planning how best to build on accomplishments. Between meetings, communication among the group has been largely through telephone and fax, although group members may meet for specific planning purposes and see each other at field-based events. Membership in the Planning Group has changed somewhat over the time of the Learning Consortium. In Year 3, only the Coordinator and two board representatives were in the original group. Although the transitions associated with changing membership have been relatively smooth, the new representatives often needed considerable time to 'catch up' with the history and purposes of the group.

Beyond the Partnership

Learning Consortium involvement in joint initiatives, through exposure to new ideas and commitment to common enterprises, in turn contributed to other significant changes in the partner organizations. We will argue that over the period of Consortium involvement the school boards, through processes both deliberate and fortuitous, shifted their professional development and school improvement practices in the direction of a more coordinated and focused human resource system.

3   A Progress Report: Learning Consortium Activities

Joint Initiatives

Summer Institutes: The Summer Institutes—held each year—have been a major joint programme initiative. Over 350 educators from Consortium organizations have participated in five-day intensive residential workshops on *Cooperative Small Group Learning, Coaching,* and *The Management of Educational Change*. The emphasis was on helping educators broaden the range of teaching strategies used in classrooms and schools (For a fuller account, see Watson, 1988; Watson, 1989).

Follow-up from the Summer Institutes: Ongoing follow-up throughout the implementation process has been a key feature of the Learning Consortium work. Planning Group representatives worked together to ensure support at the local, system, and Consortium levels. Follow-up activities in schools were wide-ranging: support came from peers, from the administration, from consultants visiting schools to provide assistance, and increasingly from participants in previous summer institutes. Through such ongoing support, educators were encouraged to implement what they had learned, and to work with their colleagues in the process. In addition to these board (or faculty) specific activities, Consortium-wide support was provided—both to strengthen learning and to infuse relevant new ideas. Such central support included follow-up workshops and a regular newsletter. (For more detail, see Fullan, Bennett & Rolheiser-Bennett 1990, Watson *et al.*, 1989, Scane and Watson, 1990).

Other Programme Initiatives: Although they will not be discussed in detail, several other programmes were in place by 1990–91, all of them related to linking the phases of the teacher development continuum, and to linking teacher development and school improvement. *Cadre*: One initiative aimed at building the professional development capacity of school systems by developing a cadre of instructional process specialists. Following training, participants have been taking an active role in providing workshops and informal support for other colleagues, both beginning and experienced teachers. *Pre-service and induction*: A Learning Consortium field-based programme for pre-service students at the Faculty of Education aimed at helping students integrate theory and practice in a collaborative field-university setting. In the area of induction for beginning teachers, two working conferences brought universities and schools together, while in Year 3, through the Faculty of Education at the University of Toronto, we have initiated an induction project combining informal support from two faculty members, a series of one-day workshops, and a computer conferencing network enabling the beginning teachers to discuss issues with each other and with the faculty members. *Graduate Studies*: A new OISE/Learning Consortium doctoral programme will, by integrating field development and research inquiry more closely than has been possible to date, foster the development of more sustained research initiatives within the Learning Consortium. In collaboration with the Consortium school boards, graduate student dissertation research will be closely tied to Learning Consortium and board priorities as well as their professional interests.

Our success in launching such common projects should not obscure the difficulties and limitations involved in the process. In the words of a Planning Group representative, 'When you're committing to collaboration, you're committing to conflict'. For example, within the Planning Group, difficulties in communicating between meetings often led to delays in making decisions or in responding to requests, as well as to some misunderstandings and disagreements. These were exacerbated by lack of clarity concerning the role of the Planning Group and that of the Coordinator. Examples of such difficulties include an occasion early in the partnership in which the Coordinator encouraged a group of subject coordinators from the four school boards to approach the Learning Consortium for assistance with a project; the request raised concerns in the school boards about people doing 'end-runs', and not going through the appropriate channels. Such difficulties have for the most part been resolved through ongoing discussion, and appropriate procedures have been developed for dealing with potentially difficult issues. In this particular instance, we have developed a system of mini-grants to support cross-board or board-Faculty collaborative projects.

Extensive negotiation was normally required before a project could be launched as a joint initiative, and many proposals were rejected for one reason or another. Relevant to decisions were factors such as: anticipated benefits to each organization, consistency with the Learning Consortium mandate, and the possibility of conflict with policies or procedures in the partner organizations, as well as concern with spreading ourselves too thin and losing focus. Logistical questions also were involved (large numbers of participants, difficulty in gathering people together over larger distances and so on). In some cases, school boards felt their interests were best served by an individual rather than a common venture. We had, for instance, discussed the development of joint Learning Consortium programmes for induction of beginning teachers, and for preparation of school administrators, but for a variety of reasons, the school boards concluded that their needs were best served by each developing its own programme in these areas.

The different priorities of school systems and universities also had a bearing on the discussions and decisions about joint initiatives. School systems, particularly in the early stages of the Learning Consortium, were more concerned with visible short-term benefits than were the university partners, and also were more focused on programme rather than research or dissemination activities. In initiatives such as the cadre of instructional specialists or the field-focused doctoral programme, it became clear that each school board has quite different procedures for making decisions, for soliciting applications from interested staff, and for selecting participants to represent the school system. Such organizational differences inevitably add to the complexity and time lines of Consortium ventures.

However, even in cases where an idea did not result in a common project, discussion in the Planning Group may have had an impact— such negotiations demonstrated the truth of Gray's (1989) observation that collaboration is an emergent process, and that negotiations shape the nature of future interactions. As the partnership developed, Planning Group representatives were increasingly apt to acknowledge the perspectives of the other partners, and even individual school board programmes were more likely to be influenced by ideas and resources gained in the partnership. Each partner represents a large complex organization. To be successful, the partners needed to be committed in principle to the value of working together, and be willing to trust that it could be worked out. A willingness to treat inter-institutional problems as 'normal', especially at the early stages of development, was required.

'Spin-offs': Within each partner organization, a number of additional initiatives emerged, closely related to Consortium activities and influenced by Learning Consortium work, yet outside the partnership framework. Related activities include induction programmes for newly hired teachers and mentors, in-service workshops or courses jointly taught by faculty members from the university and school board personnel, and leadership programmes for principals and vice-principals. We maintain that the Consortium provided the catalyst for such spin-offs to occur, as school systems attempted to bring about new institutional developments and coordination.

Another spin-off has been the growing cooperation and exchange across the four school districts. Districts rarely have access to each other's internal planning and policy considerations, or to each other's internal expertise and external resources (such as the use of outside consultants). In the Learning Consortium, school boards now issue invitations to participate in or find out about each other's work. When an outside consultant is brought in, for example, other boards are often invited to send participants. These and other examples of mutual exchange are above and beyond the joint activities carried out collectively by the Learning Consortium.

A third spin-off is the changing attitude toward research on the part of the school boards, which suggests how values and priorities have shifted over the two years. One school board representative spoke of how research on Consortium programmes has provided 'a mirror on our work', giving information that is only available from such a perspective, and stressed the value of having such feedback not about professional development in general, but about 'our own programmes'.

Other Planning Group representatives spoke spontaneously and powerfully about becoming avid and discerning consumers of research, and have described how research literature to which they had access was influencing work within the school boards. In one case:

> I was given a lot of resource material...that I brought back and shared with supervisory officers and principals. There was a sharing and a build-up of understanding...People saw that what we were suggesting about school-based improvement was conceptually sound. It was helpful to know that these ideas that we were talking about were being tried in various areas and jurisdictions in North America with a lot of success.

All these developments demonstrate a growing interest in improving schools, and all of them demonstrate the growing acceptance of the importance of career-long learning for education professionals. Although some of these developments are not formally part of the Consortium, they would have been less likely to occur without the impetus of the collaborative work. In the next section, we will explore how involvement in the Consortium encouraged such 'spin-offs' to occur, and how Consortium members were able to pick up threads and weave various related initiatives together to articulate and support core policies around teacher development and school improvement.

Meaning of Consortium Membership for Partner Organizations

Although much of the activity spawned by the Learning Consortium has been directed at classroom and school improvement (see Fullan, Bennett and Rolheiser-Bennett, 1990; Watson, 1989; Watson *et al.*, 1989), the emphasis of the current paper is more on institutional coherence and institutional development. In this section we will try to look at what Consortium membership has meant for each organization. We will argue that the Consortium organizations, in processes

both serendipitous and deliberate, are integrating the various initiatives inside and outside the Consortium, thereby achieving greater
coordination and impact.[1]

Each of the six Consortium organizations entered the Consortium with somewhat different expectations and priorities, and of
course each brought different organizational realities to the partnership. As noted earlier, from the perspective of the four school
boards in particular, Learning Consortium ideas, initiatives, support,
and research weave in and out through system plans and programmes,
making it difficult to say what is a Learning Consortium venture and
what is not. It is not any one initiative or programme that has had the
impact on staff development, but rather the cumulative effect of
Consortium and Consortium-related initiatives linking up with and
supporting other developments in the system.

In two school boards, Dufferin-Peel and Durham, the Consortium served to support and perhaps suggest a focus and possible
direction for a strengthened staff development programme. The situation in the other two boards was somewhat different. Halton and
North York had, prior to the formation of the Learning Consortium,
more developed policies, plans and programmes in the area of professional development. Since both systems realized that an 'add-on'
would be of no benefit, the issue has been how to integrate initiatives
arising from the new partnership with ongoing policies and programmes. For both university partners, the impact has been more to
encourage programme change in the direction of a greater field focus.

For the school boards, some of the key areas of impact are as
follows:

- *Cooperative learning*: In all four boards, cooperative learning
  emerged as a major focus and an integrating theme. This was
  particularly notable in boards such as Durham and Halton,
  where cooperative small-group learning became a high priority not only for schools which had participated in the summer
  institutes, but for the entire system. In Durham for instance,
  the Consortium served as a vehicle for helping to develop a
  coherent set of professional development and school improvement initiatives out of what had been a substantial but somewhat fragmented collection of activities. One Planning Group
  representative noted that cooperative learning:

  > seems to be a tying together kind of strategy that
  > allows people to do each one of those things better.
  > New curriculum guidelines call for students to work
  > in small groups, with student evaluation to reflect
  > this...Up to the point of the Learning Consortium
  > [we didn't know] how to go about training teachers
  > so they could do effective small-group learning, and

yet here it was in the guidelines. My God, how were they going to do it?

- *Instructional strategies*: Just as school systems were refocusing staff development on improving instruction in the classroom, Consortium programmes were providing assistance with instructional strategies, but within a context of collegiality in the workplace.

  The North York Board for instance was interested in developing and refining strategies for implementing coaching and mentoring programmes within the new framework. After some initial struggles about how the Learning Consortium could support this, North York was able to see an emphasis on instruction as providing additional content for their coaching programme—in the words of the Planning Group representative: 'It has given us a good answer to the question, "coaching for what?" We hadn't been clear exactly where we were going, and the Consortium has helped us.'

- *Supporting beginning teachers*. This has become a focus for all the school systems, but each has used the Learning Consortium somewhat differently. In Dufferin-Peel, the need for large numbers of new teachers (upwards of 600 needed each year) has meant that provision of new teacher support has become the key around which many other programmes develop. Learning Consortium involvement assisted the board in developing support for beginning teachers, while again an emphasis on a more collegial workplace has provided a framework for such programmes. In Halton, the group of teachers and consultants who attended the first Summer Institute were responsible for planning for a system-wide mentor teacher programme which has developed into a solid introduction to a process of career-long collaborative growth.

- *School-based staff development*. The Learning Consortium emphasis on the collaborative workplace reinforced school-based development, and helped to clarify the role of the principal in such efforts. In Halton, such efforts were linked to the system strategic plan, which in turn emphasized 'school growth plans' developed within the framework of system priorities.

- *A model of professional development as a continuing process*. The pattern of Summer Institutes followed by ongoing support has influenced how teachers and administrators view professional development. School board representatives report that participants are now more apt to see a workshop as simply the first step in making a change in their practice in schools. Educators are thus bringing a more sophisticated approach to both professional development and school improvement, as teaching is becoming synonymous with 'life-long learning'.

- *Increased professional development capacity in the system.* Through involvement in the summer institutes, the cadre, and the work of Learning Consortium consultants, school boards developed greatly increased capacity for promoting growth within their own systems. In Halton for instance, the original Summer Institute team have been particularly effective as leaders in the system. The common focus and frequent networking increased their impact beyond what might have been anticipated, given their dispersal in a range of different locations throughout the region. In Durham, teachers increasingly took a leadership role in introducing and sustaining cooperative learning within their schools, while in North York a group of Science teachers has taken a similar role in the school system.

- *Impact of outside ideas and resources.* On the interaction with other Consortium organizations, one Planning Group representative noted: 'Of great benefit...have been the collegial relationships with the staff of our other partners in the Learning Consortium. The synergy that has come from sharing, discussing, and observing has given us professional growth opportunities beyond what we could have done alone.'

- *System-wide linkage among different programmes.* This last factor may be the most crucial factor in determining the meaning of Consortium membership for each school board. In Halton for instance, the focus on instruction and on collaborative work cultures was consistent with the new board plan in which consultants work on helping schools identify and meet their needs within the framework provided by system priorities. North York has integrated much of the Learning Consortium work with its 'Supervision for Growth' framework to ensure that it supports system priorities. Durham has strongly supported the expansion of cooperative learning as the focus of much of the expanding professional development. In Dufferin–Peel, on the other hand, there has been less system coordination of Consortium activities. This is due to factors such as the rapid growth-rate of new teachers and schools, a changeover in several leadership positions at the central level, and serious financial problems. The direct impact of the Learning Consortium has been restricted to a limited number of schools, and Learning Consortium initiatives are not seen as closely linked to other system priorities.

In summary, the key for Consortium impact has been in finding ways to link existing and new initiatives, as well as to capitalize on the opportunities presented by the Consortium partnership. The meaning of Consortium membership depends on the extent to which boards shape the partnership to support their own priorities, and the extent to which they can shift their priorities in response to what they learn through the Consortium.

In the case of the university partners, the impact of the Learning Consortium has been less direct. However, membership of the Consortium has contributed to programme changes in both organizations, while opportunities for field research have also increased.

The Faculty of Education, University of Toronto, has been involved in a process of change and renewal over the past three years, during which programmes have been reviewed and expanded, new tenure stream faculty have been hired, and personnel are involved in more joint work with school boards, with an increased emphasis on research. The Learning Consortium both supports and provides a vehicle for such organizational changes. A large proportion of the faculty have participated in Consortium programmes, with considerable impact as faculty expand their range of teaching methodologies for their own Bachelor of Education students. The pre-service programme that operates in collaboration with selected Consortium schools represents a powerful model for linking teachers' preparation with school development. Several faculty members have also been involved in research and evaluation within the Learning Consortium. One acted as an evaluator with the Planning Group (Thiessen, 1989), while another conducted a study in Consortium schools, examining how prior norms of collaboration in schools were related to the implementation of cooperative learning (Anderson, 1991). Data have also been collected on student-teacher development in the pre-service programme (Rolheiser-Bennett and Hundey, 1990). In a variety of ways, then, involvement in the Learning Consortium has supported the Faculty in working toward a set of goals that represent the organization's expanded mandate.

The Ontario Institute for Studies in Education joined the Learning Consortium several months after the other partners, a delay which exacerbated the difficulty of integrating Consortium membership with the OISE mandate. However, during Year 2 the Learning Consortium became an internship site for a doctoral programme, OISE personnel worked on the evaluation and research, collaborating on planning, data gathering, and reporting, and several OISE faculty were involved in Learning Consortium conferences and workshops. The most significant OISE participation is a programme change, a pilot project representing different ways of preparing doctoral students from Learning Consortium school boards. The new field-focused doctoral programme is now in the final planning stages, with implementation scheduled for the Fall of 1991. The programme, designed to integrate field development with research inquiry, will further the aims of the Learning Consortium and its members by closely tying students' dissertation research with Consortium and school board priorities.

Much more could be said about the role of faculties of education and universities in school reform, but that is beyond the scope of this paper (see Fullan 1991; Goodlad 1990). In many ways, universities have lagged behind school districts, teacher unions and governments in addressing issues of educational reform. Through active partnerships, universities can ensure that they become centrally involved in reforms in teacher education and school improvement.

4   Issues and Dilemmas

At the institutional level, a number of issues emerge from consideration of the first three years of the Learning Consortium's development. There are four powerful implications that we have observed (and to some extent, planned for, as a partnership)—greater coordination, simultaneous centralization–decentralization, synergy, and changes in the cultures of school boards and universities. After considering these implications we highlight several ongoing dilemmas relating to cultural differences between school systems and universities, and aligning the rhetoric and reality of partnership.

Issues

(a) Coordination. In each organization, there is evidence of moving from a piecemeal, uneven set of activities to a more coordinated system. Although early Learning Consortium activities were highly specific, and not yet strongly linked to other board initiatives, over the course of the three years they have become more closely integrated, supporting other professional development activities in a variety of ways. This evolution was intentional, although the pathways were different and unpredictable. We would argue that coordination was more likely to occur given the strategy used, which:

- started with specific activities to demonstrate early action and success (not just abstract planning)
- emphasized two basic assumptions (the continuum, and the link between teacher development and school improvement) which pointed to the necessity for linking various activities
- established a planning structure for ongoing coordination and development
- avoided trying to force premature coordination, but fostered its development around specific decisions over time.

(b) Balancing centralization vs decentralization. In planning for educational change, neither centralization nor decentralization works

effectively (Fullan 1991). The issue is not choosing between two contradictory approaches, but rather developing a simultaneous top-down, bottom-up strategy. It could be said that the Learning Consortium began with a top-down approach, with the Summer Institutes and other professional development programmes. Indeed, an early Learning Consortium evaluation report (Thiessen, 1989) noted that the Planning Group determined major programme directions and details, rather than these emerging from the schools. The programmes differed from much professional development, however, in that participants in Consortium programmes came voluntarily, and follow-up support stressed the importance of school-level involvement as participants adapted the newly learned strategies to suit their own schools and teaching situations. As the initiatives became integrated into system priorities, more support was provided for school-based follow-up, as these districts, like many others, are moving toward greater school-based planning. The Learning Consortium was used by school teams and by the systems as a vehicle for school improvement planning and associated professional development. In this way individual professional development needs, school needs, and system needs were increasingly interwoven in an integrated framework. Since there will always be a tension between school-based and system-based needs, what is needed is a mechanism for sorting out and negotiating these relationships. The Learning Consortium has served as one such mechanism.

Earlier in the paper, we noted that in successful school–university partnerships, the agenda must be 'specific enough to bind participants in a common enterprise but general enough to allow for individuality and creativity' (Sirotnik and Goodlad, 1988:219). In the Learning Consortium, when partners engaged in joint initiatives, they were able to shape their participation to suit their organizational needs, and the spin-offs show the diversity with which they developed the common themes.

(c) Synergy. Another factor emerging from Consortium accounts might be referred to as synergy, in most cases growing out of the coordination and consistency described above. When initiatives are perceived as mutually consistent and supportive rather than at cross-purposes, each individual initiative may have a greater impact. One school board representative used these words:

> Once we saw the possibilities and potential of the Consortium, it was possible to make links between different initiatives and put them together...We were working on all fronts with similar themes...and the Consortium enhances the directions in which we are going.

This quote points to a new way of looking at partnerships. The more conventional view would suggest that the success of a partnership would be judged primarily by the extent to which the partners commit to joint ventures, and by the success of such ventures. An alternative view is the extent to which individual organizations change their own organizational policies and programmes through involvement in the partnership. In this way, the mark of success is the extent to which partner institutions 'use' the Learning Consortium as a vehicle for refocusing their own improvement efforts, and in so doing learn from and contribute to the learning by other partners.

(d) Cultures of school boards and of the universities. As noted earlier, the organizational cultures of school boards and universities are quite different from each other. Within the Learning Consortium, we have variation not only between the university and school board partners, but also between the two university partners and among the four school boards. Such cultural differences have led to many misunderstandings, and have necessitated ongoing negotiation and adaptation as the Learning Consortium has developed. Both school board and university participants agreed that school boards were more preoccupied with 'front line' issues of budget and accountability, and were more likely to be subject to shifting pressures from their organizations. It was understandable then, that school board representatives were eager for programmes with short-term results and high visibility. They are interested in possible long-term benefits, but rarely have the luxury of waiting.

At the beginning of the Learning Consortium partnership, school system participants saw university personnel as somewhat unrealistic (and almost self-indulgent) in their concern for research and knowledge production, while university participants were often insensitive to the need of school systems for immediate and concrete results. Since the systems of accountability in the two settings required different timelines and different kinds of reporting, it has taken time, and considerable patience, for the partners to recognize the value of incorporating elements of each other's priorities. As Thiessen (1989) notes:

> a key influence on the possibilities of partnership was the history of perceived and real differences among the six organizations. Underlying the support for a common venture were six distinct agendas of the partner organizations... Complicating the existence of multiple agendas was the traditional split between the school and university communities. Both communities were perceived to have different aspirations, ones that were largely irreconcilable. (p. 29)

Over the three years there has been considerable change. The early professional growth opportunities offered within the Consortium framework (for instance, in cooperative learning) were strongly focused on development of teaching skills and strategies. Such an approach, well executed, showed early and positive impact on teachers and on schools, and thus was particularly attractive to the school boards. School board representatives were then reluctant to consider less defined (and more risky) alternative approaches to professional growth. However, over time, and through ongoing negotiation, the Learning Consortium has recently broadened its programme to include a wider variety of alternatives (school improvement frameworks, more reflective approaches to adult learning, examining ways of building collaborative working cultures), while still strongly supporting the earlier successful initiatives.

Over the same time, the Faculty of Education has become much more involved in field-based programmes and front-line delivery, while OISE is instituting the field-focused doctorate. The school boards, on the other hand, as was noted earlier, are much more appreciative of research as a source of valuable information to improve Consortium efforts. Practitioners are increasingly involved in research, and in writing about and presenting their experiences at local, national and international conferences. Some tensions remain, however.

University experience confirms that field-based programmes are more labour intensive than traditional teacher education methods. The university incentive system and the habits of professors of education often work against field-involvement, though contribution to field development is a criterion for promotion at both OISE, and the Faculty, and new priorities and tendencies push in the direction of increased involvement with school systems. All partners find the mutual problem-solving and decision-making in the planning group very beneficial, but some found that it encroached on their ability to make fast, individual decisions. All found it time-consuming, particularly problematical when all representatives have overly full work schedules.

Although considerable growth in understanding has occurred within the Consortium, the different priorities, structures and ongoing work processes in school systems and universities continue to create barriers to collaborative work. The nature of partnership involves ongoing negotiation around such issues. The issue is how to both modify and then transcend cultural differences in developing commitment to a common enterprise. In the Learning Consortium, shortage of time has limited opportunities for educators to explore such learning, but we have overcome the difficulties and become engaged in common initiatives. Our own experience confirms what other writers have stressed: solid and successful university partnerships require nurturing and persistence. They develop slowly but significantly over a period of years, experiencing both stagnation and quantum leaps along the way. They are never easy.

Dilemmas: Rhetoric and Reality

There are steady tensions between the rhetoric and the reality of partnership, as enthusiastic talk of partnership ventures and of the benefits of collaboration is often accompanied by more limited achievements. Although such tensions have often been healthy, they also highlight the recurring difficulties with collaborative projects. We will discuss three issues: collaboration and control, practical difficulties, and overload and focus.

Collaboration and Control

By the third year of the Learning Consortium, the number of 'spin-offs', initiatives related to the Learning Consortium but separate from it, had increased dramatically. On the one hand, such growth indicates the strength of the Consortium's impact, and represents increasing integration of staff development initiatives in the member organizations. There is no need to try to control everything within the partnership umbrella. Such activities are by and large natural derivatives of the partnership, but there needs to be room for the distinctive needs of each partner to be addressed—for some, school leadership training may be a priority; for others, programmes for new teachers may be the most pressing need. On the other hand, the growth of related projects outside the Learning Consortium framework could also represent a reluctance to move further toward a common agenda, and a desire to have more control over individual system programmes. Certainly each of the partner organizations constantly weighs the benefits and drawbacks of common versus individual initiatives, and organizations may prefer to have their own programmes for a variety of reasons—because they have already started a programme and do not wish to change it, because the numbers of participants will be unwieldy if other organizations are involved, or because they believe their needs can best be met in a programme they design themselves.

In looking at the question of individual and common initiatives, it may be helpful to think of different ways of working together. Depending on the context and the needs of the participants, it may be appropriate simply to share ideas about each other's programmes. At other times people may ask for assistance, or solve problems together. Finally, they may be involved in joint work or a common project. In a partnership framework such as the Learning Consortium, we would expect a variety of forms of collaboration, which indeed is the case.

Practical Difficulties

When the Learning Consortium was established, it was hoped that links among educators in the six different partner organizations would increase, and that joint initiatives would flourish. However, practical difficulties have limited the reality of the collaboration, and the ongoing links among staff from the different organizations are not as developed as had originally been anticipated.

There are several reasons for this state of affairs. First, geography is a factor. The districts are not contiguous, and travelling time is lengthy (frequently over two hours). Such an issue may appear trivial, but distance represents time, and for teachers and school administrators, time is the most scarce resource. Plans for common programmes have repeatedly foundered on this issue. Another reason for the lack of contact may be a sense that teachers and school administrators need time to feel comfortable with using new practices in their own settings before they are interested in interacting with those from other organizations. Infrequent gatherings of groups from more than one Consortium organization have been seen as valuable, but the cross-board conversations occasionally seem somewhat contrived. Such personal and school links with other organizations, although supported by school boards, may not be a high priority compared to activities that are focused on immediate school and system issues. Nonetheless, the idea of fostering cross-board and board-university linkages (beyond those already operating within the Planning Group) is still seen as a powerful strategy. And despite these difficulties, members from the partnership organizations—central and school staff alike—do spend considerable time together over the course of a year.

The challenge is to overcome the practical difficulties, and to organize such links in order to meet genuine needs. Awarding mini-grants for school-based joint projects is a strategy that seems to have considerable potential for overcoming some of the these problems.

Overload and Focus

This is a familiar problem at the school and system level. The increasing number of competing priorities means that educators must focus their energies to avoid overload and burn-out. The same problem is seen at the level of the Learning Consortium. School boards are experiencing such great and dramatic changes that they may need to focus their energies within, thus being less eager to take on more joint initiatives. The diverse needs and organizational directions of the Consortium organizations also influence the partnership initiatives. In attempting to address the range of needs, the Consortium is in danger of overloading its own agenda and blurring its focus. On the other hand, the synergy generated by Consortium activities has provided a forum for school boards to coordinate and focus their activities in a manner hitherto neglected.

Conclusion

School–university partnerships, like other collaborative ventures, need to develop a shared vision, an agenda that fulfils yet transcends self-interests. In the case of the Learning Consortium, the vision that guided initial efforts was that of 'career-long professional growth for educators', linked with school improvement. This vision encompassed and indeed transcended the more specific mandate of each partner organization, and could be interpreted in different ways.

Planning for the Learning Consortium involves both short-term and long-term questions. While the focus for Year 3 was being pursued, decisions needed to be made about whether to continue the partnership beyond the agreed-upon time, and if so, what form such a continuation should take. We are building on the foundation of our current initiatives, and also broadening the scope of our work some-what, continually coming back to our two basic unifying themes: the teacher education continuum, and the linking of school and system improvement. We are also concerned about understanding more about the culture of the school and how it impacts on both students and teachers, since such understanding provides a productive context in which to build on our work on teaching strategies and collegial support.

Keeping the 'collaboration agenda' alive and vigorous is a major challenge. This is not due to a shortage of ideas for further activities, but rather because maintaining present initiatives requires such a high level of support that starting new ones is difficult.

We hope to continue to develop an agenda that includes yet transcends self-interests. Within the framework of the Consortium, the vision is one of collaboration, a partnership in which schools and universities will work closely together, taking joint responsibility for preparing the teachers of tomorrow, for supporting beginning teachers, for encouraging continuous professional growth among all educators, co-authoring articles, conducting research. In the course of pursuing the vision, we would expect the increasing coordination and integration of system initiatives and priorities noted in this paper. As more links are forged among the different strands, and organizations become more conscious and deliberate about making the connections, we anticipate ever-increasing impact.

All educational institutions have overloaded maintenance and re-form agendas. Attempts at innovation often increase the overload, not only because they are more work, but also because they are typically grafted on to existing plans. Fragmentation and 'ad hoc-ism' is the result. What we need instead are approaches which attack several parts of the problem simultaneously, which build on previous efforts, and which increase the capacity of the system.

There is a great deal of other evidence being assembled to document the impact of the Consortium, which we have not been able to present in this chapter. This evidence shows that most partners have made enormous strides over the first three years. The partnership is about to be renewed for a second three-year term. Through the experience it has become clear to most participants that neither school districts nor universities can solve the problems of overload, fragmentation, teacher development and school improvement if they work alone. It must also be recognized that negotiation and problem-solving are permanent features of successful partnerships. The result, as we are experiencing it, is that activities begin to intersect to create significant pay-offs for all partners. Given the failure of most attempts at educational reform, school–district–university partnerships represent a potential solution worth seriously attempting and monitoring.

Note

1 Material for this section is drawn from the experience of the Learning Consortium Coordinator and from interviews with the Planning Group representatives.

References

ANDERSON, B.L. and COX, P.L. (1988) *Configuring the Educational System For a Shared Future: Collaborative Vision, Action, Reflection*, Andover, Mass., The Regional Laboratory for Educational Improvement of the Northeast and Islands and The Education Commission of the States.

ANDERSON, S.E. (1991) 'Building collegiality: Innovation or school improvement strategy', Paper presented at the Annual Meeting of the American Educational Research Association, Chicago.

BROOKHART, S.M. and LOADMAN, W.E. (1989) 'Work perceptions of university and public school educators', Paper presented at the Annual Meeting of the American Educational Research Association, San Francisco.

CLARK, D.L. (1980) 'In consideration of goal-free planning: The failure of traditional planning systems in education', in CLARK, D.L., McKIBBIN, S. and MALKAS, M. (Eds.) *New Perspectives on Planning in Educational Organizations*, San Francisco, Far West Laboratory for Educational Research and Development.

CLARK, R.W. (1988) 'School-university relationships: An interpretative review', in SIROTNIK, K.A. and GOODLAD, J.I. (Eds.) *School–University Partnerships In Action: Concepts, Cases, And Concerns*, New York, Teacher's College Press, pp. 32–65.

CONYERS, J. (1988) 'The Glenview public schools–University of Illinois at Chicago professional development school model', Paper presented at McRel International Conference, Snowmass, Colorado.

ERVAY, S.B. and LUMLEY, D. (1988) 'School/university partnerships—A time to disenthrall ourselves', in *Educational Considerations*, Fall 1988.

FULLAN, M.G. (1990) 'Staff development, innovation, and institutional development', in B. JOYCE (Ed.) *Changing School Culture through Staff Development*, Virginia, ASCD, pp. 3–25.

FULLAN, M.G. with STIEGELBAUER, S. (1991) *The New Meaning of Educational Change*, New York, Teacher's College Press.

FULLAN, M.G., BENNETT, B. and ROLHEISER-BENNETT, C. (1990) 'Linking classroom and school improvement', *Educational Leadership*, May 1990, pp. 13–19.

FULLAN, M.G., CONNELLY, M.C. and WATSON, N. (1990) *Teacher Education in Ontario: Current Practice and Future Possibilities, Final Report to the Teacher Education Review Steering Committee*, Toronto, Ministry of Education.

GOODLAD, J.I. (1985) 'Reconstructing schooling and the education of educators', Paper presented at the Conference of Chief State School Officers, Wisconsin.

GOODLAD, J.I. (1988) 'School–University partnerships for education renewal: Rationale and concepts' in SIROTNIK, K.A. and GOODLAD, J.I. (Eds.) *School–University Partnerships In Action: Concepts, Cases and Concerns*, New York, Teacher's College Press, pp. 3–31.

GOODLAD, J.I. (1990) *Teachers For Our Nation's Schools*, San Francisco, Jossey-Bass.

GRAY, B. (1989) *Collaborating: Finding Common Ground For Multiparty Problems*, San Francisco, Jossey-Bass.

GROSS, T.L. (1988) *Partners In Education*, San Francisco, Jossey-Bass.

HARGREAVES, A. (1989) Personal communication.

HATHAWAY, W.E. (1985) 'Models of school–university collaboration: National and local perspective on collaborations that work', Paper presented at Symposium at the Annual Meeting of the American Educational Research Association, Chicago.

HAVELOCK, R.G. (1985) 'Linking universities and schools for curriculum change', Presentation prepared for the Danforth Foundation Consultation on International Education, St Louis, Miss.

KENNEDY, R.L. (1987) 'Collaborative inquiry into the Arkansas Educational Renewal Consortium', Paper presented at the annual meeting of the American Educational Research Association, Washington, DC.

McINERNEY, W.D. (1987) 'Establishing university–school district collaboration in the education of teachers', Paper presented at the annual meeting of the American Educational Research Association, Washington, DC.

MICKELSON, D.J., KRITEK, W.J., HEDLUND, R.D. and KAUFMANN, A. (1988) *Urban School–University Collaboration*, Paper presented at the annual meeting of the American Educational Research Association, New Orleans.

ROLHEISER-BENNETT, C. and HUNDEY, I. (1990) 'A case study of a collaborative teacher preparation program: Student learning in professional settings', Paper presented at Canadian Society for Studies in Education Conference, Victoria, British Columbia.

RUDDUCK, J. (1992) 'Universities in partnership with schools and school systems: Les liaisons dangereuses?' in FULLAN, M. and HARGREAVES, A. (Eds.) *Teacher Development and Educational Change*, Basingstoke, Falmer, pp. 194–212.

SARASON, S.B. (1990) *The Predictable Failure of School Reform*, San Francisco, Jossey-Bass.

SCANE, J. and WATSON, N.H. (1990) 'One year later: A report on the implementation of cooperative learning and peer coaching following Summer Institute '89', Unpublished report, the Learning Consortium.

Nancy Watson and Michael G. Fullan

SINCLAIR, R.L. and HARRISON, A.E. (1988) 'A partnership for increasing student learning: The Massachusetts coalition for school improvement', in SIROTNIK, K.A. and GOODLAD, J.I. (Eds.) *School–University Partnership in Action: Concepts, Cases, and Concerns*, New York, Teacher's College Press.

SIROTNIK, K.A. (1988) 'The Meaning and conduct of inquiring in school–university partnerships, in SIROTNIK, K. and GOODLAD, J. (Eds.) *School–University Partnerships In Action: Concepts, Cases and Concerns*, New York, Teacher's College Press, pp. 169–90.

SIROTNIK, K.A. and GOODLAD, J.I. (Eds.) (1988) *School–University Partnerships in Action: Concepts, Cases, and Concerns*, New York, Teacher's College Press.

SOCKETT, H. and ENDO, T. (1989) 'Collaboration in professionalism: The case of the center of applied research and development in education (CARD)', Paper presented at the annual meeting of the American Educational Research Association, San Francisco.

THIESSEN, D. (1989) 'Formative evaluation of the Learning Consortium: Year 1 report', Toronto, Unpublished report.

WATSON, N.H. (1988) 'Summer Institute 1988: A first collaborative venture', *Orbit, 19* (5).

WATSON, N.H. (1989) 'The Learning Consortium: Coordinator's report for Year 1', Toronto, Unpublished report.

WATSON, N.H., DAWE, R. and SARACO, J. (1989) 'Summer Institute participants one year later: A summary of responses', Unpublished report, the Learning Consortium.

WILLIAMS, D.D. (1988). 'The Brigham-Young University-public school partnership', in SIROTNIK, K.A. and GOODLAD, J.I. (Eds.), *School–University Partnerships In Action: Concepts, Cases, and Concern*, New York, Teacher's College Press, pp. 124–47.

Notes on Contributors

Johan Lyall Aitken
Johan Lyall Aitken, Professor, The Joint Centre for Teacher Development, Faculty of Education, University of Toronto/Ontario Institute for Studies in Education, is the author of *Masques of Morality: Females in Fiction* and numerous books and articles in literature, literary theory, teacher development, values education and feminist studies.

E. Patricia Crehan
E. Patricia Crehan is an Assistant Professor in the Department of Administrative, Adult, and Higher Education at the University of British Columbia. Her research interests include teacher development, collegial consultation, instructional supervision and educational leadership.

Michael G. Fullan
Michael G. Fullan is the Dean of the Faculty of Education, University of Toronto and former Assistant Director (Academic) of the Ontario Institute for Studies in Education. He has participated as a researcher, consultant and policy advisor on a wide range of educational change projects, and has recently been awarded the first Award of Excellence by the Canadian Association of Teacher Educators for outstanding contribution to his profession and to teacher education. His most recent book is *The New Meaning of Educational Change* (Teachers College Press, 1991).

Peter P. Grimmett
Peter P. Grimmett is an Associate Professor in the Faculty of Education at Simon Fraser University. Formerly Director of the Centre for the Study of Teacher Education at the University of British Columbia, he now works in the newly-established Institute for Studies in Teacher Education at Simon Fraser University. His research interests focus at the pre-service and in-service levels on the relationship between teachers' development of their craft and such processes as reflection, supervision, and collegial consultation.

Andy Hargreaves

Andy Hargreaves is Professor in Educational Administration at the Ontario Institute for Studies in Education, Toronto. He is the author of many books on education including *Changing Teachers* (Cassells/ Teachers College Press, forthcoming), *Curriculum and Assessment Reform* (Open University Press/OISE Press) and *Two Cultures of Schooling* (Falmer Press, 1986). He has researched extensively on teaching and school culture and is currently directing two projects on the relationship between school culture and restructuring in secondary schools.

Edward S. Hickcox

Edward S. Hickcox is a professor in the Department of Educational Administration at the Ontario Institute for Studies in Education. He has done research and written extensively in the area of performance appraisal for educational personnel.

Kenneth Leithwood

Kenneth Leithwood is professor of Educational Administration and Head of the Centre for Leadership Development at the Ontario Institute for Studies in Education. He specializes in issues concerned with planned change, leadership, school improvement and administrative expertise.

Denis A. Mildon

Denis A. Mildon is a twenty-three year career department head of secondary school English and a researcher involved with teacher development for Simcoe County Board of Education, Ontario. He is completing a doctoral thesis on narrative inquiry and contemporary fiction at The Ontario Institute for Studies in Education.

Donald F. Musella

Donald F. Musella is the Chair, Department of Educational Administration, The Ontario Institute for Studies in Education. He is a teacher, researcher, author, and consultant working primarily with organizational change and culture.

Jean Rudduck

Jean Rudduck is Director of the QQST (Qualitative and Quantitative Studies in Education) Research Group and Professor of Education at the University of Sheffield. Her research focuses on different aspects of innovation and change in schools, including teacher research as a basis for professional development; she is also interested in the student's perspective on learning. Her most recent book is: *Innovation and Change: Developing Involvement and Understanding*, Open University Press (1990).

Patricia J. Sikes
Patricia J. Sikes is a lecturer in the social aspects of education at the University of Warwick, England. She is particularly interested in studying teachers' lives and careers using life history and methodology.

Louise Stoll
Originally a teacher in London, England, Louise Stoll began her academic work with Peter Mortimore on the Junior School Project in 1980. She worked as a researcher in the Inner London Education Authority, and is now Effective Schools Consultant and Coordinator of Research and Assessment in the Halton Board of Education, Canada. She is co-author of the book *School Matters* published by the University of California Press, 1988, and a variety of articles on school effectiveness and school improvement.

Judith Warren Little
Judith Warren Little is Associate Professor of Education at the University of California, Berkeley. Her research and teaching interests centre on the school as a professional environment, with special attention to teachers' careers and collegial relationships. She has published widely on the topics of professional development and collegiality.

Nancy Watson
Nancy Watson, from the University of Toronto, is a Coordinator of the Learning Consortium, a school/university partnership focusing on teacher development issues. She has been involved in educational research and writing in such areas as teacher education, induction of beginning teachers and school improvement.

Marvin F. Wideen
Marvin F. Wideen is Professor in the Faculty of Education at Simon Fraser University. Prior to his becoming involved in teacher education, he worked both as a teacher and as a principal in public schools. He writes and conducts research in the areas of teacher education, science education and school improvement.

Index